THE AMERICAN ORCHESTRA
AND
THEODORE THOMAS

THEODORE THOMAS
In the full tide of his first success

THE AMERICAN ORCHESTRA
AND
THEODORE THOMAS

By
CHARLES EDWARD RUSSELL

Illustrations from Photographs

GREENWOOD PRESS, PUBLISHERS
WESTPORT, CONNECTICUT

PREFATORY NOTE

WITHOUT sounding the ever-ready pipe of vainglory, we may justly affirm that in one division of representative art the American achievement has gone beyond debate. The grand orchestra is now more than our foremost cultural asset; it has become our sign of honor among the nations. Even if sceptical or scornful about our other endeavors, the world assigns to this a verity of excellence. Starting so much later than the rest and starting handicapped, we seem, despite shortcomings and our own incredulities, to have developed the orchestra above the average attainment. If we lag about other arts, we lead in this.

Forty years or so have set down most of the visible signs of this gracious growth. Only so far back as 1876 they were not known to mortal sight, certainly, and otherwise had been scouted as impossible. Two bands, one leader, and an interest so small it seemed to pessimists a higher power of nothing may be counted as the sorry whole of our performance in that year. In many places were small groups of instrumentalists that played together unstably and were regarded by most of their fellow townsmen as partly insane; in many places there was for vocal music a large, sincere, and always expanding devotion. But beyond two bands and one leader, the thing we know now as the grand or symphony orchestra functioned chiefly to the ear of hope.

Even the one leader and the two bands, with all the most audacious of the casuals, played little music that would now be thought fitted for the symphonic dignity and much that to-day is sent down to the nursery. Besides, they were sustained (if at all) by the part of the public that was musically trained, professional or amateur. To the mass of mankind they had nothing to say—except now and then something provocative of jeers. Even among the cultured, the educated, and the thoughtful, aside from that small class of musicians, the marked absence of musical insight moved many visitors to laughter and a few to grief.

Fifty years later, and the grand[1] orchestra had become our most familiar artistic treasure. Music that at the beginning of this period had been filliped as beyond human understanding had become the easy possession of a great constituency. Forty-six cities and towns in the United States were supporting grand orchestras as not only habitual but necessary sources of intellectual and spiritual delight. If the goal of a musical America was still far ahead, statistics and other evidences were at hand to set up a singular progression. Over large communities and small, a notable transformation had come; over New York with its almost daily symphonic concerts, and over remote places where in 1876 orchestra meant two violins and a bass fiddle to which one could dance. In 1926, the observer had to note, as a philosophical fact and not as a nationalistic vaunt, from New York, Boston, Philadelphia, to Rochester, Cincinnati, Cleveland, Detroit, Chicago, Minneapolis, Duluth, St. Louis, Denver—a long line of communities, great and small, clear to the Pacific coast and up and down it, maintaining ambitious symphony or symphonic orchestras that played regular seasons to audiences always growing in numbers and always manifesting deeper interest with the better knowledge.

The influence of these so many organizations, interpreting, enforcing, and bringing home the art that comes closest to the lives and souls of men, is a great potentiality—perhaps of the greatest! Slowly the results begin to appear, like meadow grass

---

[1]The name is technically correct but laically unlucky—the word has been so sadly abused! What is meant is an orchestra containing all the instruments necessary to the adequate performance of the standard symphonies and players competent to play them.

in the spring. Music in its most exalting and valuable phases is coming down from the heights to dwell with the generality of men and to be among them and of them. In many American cities, each public school must now have its student orchestra. Systems planned with research are at work in other communities to find out and encourage among children all latent taste for instrumental music. Every public school is becoming, or likely to become, a central station that picks up musical energy from the grand orchestra and transmits it into hundreds of homes where before all such vivifying currents were rarer than the visits of angels.

From the home to the school, therefore, and from the school to the grand orchestra, it is easy to follow the trail backward. But where did the grand orchestra come from?

So far as one could see in 1926, what was at work was a cultural revolution. For the first time there was being established for great toiling populations a direct connection with pure expressions of musical beauty; a direct personal interest in maintaining and repeating them; a direct connection with the greatest minds that have felt and created such beauty; even more, a contact with the spiritual things that belong to such creations! When before have we been aware of any such force at work on such a scale among us? Suppose it to keep on for another generation, gathering head. It might produce in this country the greatest change ever known. Not about art alone; I mean about life and about thought translated into life. Two generations of it might change the whole American character; it might in the end scourge us of materialism. Is this fantastic? Not if what we believe about the power and the ethics of art has any foundation. But even if we turn from these delectable mountains of hope to things here and now, consider that in the sour commentaries of European visitors this was long celebrated as the land without art. So, then, we have lived to see that jibe transmuted into a common prediction of an American greatness in the art of music, at least, and here is the beginning of the coming true of that promise.

No such advance has been made in any other direction. Without disparaging other arts or their practitioners, or implying that any of them have stood still in this much derided and often much misunderstood land of ours, none of them has leaped ahead like this.

Certain conditions have much helped the new orchestral day, that is true. The extraordinary wealth of America has enabled it to secure the best performers and to pay them to concentrate upon the one object of the best performance. Everywhere the grand orchestra must be a kind of artistic pauper; nowhere, so far as I can learn, is it a self-supporting business enterprise. In Continental Europe, the inevitable gap between expenditures and receipts is bridged by a subsidy from government, municipal or national, or both. In America it is met by a public subscription. But as America has so large a supply of the rich, whether idle or otherwise, and as its people are accustomed to so large a scale of giving and doing, there is an abrupt end to any comparison. Orchestra players in Europe are paid so little they must seek other engagements, to the detriment of their ensemble work; more and more in America the subscriptions of the public and the gifts of the wealthy tend to develop exclusive centering upon the one clean aim.

But this makes the musical revolution in America seem only the more remarkable. Before there can be money subscribed to support an orchestra, there must be a widespread demand for such a thing; before such a demand, a widespread interest in orchestral art. Of old, experience showed these to come slowly. In America, in the last decade, they have come swiftly. Conditions again, but also many men, have contributed to the evolution. The German, Italian, Bohemian, and Polish elements in the population have been invaluable counter irritants to the Anglo-Saxon indifference. Wherever there are Jews there is music; the art instincts that their religion chained up from other expression has turned headlong to this, and with the rest of the world we have gained from the addiction. A long list of admirable names belongs to the story. Even eighty years ago in many communities there were in music devout men that dreamed of something like this and usually broke their hearts in trying to make the dream true. There came a time in our urban history when to average persons an orchestra signified twelve men (or fewer) sawing away unheeded down there in front between the acts of a play, or furnishing the true melancholy incidental to the death of Little Eva. From that abysmal epoch up to this more genial day, when so many complete grand orchestras, sixty to a hundred players in each, make every week for so many regions the common air to blossom with things celestial, all the road is lined with the records of the pioneers and with their tragedies.

U. C. Hill, who in 1842 founded the New York Philharmonic Society, our oldest and most honorable effort upon this field, was one. Carl Bergmann, who led it so long and so well; Theodore Eisfeld, the earliest leader of the Brooklyn Philharmonic, founder of a noted string quartette; Carl Zerrahn, who labored so hard and so many years in Boston; William Mason, who helped so much to develop chamber music; Otto Dresel, Theodore Ritter, Henry Ahner—these were typical apostles of the early church, often of a noble zeal and usually unsung. Almost every considerable city had someone like Zerrahn and Bergmann; somebody that toiled away, neglected and unrewarded, to redeem at least a strip of the artistic wilderness. In Chicago, so far back as 1850, Julius Dyhrenfurth[1] was such a man, giving orchestral concerts whenever he could get the players, the listeners, and the means. Ten years later, Hans Balatka was the Chicago hero, and in eight years seems to have ruined himself thrice in the effort to create a genuine musical

[1]Philo. A. Otis, *The Chicago Symphony Orchestra*, p. 9.

interest. Providence was kind beyond our deserving. In 1849 came the Germania, the first orchestra to travel in America, all good musicians and fresh from good training. After five years it went to wreck, leaving its members widely scattered through the American cities. Like Carl Bergmann, for one example, each became a nucleus of musical energy and figured commandingly in local band or orchestra. Many great singers came; the opera suddenly attained to a center of fashionable concern; and at all times there were the Dodworths, wonderful Dodworths! Working hard and apparently without reward, the whole numerous family, with pipe, tabor, trumpet, or other handy thing, contributed among the masses to imitate the dawn. Nor from this brief and inadequate list would any one wish to omit that Patrick Sarsfield Gilmore of a later day whose brass band amazed Europe and introduced many a piece of classicism where it had been but a drooping stranger. Many forces were at work, that is clear, and among them the happy circumstance of a body of conscientious writers on musical topics. Effectual, fervent beadsmen they, too, did much. So far back as 1849 there was a periodical in New York devoted to the service of the fine arts, but especially of music, and it was not long alone.

But when all other influences together have been recounted and reviewed, great artists, great leaders greatly persisting, good fortune and all, there is one man whose contribution went incontestably beyond all the rest. Forty-three years he devoted himself to this work and traveled up and down the land to originate and prosper it. When once he had been led to choose this as the one purpose of his life, he chose with equal and inspired care the means by which he might achieve it. Wherever he went in his restless wanderings he left his mark. To a great and always expanding constituency he gave the first real conception of musical elations and gave it in ways that made it permanent.

His life was a strange succession of vicissitudes, adventures, poignant sacrifices, apparent disasters, and triumphs unseen. He had great and unaccountable gifts in his art, native gifts largely untrained, but indomitably efficient for the work he was to do. He was equipped with resources of character that made him seem almost mysteriously fitted to his task. Circumstances drove into his consciousness when still young and impressionable an intimate knowledge of the mentality of the people he was to serve; such a knowledge as no other musician of his day possessed. Often at the great crises of his career he was swept against his will or inclining to the very course that proved most helpful to his aim. When he desired to stay at home, he was compelled to travel; when his work was done in one field, conditions pushed him, over his protests, into another. Whenever the ground was ready anywhere for the peculiar seed-sowing he was engaged in, some circumstance arose to lead or drive him to that one glebe land.

Where did the grand orchestra come from that we found as the originating dynamo in these communities where the musical ardor spreads and spreads?

It came to a certain extent from this man and his labors. Before his advent was one real orchestra in America; he saved that from oblivion and made it great and impregnable, while he planted or promoted others.

For more than thirty years he traveled to and fro upon his mission, East, West, North, South, and wherever he halted there appeared afterward the signs of his fructifying husbandry. Where did the interest come from that sustains the grand orchestra that produces the central station of the school that sends musical energy into these homes? From this man; he chiefly developed it. Year after year he went along a Musical Highway between the coasts. Go over that Highway now and note the luxuriant tilth of his sowing.

He was a great conductor of orchestras. But have there not been in America other great conductors of orchestras?

Assuredly; before him, in his time, after him—great men.
How did it happen that he conspicuously was the gardener, he
tilled all this soil and so started a revolution so remarkable?
What was the difference?

The difference was this, that his was the first dominant and
mobile orchestra to exist primarily for educational purposes; to
play programs that had been invariably and adroitly composed
to a purely educational end. This distinction was great, and great
the power it wrought upon the thoughts and ways of men.
Every program played by this orchestra in the course of many
years of ministrations to and fro, had place in a vast scheme
for musical education, and it is to be supposed that of not another organization of so wide and so long a career can this be
said.

It was true, too, about the man that made these programs
and conceived and directed this work. Other conductors gave
beautiful concerts, produced excellent music, interpreted great
thoughts to entranced audiences. This man alone had his mind
fixed upon a sequence of public instruction that extended over
the span of his life and beyond it. In forty-three years he led
more than ten thousand concerts for which he made all the
selections. Among all these is virtually none that was not fitted
thoughtfully into his great design. Other conductors played for
to-day and often played magnificently; he alone played for to-
morrow and all the to-morrows that are to be.

He did the work, in great measure without knowing how
much of it he had done; and he paid the price. All men that
enlist in any way to secure a better condition pay the price.
In this instance, it was high. He paid it in ways that were open
to the world's notice, ways that only his intimates divined, and
ways that only his own tortured soul could know. Throughout
a life abounding in trial and bitter discomfiture, he turned to
the light a face of such mastery and calm that men called him

impenetrable or indifferent. Black care rode behind the horse-
man, and few discerned the somber presence.

For years he fought single-handed against indifference, prejudice, and open hostility. Beyond the common lot of man he
seemed doomed to crushing disappointments. He was often discouraged; he never gave up. Out of every reverse he seemed to
come with stronger resolution. When he was most defeated he
most won.

Few men of whom there is record so strangely combined
dreamer and executive, visionary and relentless performer,
conceiver and doer. All his life he was led through gain and
loss and glory and defeat by certain dreams. After forty-three
years of tireless pursuit of these, one came true. Just inside its
threshold he died.

The lives of millions of people are the brighter or the more
endurable because of the work to which Theodore Thomas gave
himself with all his heart and with all his soul and all his mind
and all his strength; some millions to whom he is only a vague
figure, other millions to whom he is not even a name. All their
days they will be affected by what he did and the manner of it;
their children will be affected after them and other generations
after that. What kind of man was this and how did he work to
his ends?

As to these matters no one will learn much from any words of
his. About himself he had a reticence almost singular. Near the
end of his life he was hardly persuaded to undertake a sketch
of his career, called in the succeeding pages of this volume the
Autobiography. It is of about one fourth the bulk of an average
book and is managed in that space to say as much as possible
about music and as little as possible about Theodore Thomas.
His close personal friend of so many years, George P. Upton,
at whose entreaty he assumed this labor, edited it and tried
to make up its defaults with recollections of his own, called

Reminiscence and Appreciation. This, though abounding in interest and side lights, does not and could not tell the story of Theodore Thomas. The one satisfying source of information about this remarkable man is the almost monumental *Memoirs of Theodore Thomas*, by Mrs. Rose Fay Thomas, published in 1910 and long out of print, a careful and conscientious biography. Much light upon his methods and their effects is to be had from the periodical press, especially the musical press, which for the present undertaking has been examined for all the crucial periods of his career. William Mason, who knew him well, disclosed many of his unusual characteristics in *Memories of a Musical Life;* so did George P. Upton in his *Musical Memories.* An unexpected and delightful well-spring of knowledge exists in the singularly interesting volume that Philo A. Otis has compiled of the history of *The Chicago Symphony Orchestra,* much of which is made from the invaluable diary that Mr. Otis kept through the years of Theodore Thomas's greatest activities. W. S. B. Mathews knew Thomas well and has left testimonies about him in *One Hundred Years of American Music.* Dr. F. L. Ritter's *Music in America* reveals the nature of the field upon which Thomas launched himself. The musical dictionaries, Grove's and the *American History and Encyclopedia of Music,* edited by W. L. Hubbard, are helpful. All have been drawn upon for the present volume.

Acknowledgment is due to Mrs. Thomas for infinite kindness and invaluable assistance in compiling these records, for permission to examine Mr. Thomas's letters and to use the material in her book. I am indebted to Mr. Hector W. Thomas for reminiscences of his father and for sympathetic suggestions, ungrudgingly given. To Mr. Frederick J. Wessels, so long Mr. Thomas's close friend and confidant, I owe much for counsel, suggestions, and many facts not heretofore made public. I should be remiss if I did not own with sincerest gratitude the generous help given to me by Mr. Albert Ulrich, for twenty-seven years associated with Thomas, much of the time as orchestral manager, and by other surviving members of the Theodore Thomas orchestra that have corrected or confirmed my own memories of their leader and added many more.

Since Mrs. Thomas wrote, the situation of orchestral music in America has undergone a memorable change. Tendencies and developments imperceptible when Theodore Thomas died, and for years afterward, seem apparent now. In view of this evolution, the time has seemed fitting to attempt a survey of his work and the means by which he sought to accomplish it.

CONTENTS

LIST OF ILLUSTRATIONS

THE AMERICAN ORCHESTRA
AND
THEODORE THOMAS

THE AMERICAN ORCHESTRA AND THEODORE THOMAS

CHAPTER I

The Sower and His Ways

AT THE Centennial Exposition, city of Philadelphia, year
1876, about noon of an early summer day, a boy was
threading the main building when there fell upon his hearing
the strains of the "Tell" overture, now dust covered in the discard, then a classic of chaste renown. He had heard it often;
played by orchestras, played on organs, played on everything
else from an old-fashioned Emerson square piano to a pair of
cymbals, but never like this. It was not merely the unwonted
and plethoric riches of tone that caused him to stop and listen,
but a clutching revelation of things before unsuspected. He
felt that for the first time he was really hearing that composition, and really hearing music.

With a boy's curiosity he worked his way around until he
stood where he could see the conductor's face. It seemed as remarkable as the music. A man of unusual dignity, with a certain
manifest poise of command, was moving all the players to his
will and yet without effort. An expression of confident and competent authority seemed to belong to that face; the expression
of a man that knew exactly what he wanted and how to get it.
Yet in him appeared no sign of the nervous tension and concern
that had always seemed a part of such generalship. By searching
out a program the boy discovered that the man was Theodore

Thomas and the orchestra that great band of which the fame had gone wherever music had its worshipers.

The next year, 1877, Theodore Thomas came to the town where the boy lived; came with all that company of expert musicians, to give a concert. The boy's father, being the editor of the local newspaper, entertained this prodigious visitor. The boy sat and listened to him. Just a few words he spoke, in a quiet, reserved way; something about music, what it meant to life; something about music all new to his hearers.

The concert was in the afternoon. For fear he might lose a note or two, the boy was in his seat half an hour before the appointed time. Sixty-two men came out and quietly took their places. When the last man was seated, Theodore Thomas appeared at the lower right entrance of the stage, walked quickly to the leader's stand, seized his baton, raised both hands. Then the orchestra started upon the ethereal strains of the "Midsummer Night's Dream" overture, and at least one listener seemed to float up, and be lost to all the world.

Fifty years slipped away from him sooner than the memory of that afternoon. The program, without ever looking at it again, he could always recall:

Overture to "Midsummer Night's Dream"........Mendelssohn
"Funeral March of a Marionette"................Gounod
Symphonic Poem, "Danse Macabre".............Saint-Saëns
"Träumerei" ....Schumann
"Invitation to the Dance" ....Weber-Berlioz
Hungarian Rhapsody No. 2.....................Liszt

The playing of the "Träumerei" seemed something unbelievable. Theodore Thomas had orchestrated the piano score and united with it as a trio the Schumann "Romanza." Only the strings were used without the basses. At the end, the beautiful melody grew softer and softer, slowly fading until it seemed to be drifting in the air, first into Shelley's shadow of all sounds, then the daintiest gossamer and filament of elusive and faëry music, something never made by human hands or human means, floating away into the distance and slightly luminous; one could see it as one heard it. Then it grew fainter, and still slowly fainter as it rose—fainter—fainter—at last, with all intension, rapt, leaning forward, the listeners were following it. Of a sudden they awoke to the fact that Mr. Thomas had laid down his baton and there was no sound. For the last minute there had been none. The violinists had continued to move their bows without touching the strings, but so strong was the spell, these thralls had believed they still heard that marvelous elfin melody. A strange gasping noise arose as two thousand people suddenly recovered their breath and consciousness, and then looked at one another to see if all this were real.

Evidence still exists that to all impressionable persons hearing that concert, life was never the same afterward. It was not alone that they had heard something beautiful; there had been shown to them things and potentialities they had never suspected. So then there really existed as a fact, and not as something heard of and unattainable, this world of beauty, wholly apart from everyday experiences. Anybody could go into it at any time; the twofold world of memory and sweet sound. The door was open; this man had opened it.

Not only music had a new meaning; so had everything else that was beautiful. The place was on the shore of the Mississippi River. There was a spot where one could stand and look from the green curve of one great bluff, far over to the green curve of the other great bluff, with the river between and below, bordered with towns and meadow. It was a beautiful sight. The boy with careless glance had seen it a thousand times and never once noted it, seeing with physical, not the mental eye. The first time after that concert that he came face to face with this great scene, there popped into his mind the opening bars of the Mendelssohn overture:

The two went together. For the first time he perceived that the prospect had beauty. Music had opened that door, also. For the first time he laid hold, however vaguely, of some notion that everything beautiful has its normal musical chord, and the chord of the thing beautiful makes the beauty real.

There were ancient, stately woods along the river bluffs. The first time now that he went into them, the summer leaves on the trees were all going:

Sunday morning at church the voluntary, not essentially different from other voluntaries, started off a phrase of the Rhapsody and kept it going all day through one poor noddle, inexpressibly happy.[1]

In the town where he went to a preparatory school hung Bierstadt's Valley of the Yosemite. The addlepate had seen it before and marked it not except as something big. Now the first time he looked at it, the "Träumerei" came back:

[1]Finck relates a similar experience after the first time he heard "Tristan und Isolde." See *Chopin and Other Musical Essays*, p. 157. It is doubtless among our common sensations, only we do not often speak of it.

Afterward, he never looked upon any prospect of distant and beautiful mountains without hearing the same air.

First and last, in one way or another, the whole town where he lived came to be affected. It had always been notable among its compeers for a musical interest, due to the happy possession of a large German element that in an Anglo-Saxon wilderness insisted upon music as the food of veritable life if not of love. To the rest of the population, this had been an occasion for mirth, slightly tinged with scorn. In especial, one man had striven to instruct Philistines for their own good. Jacob Strasser was his name, long gone to his reward, which ought to be rich, for rich was his deserving. The Hans Balatka of this community, he had labored with the zeal and sometimes, I think, with the tortures of the early martyrs to keep open the musical sanctuary. By his own wit and energy he held together an orchestra of enthusiastic amateurs among his countrymen, an orchestra respectable in size and admirable in performance. He led a brass band. He organized and kept life in a quartette for chamber music, the De Beriot Quartette, keen Dr. Braünlich playing the violoncello and putting all his soul into its strains. He gave Sunday night concerts, he led the orchestra at the German theatre. A kind of amiable lunatic he had seemed to the other end of the town. Now it dawned there that he might be the sanest man of all, since what he had been trying to teach was shown to be everlasting truth; music was indeed the best thing in the world and its own exceeding rich reward, as he had set forth. Dr. Braünlich and his violoncello took on a new and interesting significance. Before, the two had seemed an inexplicable dumb show, and small boys used to throw cabbage stalks at the excellent doctor's sign.

To the soil that these worthy men had plowed and harrowed came Theodore Thomas to plant.

In later years, he returned to water and to nourish. Musical interest passed out of the bounds of "Dutchtown" where before it had maintained an almost exclusive habitat. Slowly it grew and multiplied and at last flowered into one of those grand orchestras that have so honorable a place in the country's musical history, an orchestra of high and sustained excellence, giving regular seasons of concerts, playing admirably. Yes: and who led it and made it admirable? A masterly musician that among the first violins had sat for years under the baton, instruction, and inspiration of Theodore Thomas.

Direct cause; direct effect.

This is the story of one community. As we shall see now, he visited hundreds of communities as he visited this. He visited none without planting to some such growth.

CHAPTER II

The Boy Violinist

THE metropolitan city of New York in the year 1845 seems to have presented to the visitor from foreign parts many aspects likely to astonish him. By all accounts it must have been fairly raw and dreadful, sprawling on either side of Broadway three miles from the Battery to a country lane; rowdy, bustling, two-storied, two-fisted, unkempt and unashamed, full of business, full of self-conceit, and to all the arts harder than granite. Chroniclers came, verjuiced like Dickens, vitriolic like Mrs. Trollope, observed all this with a spiteful pleasure, and went away to write of it immortal scorn. Dickens, who had arrived in 1843, found the city to abound in "leprous houses," standing in "lanes and alleys paved with mud knee deep." In the most pretentious thoroughfares ran the pigs in droves, preying upon garbage. They were the only scavengers, Dickens averred, and specially bred to dispose quickly of potato rind and other midden.[1] He is never done gaping at them.

"Once more in Broadway!" he writes. "We are going to cross here. Take care of the pigs! Two portly sows are trotting up behind this carriage and a select party of half-a-dozen gentlemen hogs have just now turned the corner." Their "scanty brown backs" seem to him "like the lids of old horsehair trunks" and he marvels at their long gaunt legs. "At this hour," he says, still of Broadway, "just as evening is closing in, you will see them roaming toward bed by the scores, eating

---

[1] *American Notes for General Circulation*, Chap. VI.

7

their way to the last, perfect self-possession and self-reliance and immovable composure being their foremost attributes."[1]

All the crudity of a mining camp was here, but none of a mining camp's romance and saving grace in the spirit adventurous. Rational amusements and entertainments Dickens found to be in a state of sad neglect. Three principal theaters, so far as he could see, composed the city's effort in dramatic and musical art. Two of these, the Park and the Bowery, were "large and handsome" but generally deserted. There was a small theater, called Niblo's, "with gardens and open-air amusements attached; but it was not exempt from the general depression under which Theatrical Property, or what is humorously called by that name, unfortunately labors."[2]

Into this mad place immigrants were thronging in great numbers. *Martin Chuzzlewit*, if anyone now remembers it, contains vivid pictures of the sufferings they endured on the passage and the horrors that attended their landing in the new country. It was probably the last place in the civilized circuit a musician of delicate nerves and perceptions would select for a career, but among the immigrants in that very year of 1845 came from Europe in a sailing vessel six weeks upon the voyage, such a visitor with such a purpose, and brought with him his large family.

Johann August Thomas was his name; the town of Esens, capital of the great marshy East Friesland province of Northwest Germany, the place whence he had come so far. In Esens

---

[1]The pigs seem to have drawn the comment of every visitor. Mrs. Trollope (*Domestic Manners of the Americans*, Chap. IX), says of them in Cincinnati:
"But the annoyance came nearer than this; if I determined upon a walk up Main Street, the chances were five hundred to one against my reaching the shady side without brushing by a snout fresh dripping from the kennel."

[2]Indeed, all amusements seemed strangely to languish at this period. Mrs. Trollope wrote of the Cincinnatians: "I never saw any people who appeared to live so without amusement. Billiards are forbidden by law; so are cards. To sell a pack of cards in Ohio subjects the seller to a penalty of fifty dollars. They have no concerts, they have no dance parties." (Chap. VIII.) Of the theater she said that "either for economy or distaste, it is very poorly attended."

he had been a musician of ability and some renown. He had even been Stadtpfeifer, a point in his history worth a moment's noting.

Stadtpfeifer—that was a post of ancient origin having veritable honor in Germany's old-time musical world; eminent men had been glad to hold it. Johann Ambrosius Bach, father of Johann Sebastian, was Stadtpfeifer of Eisenbach, and his twin brother, Stadtpfeifer of Arnstad.[1] A chief town musician, selected and paid by the municipality, was the meaning of the word then. The Stadtpfeifer's job was to furnish music for state occasions and to lead the town band. Later it shifted more and more into band leading. Finally, as the dukes disappeared and state occasions lessened, it fell upon the leading of one particular kind of band.

Before Bismarck blighted Europe with his devilish device of universal and compulsory military training, the Schützen Corps was a famous institution throughout Germany. It was voluntary and comparatively innocent; it took people out into the open to shoot merrily at wooden and woundless targets. Besides its zestful patriotic note, it appealed to local pride and to the competitive fervor. Every Schützen Corps, to be up to date and in the best form, must march to the shooting place headed by a brass band. Every band must have a leader, and in most places this honor fell to the Stadtpfeifer, recipient of an amazingly small stipend from the municipality and performer in the band upon some instrument, say the E flat cornet.

In Esens, Johann August Thomas, Stadtpfeifer, leader of the Schützen Corps band, performer on the cornet, lived in a small house in the Lilienstrasse. This is about all the world is likely to know authentically about him and his story, because in 1860 a fire destroyed all the town records, and otherwise in Esens the traditions of 1835 are fairly extinct. He had to wife the daughter

---

[1]Forkel's *Life of John Sebastian Bach*, Terry's Edition, p. 9. These were the famous twins that nobody could tell apart.

of a physician in the good old university town of Göttingen[1] a woman of culture and of a notably sweet and gentle disposition, so that the fame of her goodness long lingered after her. In Esens to-day the opinion will be freely offered to one making inquiries that her husband must have been an outsider, for Thomas is not a Friesland name. In this instance opinion is singularly correct; he came from Erfurt in Thuringen, where his father had been a bookseller. In the little Lilienstrasse house, now destroyed, his first child, a son, was born October 11, 1835, and laden with the names of Christian Friedrich Theodore Thomas.

It is a sleepy old town, Esens, but nice enough; dozing about two miles from the North Sea in a country as flat as a board and not much more interesting, bitterly cold throughout a long winter and hardly thawing out in midsummer. It has about three thousand inhabitants and no more kudos for music than hundreds of other towns in Germany, all silent in the trump of fame; it is no Baireuth and no Weimar. Here Stadtpfeifer Thomas seems to have thought that with the blessing of God, Christian Friedrich Theodore might make a good village physician and be like his grandfather.

The first shadow upon this fair hope came when the boy was two years old and demanded a violin for a plaything. There is an ancient and highly libelous story that at this age every Hungarian father puts before his child a watch and a fiddle and according as choice is indicated knows whether his offspring is destined to be a musician or only a bandit. The elder Thomas must have known this story well and thought he heard the voice of fate when Christian Friedrich Theodore raised his for a violin. One was found in the town, a derelict from an attic, and when it was strung, the child began to make noises on it.

In the household, expectation now looked to see this the end

---

[1] *Theodore Thomas: A Musical Autobiography*, edited by George P. Upton, pp. 19–20. *Memoirs of Theodore Thomas*, by Rose Fay Thomas, p. 1.

of the matter. On the contrary, the boy next insisted that he be taught to play. To keep him still, Papa gave him a few lessons. It appears that in a few weeks the infant was playing all over the place. He grew up with a violin in one hand and a bow in the other. Music he could read before print. When he was five he was playing at sight; at seven the members of the Schützen Corps band used on wagers to try to put before him music that he could not play offhand. One such piece was an "Air Varié" by De Beriot.[1]

When all allowance has been made for the amiable excesses of tradition and the magnifying halo of years, the fact stands out clear enough that this was one of those strange unaccountable beings born into the world already possessed of a facility full fledged that others must toil years to attain. The psychology of such a thing seems worth attention. Observe then. This boy said long afterward that when he was being taught anything of music, he seemed to be recalling something he had known before rather than acquiring anything new.[2] He never had to exert himself to master a phrase; it came to him intuitively. When he was seven he was a child wonder, starred in concerts through his native Friesland and beyond. Once he played before the King of Hanover,[3] when the first clear indication of destiny seems now to have been the fact that he escaped that aged potentate's purpose to make him of the royal household.[4]

He was mad for music and indifferent to everything else, including the school to which he was early sent in the old red brick building back of the Lutheran church. Nicholas Hickens, the oldest man in Esens, long afterward recalled that Christian

[1]Autobiography, p. 20; Mrs. Thomas, p. 2.
[2]Mrs. Thomas, p. 4.
[3]Ibid.
[4]Stephen Fiske says of the Hanover performance, "The audience laughed as he came forward, for his fiddle was nearly as large as himself, but they laughed no longer when the little Theodore began to play." (Offhand Portraits, p. 314.) He adds that "the little Theodore became a feature of the Hanover concerts."

Friedrich Theodore was reputed to be a poor scholar but an imp for playing tricks and always in trouble. His copybook he filled with bars of music and his idea of doing sums on his slate was to demonstrate how many notes could be put into a measure of $\frac{3}{8}$ tim᷄ Brothers and sisters came in the Thomas house, and not one of them indicated unusual capacity for music or strong interest in it. But this is a phenomenon with analogues; Shakespeare had a brother, although the world knows not the fact, and Napoleon a fraternal handful the world has been glad to forget.

The earnings of a Stadtpfeifer in Esens, though eked out with fees for teaching and with such thalers as the young violinist earned, proved all too slender for this increasing family. At last, sheer want drove it to this desperate adventure upon the high seas, followed by the casting of a musician upon a strand uncouth and unmelodious, and then a grim struggle with the wolf.

If the father had been a carpenter, a blacksmith, or a good reliable barkeeper, all this would have been different. New York in 1845, knowing as little about music as Kairouan and caring somewhat less, offered to the Thomas tribe nothing exhilarating. There was no chance for the young violinist to get the education he lacked; he must use all his time to gain the money whereby the family might live and not starve. He had long before lightened his burden for the race by casting off superfluous nomenclature; from the age of seven he had been known as merely Theodore Thomas. Sometimes by this name, sometimes as "Master T. T.," more often unheralded and quite unknown, a broth of a boy, undersized even for his young years, he played in concerts, at dances, balls, weddings, shows, wherever he could get hiring and a piece of coin. Once, when he was particularly hard pressed, he took his violin under his coat, went into a barroom, played, and passed around the hat.[1]

[1]Autobiography, p. 26; Mrs. Thomas, p. 6.

LILIENSTRASSE, ESENS
Where Theodore Thomas was born

THE OLD SQUARE, ESENS

Where the Stadtpfeiffer often led the town band

Other musicians much more eminent than he were obliged to beat the drum in a parading band that they might keep out of the poorhouse. The dances were his chief source of revenue; the Dodworths playing the fairy godmother's part. Harvey B. Dodworth, who discoursed sweetly upon the cornet and furnished music for innumerable dances, was the leader of this interesting group. He seems to have formed a liking for the queer little bright-eyed restless boy from North Germany, and to have provided him with many chances to earn half dollars by playing the violin all night at hops.[1]

It was catch-as-catch-can then for any man that sought to make his living by music. Brass bands were in some demand, for it was the age of political military parading; but orchestral music left New York cold indeed. The Philharmonic Society, destined to play so noble a part in the development of metropolitan culture, had been launched three years before the arrival of the Thomas family, but it was a feeble and largely futile venture, meaning nothing in the city's young life. Yet in one aspect, the story was otherwise. Every theater had its orchestra for overtures and incidental accompaniment, and in the opinion of one competent judge they played better music than the theater orchestras of sixty years later.[2]

So, then, the first really coercive incident in the career of this boy was when he secured a place in one of these theater orchestras. He had a mind that hungered and thirsted for knowledge and yet by the stern exigencies of his life was deprived of every chance of schooling. His formal education might have gone as far as what would now be called the fifth grade. Providentially, the lack was in a way supplied. The theater in which he found employment, occupying a long vanished site west in Spring Street, was devoted largely to the plays of Shakespeare. In those days the theater orchestra sat where it could see the play,

---

[1]Autobiography, p. 26.
[2]*Ibid.*, p. 21.

or most of it. There Theodore Thomas saw Edwin Booth's father in the *Merchant of Venice* and so was introduced to Shakespeare.[1] He was a singularly impressionable youth; the power and beauty of the lines laid hold upon him. With agile readiness he had learned to read the new tongue before he had been a month in the strange land. He now began to study Shakespeare and so formed a predilection and habit that were lifelong upon him. After three years of this, his father enlisted in the United States navy as a musician, becoming the first horn player in the navy band at Portsmouth, Virginia. He obtained in the brass choir a place for his son, and for a year the two, side by side, played morning and night on the old man-of-war *Pennsylvania*.

The next year the family economics bettered. Theodore's help was no longer indispensable; father and son acquired their discharges from the navy, and the son started upon that strange solitary tour of the remote corners of the country that is so striking a revelation of his character. Scarcely fifteen years old, still a stranger to everything except New York and Portsmouth, he went forth as a violin virtuoso, without accompanist, backer, or guide, and for all of a year traveled from town to town, giving public performances for what money he could take in at the door of hotel dining room or public hall. His posters he made himself with a pen, announcing a coming concert by "Master T. T."[2] He was his own manager, ticket collector, and press agent. Often he traveled on horseback from town to town —preferably at night and alone!

Two things are to be noted. He seems to have played always good music at these affairs; much of it music ahead of the taste of his hearers. Second, his travels gave him an intimate knowledge of the real America, such as he could never have obtained by any length of residence in New York, or by any study. Al-

[1]Autobiography, p. 21.
[2]Autobiography, p. 22; Mrs. Thomas, p. 7.

ways thereafter he knew the American people because he had been down close to their hearthstones and habits.

He came back to New York the next year, 1850, to find the musical situation much changed. A demand for good music, chiefly as manifested in operas, was beginning to appear. A German theater had been opened; young Thomas achieved an engagement there to play among its violins. The plays of Goethe, Schiller, and Lessing[1] were the standard favorites at this house, and sitting there in the little string choir he had his second great educational impulse. To Shakespeare he added the great German classics.

It is plain enough now that the unusual gifts with which he started were many sided. He had more than the exclusive musician's mind; he had an inborn and genuine taste for culture and for all art. Goethe, Schiller, and Lessing reacted upon him with a desire for more reading. A library became his schoolhouse, then and afterward. To overcome by voluntary application the lack of elementary training is rare. He did it so well that in early manhood he had become notably well read, had taken on unconsciously that manner of speech belonging of right to the man made full by reading, and came finally to create a common impression that he must have been college bred. Better than all this, he endowed himself with an excellent, terse, and ready American style; he, the immigrant boy that had landed in New York without a word of the vernacular.

For two or three years after his return from his concert tour, he lived in New York wholly his own master while still in his teens. Father and mother had long given over the attempt to manage so untamable a spirit. He contributed to the family support but was little at home. He made his own way, ruled his own life, sought adventure and found it,[2] and seems to have had such excess of vitality and of animal spirits that the ordi-

---

[1]Mrs. Thomas, p. 9.
[2]*Ibid.*, p. 15.

nary demands of sleep and rest meant nothing to him. He went to bed late, if at all, arose early, and between times was ceaselessly active. He did everything at a tension, practised furiously, read laboriously, took every engagement he could find, and amused himself with the wild pranks of the overvitalized.

It is to be observed that from the beginning he had cherished an ambition: he wished to be the world's greatest violin player, and this goal he seems to have kept in sight, however florid his days and nights. In after years, he was wont to refer with solemn head-shakings to the wild years of his youth in New York. It appears that, in fact, the pace he traveled was nothing wonderful. A boy, brim full of fun and left without control or guidance, nevertheless he had no taste for what is called dissipation, and he kept unsullied a fine ideal of moral cleanliness. He himself admitted that he never did anything he was ashamed to have his own boys know.[1] He thought he held to his art certain relationships important enough to shut the door on vice. According to his observation, any artist that soiled his soul with licentiousness was impairing his mastery over the best of his powers of expression.

"A musician must keep his heart pure and his mind clean," said he, "if he wishes to elevate instead of debasing his art."

He thought that to see a vulgar or licentious play was to affect evilly all his playing the next time he appeared with his violin. He looked upon music as the noblest expression of the noblest emotions of the human soul and could not see how a man could effectively give himself to that expression one hour and to sensuality the next. I am speaking now of his creed as he developed it with maturity; but even in youth he seems to have felt enough of this to have an anchorage in it.

He could never have allowed his pranks to interfere with his work, for he gained steadily in reputation; the time was close at

---

[1]Mrs. Thomas, p. 16.

hand when he should have his due place in the sun of the public prints. In 1851 he was made one of the first violins of the Italian Opera Company (for Italian Opera had come to the great American desert and was doing rather well there); one of the first violins at the ripe age of sixteen years and sitting above many bald veterans. It was a company that had good singers, and while he was playing for them Thomas was struck with a thought that afterward profited him. Here was this purpose of his to be a great violinist, the greatest of the age. He noticed the powerful effects produced by the best singers when their voices were the mellowest and most sympathetic. It occurred to him that it might be possible to produce upon the violin similar sounds with similar effects, although he had never heard them.[1] He experimented and practised to this end until he learned how to duplicate the tender and searching vibrations of the human voice in its deepest emotions. This was the quality that, joined to his precision and his singularly conscientious musicianship, seems to have accounted for the success that began early to be authentic.

As to precision, however erratic about the dinner hour, he was in music as meticulous as the Strasbourg clock; and as to musicianship, we are to remember the strange fact that, violin virtuoso and all, he had little real instruction but his own. He had studied harmony with one man and counterpoint and fugue with another,[2] but of the patient, thorough, long-continued drilling that now the conservatories so happily afford he was always destitute.[3] Yet, so largely self-taught, he was evidently well taught; he amply justified the hope of fame that lightened before him.

Abundant testimony exists to his solid attainments when he

---

[1]Mrs. Thomas, p. 10.

[2]Rudolph Swillinger for harmony; William Meyerhofer, an organist, for counterpoint. See Autobiography, p. 45.

[3]See *American History and Encyclopedia of Music*, Vol. 88, article on Theodore Thomas.

was still a youth. In 1852 he was one of the star performers at Dodworth's "Grand Music Festival," Metropolitan Hall,[1] where he played as a solo Ernst's Theme and Variations from "Otello." "Master Thomas," the program called him; it was February 20 and he was sixteen years old. On April 26 of that year he appeared at the Apollo Saloon as a soloist in a benefit concert, when he was shrinkingly announced as "Master Theodore Thomas, probably the most extraordinary violinist in the world of his age." On this occasion he played Lipinski's "Concerto Militaire," and Ernst's "Carnival of Venice." He was often a soloist at the Sunday night concerts given at the German Theater. Before long the critics that wrote of these began to note wonderingly the unusual quality of his tone.

About this time there came to America an undeserved benefaction in the person of Karl Eckert, whom Thomas afterward referred to as "the only really fully equipped and satisfactory conductor that visited this country during that period."[2] In the opera orchestra of this talented man, Thomas became one of the first violinists. His unusual quality won the early attention of the commander, who asked him to become principal of the second violin choir. The boy consented without a suspicion that he was taking the first step in his real career. As principal of the second violins, he had a responsible executive post; he was

---

[1]Metropolitan Hall, where he appeared on this occasion and many times thereafter, was a place of unusual historical interest. It was originally called Tripler Hall—why Tripler, I do not know. Ernest Harvier writes of it:

"Tripler Hall was in Broadway nearly opposite Bond Street, and was built especially for Jenny Lind's début. It was not finished in time and so the sweet singer made her début at Castle Garden. Tripler Hall was the place of the first public appearance of Adelina Patti. It was burned in January, 1855, was rebuilt and reopened in September of the same year. It was the scene of Rachel's first appearance in America. Later it was refitted and reopened as Laura Keene's Varieties and still later was called Burton's Theater after W. E. Burton, the comedian. Later it was known as the Winter Garden, and in August, 1864, it passed into the control of Edwin Booth, his brother-in-law, John S. Clarke, and William Stuart, Booth's manager. A performance there of *Julius Cæsar* in November, 1864, included in its cast Junius Brutus Booth, Edwin Booth, and John Wilkes Booth. It was at this house that the famous one-hundred-night run of *Hamlet* took place. On March 23, 1867, it was destroyed by fire."

[2]Autobiography, p. 29.

virtually conductor of that part of the band. Soon afterward, he being then but seventeen years old, he was made concert master of the orchestra and actual working head of the whole body of instrumentalists; sure proof that he had developed the traits of command. Luigi Arditi was the conductor then. Everything about the daily management of the orchestra, even to the engaging of players and the keeping of them in order, he left to this smooth-cheeked boy.

The next year, 1853, vaulting ambition had a new and still more profitable experience.

The means chosen to its peculiar ends by Destiny or Fate or Overruling Providence, or whatever else directs mortal affairs, must often cause to the philosophical an endless amazement. For some years European music had been adorned with a singular creature named Louis Antoine Jullien, usually described as a musical lunatic and long afterward by Thomas as "the musical charlatan of all ages."[1] He was conductor of an orchestra, so to call it. At least, he had a large company of musicians known collectively by that name and performed with them various compositions of repute, and others. If we may trust the records, the people came not to hear these productions but to watch his gyrations, which were many and extraordinary. He dressed extravagantly and led the performance in a kind of dance. Everybody in passing used to take a hack at Jullien, his ruffles, his theatrics and his vanities, but despite them all he was a chosen instrument.[2]

He drew the people to see his amazing gymnastics, and when he had them in hand, fed them certain dosages of music they would otherwise have shunned like the plague.

Whether this was his deliberate design or something thrust

---

[1]Autobiography, p. 26.

[2]Poor Jullien died in a madhouse in 1860. It is charitable to think that his mind had been unhinged years before. But the history of music will never be done telling of his eccentricities. Not without reason. When he played "The Firemen's Quadrille" at the old Crystal Palace, Bryant Square, he set fire to the roof as a piece of realism.

upon him is among the mysteries that will never be solved. The Malvolio of Music favored New York with his presence in 1853–1854 and naturally picked Young Prodigy to play in his first violin choir. All his life, Theodore Thomas had an innate and unconquerable horror of anything savoring of sham, and now regarded with disgust this affectioned man under whose baton he must play. Yet in a momentous way the engagement shaped his life.

For the first time, the symphony was brought home to him.

The more he considered this supreme triumph of human art and intellect, the more he felt moved to fall down and worship it. He saw what it was even in the hands of a grotesque person like Jullien; he had marvelous visions of what it might be if played with feeling and insight. It seemed to him that here was the answer to the impatient quest of the soul of man, if man would only stop to listen to it, for here were strength, repose, and the direct line of connection with the power that wields the world with never wearied love. Jullien played an intolerable deal of trash to one halfpenny worth of symphony, but even on such terms the boy was glad of the bargain.

At that time the only thing in America that could be called a real orchestra[1] was still the Philharmonic, and in that case the application was not without violence. The Philharmonic was a voluntary and coöperative association of players that a few times in a year (never more than five) offered to a reluctant public the performance of works more or less classical. It was badly supported, but like Johnson's dog on its hind legs the wonder was that it was done at all. The players were members of the society and were paid *pro rata* from the receipts, if any; an arrangement that made the expenses light and was possible because all the players had other occupations, the Philharmonic being to them but an amiable diversion. Still, whatsoever the

---

[1]George P. Upton, *Reminiscence and Appreciation* (part of the Thomas Autobiography), p. 126.

defects, it represented a desire for things worthy, it had ideals, and it kept the better musical taste from going atrophied. In 1854 it elected Theodore Thomas to membership; thereafter he played in its concerts.

Among the apostolic lights of American music, and one without discount, is William Mason, the first noted American pianist. In 1855 he thought the time had come to venture in New York upon chamber music of a high grade and was bent upon forming a string quartette to play with himself as pianist. He chose Theodore Thomas to be his first violin, Thomas being then twenty years old. Mason was more than a good musician; he was a good man. Thomas had a predilection for good men; he liked their society, he liked to talk with them even when they were not musicians. He took instinctively to Mason, and they became lifelong and intimate friends. The conjunction was invaluable to the younger man. Mason, who could not teach him anything about music, in other ways put forth an influence steadying and salutary. By the sheer force of his own genius, Thomas became at once the leader and dominating power of the Quartette and it was his insatiable passion for perfection that made the venture so great an artistic success that afterward Thomas himself, a severe self-critic, admitted it to have been the corner stone of American music. The Mason-Thomas Quartette lasted thirteen years and attained to an extraordinary fame both in this country and abroad.[1] To this the programs, always made by Thomas, contributed much, for the numbers were chosen with a skill that seems now inspired. Beginning with a certain admixture of things popular, they were gradually carried to higher levels until no quartette in the world played a better grade of music.[2]

[1]They seem to have been floated on a shoe string. Once Mason and Thomas must themselves distribute the handbills in the streets.

[2]"The prevailing idea of the period was that no musical entertainment could be enjoyed by the public without some singing. We quickly got over that notion, and thenceforth, with rare exceptions, our programs were confined to instrumental music." (Mason, *Memoirs of a Musical Life*, p. 195.)

Meantime, he was laboring with tireless zeal to perfect himself in his chosen calling of a violin virtuoso. His reputation seemed to have won to the solidest foundations. He was hailed not only in New York but in other cities he visited, westward even to Chicago, as the rising hope of music. Critics dwelling upon the sincerity and thoroughness of his work and the infinite purity of his tone, said that here at last was art's true missionary. In 1859 one of them called him "America's most accomplished violinist." With reason he thought the goal he was aiming at was almost in sight.

Even then he had begun to show the character traits that afterward started so many discussions and caused perturbation to so many persons, chiefly charlatans. Merit was everything with him. When he was on an early tour with Mme La Grange he undertook, as concert master of the little orchestra she carried, to hire and control the men. The excellent Madame had a valet that she thought might as well be carried on the payroll of the enterprise, perhaps to the relief of her private exchequer. She asked Thomas to place him among the members of the orchestra.

Thomas refused. The man was not good enough.

The lady insisted; prima donna, and all that. The Thomasian obstinacy, afterward celebrated in story if not in song, came now into play.

"Have I to get down upon my knees and beg you?" asks Beauty, horribly incensed.

"I don't care whether you kneel or not," says the imperturbable Thomas. "I should think it would be more convenient to stand. But your man can't play and that's the end of it."

That night Thomas must do an obbligato to one of her songs. When the entertainment was over, Mme La Grange sought him out and said:

"You were real mean to me to-day, but you played like a god."[1]

_____

[1] Upton, _Reminiscence and Appreciation_, pp. 205–206.

The virtue had an old Roman complexion. Thomas was extremely fond of his father, whom he continued to help. He might have provided a place in the orchestra for the old gentleman, who could still play the cornet tolerably well. The son would do nothing of the kind. Tolerably well was not well enough.

Not much is known of his life in the five years from 1855 to 1860[1] except that he was wholly devoted to his ambition and allowed nothing to interfere with his study. He seems to have continued with an inexplicable enthusiasm to divide his time between studying music and reading good literature. He liked history, Shakespeare, and, strange to say, philosophy. We usually hold, and rightly enough, that music demands so much of its practitioners they can have no possible time for other main interests. It was not so here.[2] Music with Thomas overspired all other concerns of life but did not erase them. Any topic of reasonable appeal to the sane was within his scope. He was so many sided that he knew well enough what was going on in the world; nothing human was alien to him. He taught himself so well that men like William Mason, highly educated, long trained at home and abroad, felt in him a peer and were glad and proud of him. That early conquest of terse, expressive American speech, standing him so well in hand, was not strange in him; he had become so thoroughly Americanized he is a citable illustration of the efficacy of the melting pot. He took his adopted country not as a foster mother but as the reality of his passionate attachment. I have known many Americans, but few of a patriotism so lofty and sincere as his. The accident of birth was to him nothing. Americanism was not geographical; it was a matter of mind and spirit. Possibly his service on the man-of-war had something to do with this, but I think it more likely to have sprung from his extensive

[1]He was always about himself singularly uncommunicative, and as he was not yet sufficiently eminent to be much in the public prints, there are few sources of knowledge about him in this period.

[2]Upton, *Musical Memoirs*, p. 187, describes Thomas's unusual cultural attainments.

studies in history; for if I understood him aright, his was faith in the American destiny.[1]

Some men, if we believe tradition and biography, choose out their careers and batter their way upon selected trails; but all that I have known personally have had opportunity thrust upon them. Up to December 7, 1860, Theodore Thomas never had a thought of another métier than that of violinist and composer, and then, of a sudden, Fate whirled him into something wholly different. He was living in East Twelfth Street; the old Academy of Music, where the operas were given, was at Fourteenth Street and Irving Place. On that night the opera announced was "The Jewess," by Halévy. Thomas, after rehearsing the Mason-Thomas team, had settled himself for an evening's rest when a messenger came in haste to tell him that Carl Anschütz, leader of the opera, had been taken suddenly ill. The audience was all in place and impatient, but the curtain could not rise because there was no conductor. Would Thomas come and take charge?

It was a remarkable draft to make upon a man twenty-five

---

[1]Conf. also Upton, *Reminiscence and Appreciation*, p. 254.

In a collection of old programs of this period I find one of an interesting event in Philadelphia, which I will annex. "Lord Renfrew" is the name under which the heir to the British throne, afterward Edward VII, toured this country in 1860. In those days "leader" on a program meant concert master, or first violinist.

"Philadelphia. American Academy of Music. Grand Gala Night!

"In honor of Lord Renfrew by the Ullman and Strakosch celebrated Italian Opera Company, Wednesday, October 10, 1860, under the supervision of the Committee of Arrangements, when the following operatic entertainment will be presented in accordance with the wishes of Lord Renfrew, to whom the repertoire was submitted for selection, viz.,

"Flotow's Grand Opera of 'Martha' and the first act of Verdi's Opera 'La Traviata.'

"The performance will commence precisely at 8 o'clock with the English national anthem, God save the Queen, followed by Flotow's chef-d'œuvre.

"Lady Henrietta	Miss Adelina Patti
"Nancy	Signora Fanny Natali
"Lional	Signor Brignoli
"Plunkett (his original rôle)	Herr Carl Formes

"Musical director and conductor, 'Martha,' Max Maretzeck; leader, Theodore Thomas.

"'La Traviata,' musical director and conductor, Signor Muzio; leader, Theodore Thomas."

years old, almost inexperienced as a conductor, who had never heard "The Jewess" and was unfamiliar with the score. He debated with himself for a few minutes and then, more on an indefinable impulse than on reason, he said, "I'll do it," and slipped into his evening clothes. Twenty minutes later he raised his baton and started to conduct the performance of an opera all new to him. Incredible, you say. I know it; but there is the record. William Mason tells the whole story in his book, *Memories of a Musical Life*,[1] and other competent authority supports him. In *Dwight's Journal of Music*, for instance, the musical newspaper of that day. Its account says Thomas wielded the baton rather nervously, but well. It must have been well, for at once he was made permanent conductor. Some trouble was brewing in the company. Anschütz retired[2] or was bowed out and from that night Thomas had his place.[3]

He had never expected to be a conductor. "I avoided it as long as I could," he says, "for I wished all my time for study."[4] But the balance had already turned. As he went farther into the new work, he found that he liked it. Instead of one instrument on which to express his ideas, he had now forty or fifty. It was exhilarating; soon it became fascinating. So much could be done by combining different sound values! Naturally, the opera soon seemed to him a limited field. He remembered Jullien

---

[1]Mason (p. 200) tells it much better than I, because he was under the belief that this was the first time Thomas ever conducted an opera; hence an entrance upon the conducting stage, strange and dramatic. Among the old programs preserved in the Newberry Library in Chicago, is one of the Academy of Music, New York, for Wednesday evening, April 29, 1859, announcing the "last night of Mme Gazzanigo in Bonizeti's "La Favorita," Conductor, Theo. Thomas. At the side is penciled in Mr. Thomas's handwriting, "First time on programme."

[2]Upton, p. 124.

[3]The next night Thomas conducted "Stradella," with Fabbri, Stigelli, and Carl Formes in the cast.

[4]Autobiography, p. 49. Thomas says that Anschütz was "a kindly, congenial and most generous man," and adds, "I was gradually drawn into the conductor's chair by his illness." All the kindness could hardly have been on Anschütz's part. Two stories were afterward related about his failure to appear for "The Jewess." One was that he had refused to conduct until he should be paid and the other that his sudden absence was due more to his habits than his health. Thomas does not mention either.

and the symphonies, and eighteen months after that evening at the Academy of Music he announced his first orchestral concert, Irving Hall, May 13, 1862.

The conversion in him had been complete. He had come to renounce all his cherished plans of a virtuoso's career, for he had resolved to make the cultivation of musical taste in America his life work.

CHAPTER III

"Giants, Dwarfs and the Like"

SUPERFICIALLY, this was a task to daunt the stoutest heart. The New York of 1862 was not the New York of 1845, that is true enough; it had become citified to the extent of banishing the pigs and of sprucing its looks. But the deliberate judgment of many a foreign visitor[1] condemned it to a hopeless barbarism about music. The only question in the minds of these judicious critics was whether the Esquimaux had better musical taste than the New Yorkers. Joseph Gungl, who in 1849 brought hither a band of German musicians, went back to his native land and voted in favor of the Esquimaux on the charitable ground that he did not know them. Many a combination of foreign artists landed with high hopes, toured the country, and had to be helped from the financial reefs, or stayed upon them, as might be. The loud complaints of such castaways added nothing to the glamor of art life in America.

Extant records seem mostly on the side of these acetic commentaries. Years afterward, George William Curtis,[2] who had been in a position to speak with feeling and knowledge, said that the average musical taste in 1862 reached its apogee in a rhapsody for tin pans known as "The Battle of Prague." To judge by the programs of notable musical events of the best order, other classics contested for this palm. "The Skinners' Quickstep" was highly esteemed, "The Firefly Polka" had

---

[1] "Often where a liberal spirit exists, and a wish to patronize the fine arts is expressed, it is joined to a profundity of ignorance on the subject almost inconceivable." (Mrs. Trollope, *Domestic Manners of the Americans*, Chap. XXX. She is writing here about New York.)

[2] Address at a banquet to Theodore Thomas at Delmonico's, New York, April 22, 1891.

enduring charms, but above all others appeared "The Firemen's Quadrille," of which the appeal was irresistible because, when properly performed, firemen appeared in full uniform and solemnly danced to the edification of all concerned.

From time to time the Dodworths, or some other hardworking, ill-paid, and hopeful heralds of light (but it was usually the Dodworths), would give in a place like Metropolitan Hall or the Apollo a recherché and fashionable entertainment in which music was craftily compounded with other delights more to the popular taste. There might be, for example, a literal invasion of the bones and tongs, or a gentleman that did the "pedestal clog." Sleight-of-hand performers and troupes of athletes from the Turn Verein were common additions to these reasonable feasts. A violin solo by Vieuxtemps would be followed by a performance on the concertina in which the gifted artist would show how it could be played with one hand, or while it was collapsing upon his eminent forehead or nose.[1]

The brass band, sometimes called a "promenade band," sometimes a "silver cornet band," was the illustrious climacteric at all these events, enlivening and always closing the program with appropriate selections, such as the "Katydid Polka" or the "Trip by Railroad,"[2] which seems to have been another notable favorite. About 1852, easily the most renowed musical attraction in New York was "Master Marsh, the infant drummer," who at the tender age of four years (according to the advertisements) performed upon two drums at once to the inexpressible joy of his listeners. In 1853 or 1854 an orchestral gem was produced in Boston called "The Railroad Galop," brightened by the appearance on the stage of a miniature imita-

---

[1]Upton mentions some of these programs in the Autobiography, but still better examples exist in such early periodicals as *The Message Bird.*

[2]The composer of "Pacific 231" might learn from these files that he was not the originator of the brilliant idea of imitating the cacophanies of a steam locomotive. Theodore Thomas's friend, Harvey B. Dodworth, preceded him in that delightful art by about seventy years.

THE STADTPFEIFFER OF ESENS
From a silhouette preserved in the Stadthaus

BROADWAY, NEW YORK.

NEW YORK AS HE FOUND IT

Broadway and Canal Street in 1845

tion locomotive that ran around in a circle with a tuft of black wool attached to its funnel to simulate smoke.[1] Joseph Gungl, in his acrid comments on the state of American culture, relates that at a concert given by a pianist, one Hatton, he saw that gifted performer appear with a string of sleigh bells fastened to his right leg. When he reached the proper place in the composition he was playing, which seems to have been something about a sleigh ride, he agitated his right leg violently while an assistant appeared with an instrument that made a noise like the cracking of a whip. "And this thing," says Gungl, scornfully, "aroused a storm of applause, which had no end until they had repeated it several times *da capo*."[2]

Gungl asserted that what were called "minstrels" were the truest exponents of musical development in America and that their vogue lay in their ability to blacken their faces, dance, and "jump about as if possessed." "Circus-riders, rope-dancers, beast-tamers, giants, dwarfs and the like are so numerous," he added, "that they may surely be reckoned as forming a large percentage of the population."

Other infant phenomena besides "Master Marsh," the virtuoso on two drums, were beloved in that period. One of them, "Little Mlle. Petit, aged nine," was able, we are informed, "to execute with her left hand the most difficult trills and runs." Another, one Adelina Patti, destined to larger fame, was singing in public at eight years selections from "Ernani" and "La Sonnambula." At Metropolitan Hall, in May, 1852, there was a concert to introduce to an appreciative public a new musical instrument called the "Plus-Harp-Guitar," or "Bewitcher,"[3] of which history seems to have omitted subsequent mention. In June, 1862, Mme Borchard, opera singer, appearing as *Lucretia* at the Academy of Music, had crinoline

---

[1]Reminiscences of William F. Apthorpe. It was the Germania, alas!
[2]Reprinted in *Dwight's Journal of Music*, December 18, 1852.
[3]*Dwight's*, May 22, 1852.

as part of her costume, and the opinion of the day seemed to think it was all right except that in some of the scenes the hoop skirts were awkward to manage.[1]

Some years before a season of Italian opera at the most fashionable theater of the city showed this result: Receipts, $51,780.89; expenditures, $81,054.98. Whereupon it is casually recorded that the prima donna, Signora Fanti, fled from the inhospitable city and the enterprise collapsed.[2]

On April 8, 1851, a notable musical event took place at Castle Garden when a gentleman named Knaebel offered a "Grand National Concert." "On which occasion," says the prospectus, "will be presented his Descriptive Battle Symphony entitled 'The Battle of Bunker Hill,' executed by two powerful orchestras, representing the American and British armies." Among the scenes, events, and emotions portrayed by the "powerful orchestras" were "1. General Putnam's March; 2. Digging fortifications after midnight (in the meantime the British cry, 'All's Well'); 3. Astonishment of the British discovering the fortifications; 4. First cannon by the British; 5. Signal to fire," and so on, culminating in a "combat between both orchestras on the National Airs,"[3] the whole affording not merely testimony but demonstration that even in America Program Music is older than the authorities have told us. It is odd to notice that Theodore Eisfeld conducted part of this concert, the part that contained the favorite composition of the day, "General Taylor's Funeral March." Tickets were fifty cents each, which indicated entertainment of massive proportions.

Another concert program of the period announces, between

---

[1] *Dwight's*, June 30, 1862.

[2] W. S. B. Mathews, *A Hundred Years of Music in America*, p. 54, and Ritter, *Music in America*, p. 205. Ritter points out that opera performances in those years were frequently given in a way we should deem slovenly and intolerable. In the best Italian opera that had visited New York there were no oboes in the orchestra and the oboe parts were played on clarinets.

[3] Advertisement in *The Journal of the Fine Arts*, April 1, 1851. This periodical of light was started August 1, 1849, as *The Message Bird, A Literary and Musical Journal*.

operatic arias, a "comic Duet and Dialogue, written for the occasion by Mr. J. T. Harris." But the truly Alpine heights of art's glories for that season were reached in a performance of Czerny's arrangement of the overture to "Semiramide," by sixteen pianists on eight pianos;[1] at which we are reasonably informed the town marveled.

Public manners, if we may trust contemporaneous comment, were of a piece with the foregoing disclosures and must have been delightfully unconventional. Mrs. Trollope avers that at one of the New York theaters she saw men sitting in the boxes without their coats, women nursing their babies, and the tobacco chewers manifesting their presence everywhere.[2] This was some years before the exploit of Mme Borchard, but not before the days when rival fire engine companies used to stop to fight on their way to a fire, and strangers never ventured into the Five Points region even at noon without a bodyguard.

At one of the annual concerts and suppers of the Euterpean Society of amateur instrumentalists, the program powerfully reminded the guests that life had its amenities. "No gentleman," it announced firmly, "will be permitted to wear his hat in the room during the evening or dance in his boots. Standing on the seats is strictly prohibited."[3] The custom of sitting in the front row of the balcony at a theater and resting the feet upon the top of the railing had been much condemned about this time. So recently as 1857, the Rev. Richard Storrs Willis, a brother of Nathaniel P. Willis, had preached against the bad manners of audiences at the Philharmonic performances. "The inattention and heedless talking and disturbances of but a limited number of our audience," he said, "are proving a serious annoyance." He must have been justified, for the Philharmonic had extracts from his sermon printed upon its programs.[4] A

[1]Krehbiel, *The Philharmonic Society: a Memorial*, p. 51.
[2]*Domestic Manners of the Americans*, Chap. XXX.
[3]Quoted by Krehbiel, p. 26.
[4]*Ibid.*

special effort was made through a "Splendid Musical Edifice and Grand Concert" at Castle Garden to raise the beginning of a building fund for the Philharmonic. The results were a small attendance and net receipts of $390.[1] A year or two before Theodore Thomas made his plunge, distracted supporters of the Philharmonic had tried to start among the well-to-do a stock company or something of the kind to help it to a permanent home. The effort was a ghastly failure.[2]

About this time the musical instrument found to be dearest to the palpitating heart of young New York is, perhaps not inappropriately, the trumpet.[3] "The trumpet playing of Mr. Norton was a splendid affair," says one critic, summing up the glories of a concert. Mr. T. Petrie is for a time the city's idol because of his mastery of this implement. Then one Young, an artist from England, appears in New York and sets the city wild with enthusiasm by his performance upon that ancient and unlovely invention, the keyed serpent. It is made the occasion for a conscientious journalist to administer a rebuke to his age for its devotion to such gymnastics. "The uncommon partiality our citizens manifest for the noisy part of the orchestra," he says, "has been lately much commented upon by strangers. The trumpet and the trombone occupy in our concerts the post of honor"[4]—this with an emphasis of disdain. The citizens do not seem to mind. Not long afterward comes a trumpet-blowing contest at Niblo's Garden between two lusty exponents of this art and draws a deeply interested audience. When the award is made the adherents of the defeated contestant make violent protest. Whereupon a free fist fight, a riot in the pit, and the police rush in.[5]

[1]Krehbiel, p. 49. Ritter says the concert left the Philharmonic in debt despite an unusually good program (pp. 280–281).

[2]Krehbiel, p. 49.

[3]Ritter, p. 134.

[4]*Ibid.*, p. 214.

[5]*Ibid.*, p. 215.

When the really meritorious and useful Germania orchestra arrived in 1849, it met with so frosty a reception in New York that its backers were appalled and transferred the enterprise to Philadelphia. Several performances at expensive halls having drawn empty seats, the management moved to less pretentious quarters in Arch Street and advertised a grand promenade concert, hoping to attract a crowd. The total receipts were $9.50. The hall rent being $10, the proprietor turned off the gas and there was no concert.[1]

Discipline (so to call it) even in the Philharmonic was largely of a jestful significance. Thomas records that "the orchestra was often incomplete," and that if a member had another engagement he would keep it instead of going to a rehearsal. "When one of the wind choir was thus absent, his place would be filled for the occasion as best it could. A clarinet or oboe part would be played on a violin, or a bassoon part on the 'cello." Even at public performances this seemed to be the way of it. "The audience talked at pleasure," Thomas adds.[2] Mathews in his *A Hundred Years of Music in America* says that about this time "American orchestras were as yet so imperfect as to be the derision of European writers."[3] And elsewhere, speaking of the lack of rehearsals of many performed compositions, he observes significantly, "Play them with this preparation they did, and as a rule all the players got through the work at the same time."[4]

The Philharmonic concerts took place in the Apollo Hall, a ballroom in Broadway between Walker and Lispenard streets. There were no chairs; for a concert rough wooden benches were dragged in. An annual charge upon the accounts of the Society was an item of kid gloves for four members of the orchestra

[1]Ritter, pp. 317–319. Also, Elson, *History of American Music*, p. 59. Consult Elson for the full story of this valuable organization.
[2]Autobiography, pp. 50–51.
[3]Mathews, p. 48.
[4]Mathews, p. 420.

that with long wands pointed out available places on these benches. When they had seated the audience, they went up on the stage and took up their instruments.[1]

There were indications of the infantile stage of musical development in other cities than New York. When the Chicago Philharmonic Society was incorporated in 1853 the Legislature seriously entitled the incorporating bill "An Act to promote the Science of Fiddling." In 1862 it was announced that Carl Zerrahn, after seven years of desperate struggle, had been obliged to give up his orchestral concerts in Boston "because they did not pay, or rather because they entailed too great a loss."[2] Someone having ventured to bring out Beethoven's Fifth in Chicago, a discriminating critic there observed of it that "the audience bore it like martyrs, vainly trying to comprehend the grand ideas and beauties of this wonderful 'tone creation,' so called, by the diligent study of its analysis as written by some transcendental, spiritualistic Bedlamite, and printed on the back of the program."[3] About this time in Chicago Hans Balatka was carrying on a hand-to-hand conflict to introduce good music and driving toward his overwhelming defeat in 1867. Criticism in New York was not much farther advanced. On the first performance of Schubert's C Major there, one learned authority expressed contempt of its tedious length. Being mildly controverted, he returned to the attack and declared the symphony to be "overlabored, forced and overdrawn."[4]

This was the Castle of Indifference that Theodore Thomas in his twenty-seventh year set out to take by assault. It is not to be supposed that he was the panoplied new knight suddenly arrived from other shores upon a strand all hostile. Many other

---

[1] Ritter, edition of 1890, p. 276.

[2] *Dwight's*, April 5, 1862.

[3] Quoted in *Dwight's*, April 12, 1862.

[4] *Dwight's*, May 17, 1862. One is forcibly reminded of Schumann's remark about the "Heavenly length." But I can find at that time small tolerance for any such composition.

men of the admirable order of Bergmann, Zerrahn, Balatka, Eisfeld, Eckert, Strasser—sincere, unselfish pioneers—had preceded him, often to their own sorrow and the unconcern of the Castle. Yet, against all that has been or can be averred about the musical ineptitude of New York in its early days, no one can fail to see that music had been steadily advancing. A host of excellent musicians, some of them of historical fame, had visited this country in the fifteen years preceding the outbreak of the Civil War and had made a deep impression. Jenny Lind, Henriette Sontag, Mirate the tenor, Mme La Grange, had toured the country, and the memories of the revelations they had wrought were strong and beneficent. At first the evolution was more upon vocal than instrumental lines, but instrumental music began likewise to emerge from the Silurian of the trumpet and drum. German artists came singly and in companies; many remained to become wherever they might be central dynamos of devotion to music. Native leaders arose, sincerely loyal to the musical hope, like William Mason and U. C. Hill, invaluable aids to a movement that was more real than easily discernible. By 1852, at the height of the reign of Master Marsh and the "Firefly," it was recorded that in New York City, 2,685 men and women, including the marvelous family Dodworth, lived by their labors in music.

The instrumental music, even in earlier days, had not been all trumpet and keyed serpent. The Euterpean Society, upon which we have previously alighted in these annals, had a long though somewhat ineffectual career in the metropolis. It was composed of amateurs that assembled, strange to say, of summer evenings to practise ensemble playing, and gave once a year a concert, supper, and dance at the old City Tavern in Broadway. Contemporaneous criticism sniffed at these, yet they were in a way the progenitor of the history-making Philharmonic, which when launched comprised many Euterpeans. Hill, himself, the originator of the Philharmonic, was one

whose just fame has been impaired by an error about his name
that confounded him with another. "Uriah C. Hill," he is usually called, even by the highest authorities.[1] In reality he rejoiced in prenomenal distinction much greater than that.
Ureli Corelli Hill he had been christened; in spite of which
he was a musician[2] both honest and able, and the smile that
his surnames provoke is quenched by any knowledge of his
melancholy ending.[3] The inimitable Dodworths were there, and
among all that shone or starved in those inglorious days, I am
for Dodworth. Surely the literature of New York is poor,
lacking a brochure about this picturesque tribe of Bedouins
wandering about the edges of Sahara. You meet their trail at
every turn; they have been beneficently busy. Every one of the
name makes a joyful noise upon some form of instrument, be
it but a pair of castanets. Allen Dodworth plays the violin,
Harvey B. Dodworth plays the cornet, C. R. Dodworth plays
the concertina, C. Dodworth plays the trombone, Thomas
Jefferson Dodworth plays something else—I think it is the
helicon bass. They have a silver cornet band and a promenade
band and a serenade band and a full band and a band. They
have a hall, Dodworth's Hall, in Broadway next to Grace
Church, and let fly there much music on her silvern wings and
on wings of brass. The Mason-Thomas Quartette seeks its
hospitable shelter; Artemus Ward speaks there. Harvey B.
Dodworth has orchestras in assorted sizes from three to thirteen
that he furnishes for public balls and private dancing parties.
When Dartmouth College at a commencement wishes to dis-
tinguish itself in music it sends to New York and Dodworth's
silver cornet band responds, arousing great enthusiasm as it
marches to the station in its gorgeous new uniform of red and

---

[1] Ritter is one that makes this error and Elson repeats it, p. 54.

[2] He had studied abroad and been a pupil of Spohr's.

[3] After a long struggle against poverty and neglect, the poor man committed suicide in Paterson, New Jersey, September 2, 1875. Krehbiel, p. 56. He was seventy-two years old.

yellow. When the Philharmonic is born the Dodworths come near taking charge of the accouchement. Allen Dodworth is treasurer and plays in the violins, with Harvey B.; T. Dodworth is one of the trombones, C. Dodworth plays the piccolo or octave flute.[1]

It is a marvelous aggregation. When *The Message Bird* is started, the first periodical in New York devoted exclusively to fine arts and the uplift, in the first number the chief contributor is Allen Dodworth, writing about the best way to form a brass band. He is no idle singer of an empty day, either. He writes a book about dancing and another entitled *Dodworth's Brass Band School*, "containing instruction in the first principles of music." They all compose music as well as sell it in their store at 403 Broadway. Allen composes the "Cally Polka," "Devil's Hoof Quickstep," "Jenny Lind Polka," "'Woodman Spare That Tree' Quickstep," a composition modestly announced as "Dodworth's Very Best Polka," and many other works. Harvey B. furnishes "The Lament, a Great Quickstep Introducing Dempster's Beautiful Air, 'I'm Sitting on the Stile, Mary,'" the "Young Bachelors' March," the "Evergreen Empire Quadrille," and an astonishing list of other creations.[2] They move up town with the advancing tide, Broome Street, Union Square, and still farther. In 1879 one of them was playing in a band at Madison Square Garden.[3] As late as 1887 Harvey B. was still in the New York Directory as a "musician," the stout old boy. Then the tribe vanishes and leaves no trace.

[1]The Philharmonic as organized presented a respectable battery, thus:

22 violins	2 clarinets
6 violas	2 bassoons
4 violoncellos	2 trumpets
5 basses	3 trombones
4 flutes	4 horns
2 oboes	drums

piano

There were sixty-three active members. At the first performance the only vacancy was in the second trumpet.

[2]Preserved for the curious in the New York Public Library.

[3]See *Music Trade Review*, July 12, 1879.

But back in 1842 they are all playing in the Philharmonic.
Hill leads the first concert, with a program not to be jested
about. Then Hill and others are conductors until Carl Bergmann comes and gives to this démarche a new aspect.

Thus in the face of a somewhat scowling outlook, they labor
on year after year with the zeal of the ancient evangels. Conditions largely beyond their helping hampered their efforts. At
first they could give but three concerts in the year; for sixteen
years they gave but four annually.[1] It was impossible thus to
make an enduring and advancing impression. Before the second
concert came the first had been forgotten. Because the players
must have other employments, there was no chance to secure
a high degree of efficiency; adequate rehearsing, drilling, and
concentration were impossible. The programs, in themselves
often admirable, lacked all coherent educational scheme, such
as the situation demanded. Then the audiences that gathered—
they were another difficulty. Apparently, they were of two
elements, the trained musician, whether professional or amateur, and the variable crowd of curiosity seekers that came on
idle impulse and remained to talk or jeer or both. That is to
say, a part of the public appealed to was already converted and
needed no redemption, and the rest was never reached by the
efforts put forth.

What happened now was that the new man coming to this
task had a definite and thought-out plan, an indomitable faith,
an intimate knowledge of the people he was to address, a correct
understanding of the way to their interest, an unusual musicianship, and a resolution almost ferocious. An army of good
friends threw up their hands when they learned that this youth
with so brilliant a future as a violinist was determined to sacrifice himself in the pursuit of what all well-informed persons

---

[1]"The Philharmonic gave three concerts the first season. The next year the number
was increased to four and so remained for sixteen seasons, for the next ten years the
number was five in each season, and after the twenty-seventh season it was made six."
(James Huneker, *The Philharmonic Society of New York*, p. 17.)

knew was mere illusion. The leopard would change its spots before America would really care for any music above the grade of "Napoleon Crossing the Alps." Americans might be well endowed to carry on business, gouge their neighbors, sell sanded sugar, gather profits from wooden nutmegs, heap fortunes, and glorify wealth, but of art they were congenitally incapable. The support they gave to visiting celebrities was but the foolish affectation of the purse proud. At heart they cared not a hoot, and this proposed expedition is dependent absolutely upon their real interest, not upon their curiosity. Glance at the programs they make for their own entertainment—that will be enough. A foreign artist for a large stipend might be willing to appear at the same concert with the Master Marshes, snake-charmers, rope-dancers, and jew's-harp specialists that figure at these sad affairs, but it is absurd to think anything can be done to raise the taste of such a people. Look at the failures of all the men that have essayed it!

The recipient of all this remonstrance, caution, and advice was unmoved by it. His mind was made up, he believed he had a mission in life, a serious call, a task laid upon him. There was always in him some hint of the spirit of the Puritan and the men of Leyden, the Northwest Teuton,[1] a little grim, a little taciturn, and a little berserker, too, if you come to that. He believed that in his intimate observations among the people he had discovered their soul. If they liked the "Firefly Polka" it was because they had never really had a chance to like any-thing else. Underneath the superficial fondness for rubbish there was a vast possibility of music that needed only to be touched and vivified.[2] He conceived of himself as appointed to

[1]At the Church of St. Lambert, Münster, they show you the cage of John of Leyden and his two companions and give a competent notion of the things these Teutons of the Northwest endured.

[2]"I shall succeed because I shall never give up my belief that at last the people will come to me and my concerts will be crowded. I have undying faith in the latent musical appreciation of the American people." (Statement of Theodore Thomas made when he was trying to float his orchestra and quoted by Upton, *Reminiscence and Appreciation*, p. 127.)

find and animate this sleeping spirit—Dornröschen, and he the prince, if you like.

He brought to his task the strangest combination of inconsistent and even opposite qualities I have ever known in one human being. He had a strength of will that nothing could break, bend, or divert, a kind of relentless and almost savage resolution, proof against assault and most proof against the other side of himself. With this he united a sensitiveness abnormal and unaccountable; he was sensitive physically as well as mentally and spiritually. All his life the common medicinal drugs that an ordinary man could take without harm were too potent for him; he must have his medicine in minute dosage. A draught of chilled air that another man would never be aware of produced in him acute catarrh.[1] Spiritually, he was so sensitive that a single expression of beauty of any kind could send him into a state of rapture the more powerful because it was absolutely silent, uncommunicated—uncommunicable! His natural gifts of hearing were so remarkable that they seemed to make him a prodigy, and his knowledge of musical literature so great that it was said of him, with amiable extravagance, that he knew everything that had ever been written for the orchestra. One side of his nature would wince under a single unpleasant word or unjust criticism, and the other carry on in the teeth of relentless battle.

To anyone still obsessed with the old novelists' notion of man as a being all of a piece, here was something to cause gasps; for this one was a conglomerate of contradictions. In some ways he was marvelously shrewd, discerning, farsighted, and even calculating (in the best sense, I mean), and in others as simple as a child. He was always lamenting his poverty of education; in point of fact, diligent reading was making him one of the best educated men of his times. Even at this early age, he had acquired some repute as stern, austere, and reticent; in point of

[1]Philo A. Otis, *The Chicago Symphony Orchestra*, p. 19.

fact, he was among the kindest of men, wore his austerity as an indispensable mask to his essential tenderness, and, when among his friends or on a topic that interested him, was a fascinating talker. As a final curiosity I may observe this, that whereas he habitually saw every project in its greatest terms, so that he seemed to do everything upon a huge scale, he had a gift for minutiæ and followed up detail like some form of human sleuth.

Physically as well as mentally he had gifts available for his purpose. One was the born executive's way of indenting his will upon other men without really formulating it; another was a bearing so singularly expressive of strength in repose that he always seemed much taller, for instance, than he really was. This was an odd illusion, not explained by the fact that he stood upon a dais while conducting; for even when he entered upon the stage he looked rather tall. His unusual length of trunk contributed to an impression that was almost universal. Even Stephen Fiske, who had seen him often, speaks of his "tall and well-knit figure."[1] Yet he was only about five feet five and a half inches in height, his long torso being counterbalanced by short legs, as I have often noted in other men fitted for great activity and endurance.

For with his singular physical sensitiveness was combined an almost equally unusual physical prowess. He had a body that seemed insatiable of labor and incapable of fatigue. Remembering that in his youth he had had no training, no athletics, no recreation, and no exercise more fortifying than the swinging of a violin bow, his muscular strength, not alone of his arms but of all his make-up, was almost phenomenal.[2]

---

[1]Fiske, *Offhand Portraits*, p. 313.

[2]Upton, *Reminiscence and Appreciation*, pp. 244–245. Mr. Upton relates, for example, that at a supper party in Cincinnati, Andres, the pianist, gave an exhibition of the unusual strength of his third finger. With his hand flat on the table he could raise the finger and bring it down like a piano hammer. No one else at the table could do this, but Mr. Thomas quietly placed his hand on the table and much exceeded Andres's feat.

His eyes were his most extraordinary feature; blue, and more than blue. There was back of them a curious blue fire, a kind of latent blaze that on occasion burst out so that it is a fact that few persons were able to withstand them when he was aroused. Men that played long under him said that he conducted more with his eyes than with his baton, and it is true that he had an unusual power of conveying meanings with a look. A gift of graceful movement must have been his by nature; every motion of his raised arm was made with flexile ease and no one ever saw him do an awkward thing or lose in public his perfect poise. This was true and remained true even when he was conducting pieces at his own fastest tempo, which was a terrific gait and taxed his players to the utmost.[1]

Besides these advantages, his career had been so led as to supply him with experiences of inestimable value to one undertaking such a task as he had chosen. Being the foremost American violinist of his time he was, of course, the master of his favorite instrument; he knew it for solo purposes and he knew it in ensemble; he had sat in both first and second violin choirs. His year in a navy band had revealed to him the heights and depths of the brasses. Jullien, the fantastic, had assembled the greatest wood-wind choir this country has ever known;[2] Theodore Thomas, playing in the orchestra with these men, had been fascinated with their excellence, and from them he learned the possibilities and functions of wood winds. His work as a leader of operas had made him familiar with the principles of voice expression. His long experience with the Mason-Thomas Quartette had revealed a world of classicism, refined his tastes, tutored him in tone colors, in the possibilities of the most delicate modulations, and even in the steps by which mass psychology comes to master good music. He knew the ways of audi-

---

[1]Otis, p. 19; Mrs. Thomas, p. 77.
[2]Their names and glories are preserved in Thomas Ryan's book of musical reminiscences.

ences; he knew how they could be won and led and how they could not be driven. For years he had made all the programs for the Quartette, and there could hardly have been better training. He says himself that they began with "silly solos" and other stuff interspersed among the meritorious pieces and rose to a state where the musical world of Europe looked for them as models.

The pictures of him made in his youth reveal something of his phenomenal make-up. They show a face high bred and strong, the eyes of a resolution like a viking's, the mouth as sensitive as any woman's; an odd expression of cogency, self-mastery, and daring; an equally odd suggestion of the capacity to suffer and to endure. Almost at once he gained fame as a disciplinarian of stern demeanor in the rehearsal room; yet his face at that time and to the end of his life had, when in repose, a strong intimation of good-humor, a good-humor that might easily become sardonic, if need be, but not less relishable for that.

There was yet one other element in his make-up almost as potent in its results as his wide knowledge of musical literature. He had this basic belief in music as an ethical force. It seemed to him essentially impossible that men filled with the spirit of beautiful music could go forth to wrong their fellows. "I have known the Oratorio of the Messiah," says Dr. Haweis, "to draw the lowest dregs of Whitechapel into a church to hear it, and during the performance sobs have broken forth from the silent and attentive throng. Will anyone say that for these people to have their feelings for once put through such a noble and long-sustained exercise as that could be otherwise than beneficial? If such performances of both sacred and secular music were more frequent, we should have less drunkenness, less wife-beating, less spending of summer gains, less winter pauperism."[1] To Thomas, all this had the warranty of religion.

[1] Quoted by Henry T. Finck in *Chopin and Other Musical Essays*, p. 174.

He was deeply convinced that it was for this purpose that music had been ordained; to his mind the beauty of music and the beauty of conduct were akin; ethics and æsthetics were inseparable. "How great a gift God gave to the world when music was breathed into creation!"[1] he cried, and not as one intent upon grand-standing; he said it to his intimates, and so that they knew he felt it.

If he had the brooding soul of an artist he had the quick and certain eye of the experienced observer. Traveling to and fro in the land of the free, he had taken shrewd note of his American. He saw his typical fellow citizen threatened with soul submersion in the rising tide of commercialism. Many others have seen this, artists and what not, and have passed by on the other side; for what business was it of theirs? On with the dance. But there was a difference here. Theodore Thomas seeing it, felt that the American was too good to be thus lost. After a day spent in striving with all his faculties to outwit his fellows, the American business man needed something to release, refresh, and elevate his thought; something that would not only take his mind all away from business, but purify it and give it glimpses of another kind of an existence.[2] Thomas said so succinctly, "What our overworked business and professional men most need in America is an elevating mental recreation that is not an amusement."[3] It was useless to offer the medicament of other entertainment. A show might make Mercatorius laugh and for three hours forget the counting room; it would

---

[1] *Reminiscence and Appreciation*, p. 250.

[2] Some years after, Henry T. Finck wrote this:

"In America, more than anywhere else, is music needed as a tonic, to cure the infectious and ridiculous business fever that is responsible for so many cases of premature collapse. Nowhere else is so much time wasted in making money, which is then spent in a way that contributes to no one's happiness—least of all to the owner's. We Americans are in the habit of calling ourselves the most practical nation in the world, but the fact is it would be difficult to find a nation less practical. . . . Our so-called 'practical' men look upon recreation as something useless, whereas in reality it is the most useful thing in the world." (*Chopin and Other Musical Essays*, p. 180.)

[3] Mrs. Thomas, p. 50.

NIBLO'S GARDEN

The fashionable amusement place when Thomas came to New York

THE OLD CITY HOTEL

Where the Euterpeans gave their annual concert.   Trinity Church near by

not truly rest him because it would not take him into another world but keep him always in this. What was required was something that would appeal to and arouse the spiritual nature, and for that purpose was nothing in the world comparable to music. Not music that consisted of a mere concourse of agreeable noises, but music that had spiritual significance and message.

The summit of such music was to be found in the symphony, which he deemed the highest achievement of the human mind and the greatest expression of the aspirations of the human soul, so that when a symphony had been heard with understanding and knowledge it conferred upon the hearer a wealth of the purest emotions, cleansing and uplifting.[1] He would have agreed entirely with Margaret Fuller. "I felt raised above all care, all pain, all fear, and every taint of vulgarity was washed out of the world." Beyond all other forms of art, probably beyond all other forms of this art, such was its effect. The lofty intellectual concept of the symphony, the nobility of its animating thought, the varied splendor of its architecture, the just apposition of its parts, the beauty of its themes, the skill of their development—all this seemed to him to constitute a kind of means to human salvation. He set out, therefore, with first this end in view, that he would, if possible, make the symphony understood and liked in America.

Every part of the task he had chosen for himself was difficult and none worse than this. Against the mere name of a symphony existed a prejudice that amounted to a phobia. Symphony— that meant something technical, remote, darkling, abstruse, and beyond the comprehension of any except long-haired experts, music cranks, of whom the perfectly sane might well beware. It was foreign, it was unmelodious, it was muddled

---

[1]"To follow a movement of Beethoven is, in the first place, a bracing exercise of the intellect. The emotions evoked, while assuming a double degree of importance by association with the analytic faculty, do not become enervated, because in the masterful grip of the great composer we are conducted through a cycle of naturally progressive feeling, which always ends by leaving the mind recreated, balanced, and ennobled by the exercise." (Haweis, *Music and Morals*, Harper Edition, p. 59.)

and unlovely. The opinion that the blunt critic in Chicago expressed about Beethoven's Fifth was typical of the view held
tenaciously by the major part even, strange to say, of the public
that was called music loving. For nineteen years the Philharmonic in New York had been struggling along, playing many
symphonies[1] to audiences unstudious of thought and small in
numbers. Even upon these, the net results were not heartening.
With difficulty one could think that true progress had been made
in preaching the musical gospel; assuredly none with the symphony, which continued to be the object of more than mere
dislike. Again and again New York had demonstrated that it
would tolerate musical novelties even of a revolutionary character—the overture to "Tannhäuser," and other Wagnerian
innovations that Carl Bergmann had introduced. It would
not for a bribe, a hiring, a price, tolerate anything that bore
the name of symphony.

It was even sceptical (being uninformed) about orchestral
music as after all a branch of art to be followed for its own
sake. The brass band continued to be its satisfying ideal of
instrumental music. The true place of the orchestra was in
opera and to play "Home Sweet Home" softly in tense moments
of *The Stranger*. Even successful Italian opera could be well
given with orchestras of thirty-five or forty men.[2] New York
came slowly to accept the idea that an orchestra had legitimate
concert uses. Long after its public had emerged from the stage
of the Master Marshes and the dizzy deeds of him of the concertina, it must have programs in which a few orchestral numbers might be slyly introduced between vocal solos and choruses,
preferably of a religious nature. On such occasions the solo and the

---

[1] For example, Schubert's C Major, first played in New York by the Philharmonic,
January 11, 1851, Theodore Eisfeld conducting. The first number on its first program,
December 7, 1842, was Beethoven's Fifth, U. C. Hill conducting. Carl Bergmann
resolutely introduced Wagnerian compositions in the face of bitter criticism. His first
performance of the "Tannhäuser" overture, April 21, 1855, was the first time it had
been heard in America.

[2] Autobiography, p. 25.

chorus were regarded as the real events and the orchestral numbers as mere filling material to promote the art of conversation.

It was upon this field that Theodore Thomas, aged twenty-seven, ventured that May night at old Irving Hall, Fifteenth Street and Irving Place, with an orchestra of about forty men made up chiefly from the opera where he had been conducting, and a program of his own peculiar constructing.

This was his announcement,[1] in itself a curious indication of the times:

It is the intention of the subscriber to give a Grand Vocal and Orchestral Concert on Tuesday, May 13, at the Irving Hall. To this concert he would beg leave to call your attention, as it is his determination to make it one of the finest as well as the most popular Vocal and Instrumental Concerts of the present season.

The whole programme will speedily be announced as soon as the arrangements have been completed. Amongst the attractions, it will contain the whole of Meyerbeer's Music for his brother's tragedy of "Struensee." This popular and dramatic composition for full orchestra with harp obbligato and chorus, which enjoys so immense a reputation in Europe, has never yet been performed in this country. He also brings for the first time before an American audience, Wagner's original and descriptive overture, "Der Fliegende Holländer," one of the most successful works of this celebrated composer. Another novelty will be the performance for the first time of Moscheles's Grand Piano Forte Composition, "Les Contrasts," the only one originally written for Four Pianos, the rendering of which has been entrusted to Four of the Leading Artists of the world.

In alluding to these novelties, the subscriber scarcely considers it necessary to say that the solos will be rendered by Vocalists and Instrumentalists of the most established reputation.

THEODORE THOMAS.

108 E. 12th Street, New York.

Below this was the information that tickets at the price of one dollar were to be had at all the music stores of the day, and

---

[1] Original in Newberry Library, Chicago.

there was no charge for reserved seats. The newspapers were kind in their advance notices, but the *World* lamented the program. "We regret that Mr. Thomas has omitted offering some morceaux for the violin, of which instrument he is the master, to be performed by himself." Here are the offerings in full on this historic occasion, the first upon which Theodore Thomas appeared as conductor of his own orchestral concert:

Overture, "Der Fliegende Holländer" .... Wagner
        (First time in America)
Hymn, "Lord, be thou with us". .... Apel
        (The Teutonia Choral Society)
"Fantasia," op. 15 (arranged by Liszt) .... Schubert
        (First time in this country)
        (Played by William Mason.)
Aria, "Bel raggio lusinghier" from "Semiramide". ...... Rossini
        (Mme de Lussan)
Concerto for the violin in A minor, first movement. ..... Molique
        (Mr. Bruno Wallenhaupt)
Quartette, "Les Contrastes," for piano. .... Moscheles
        (First time in America)
        (Messrs. Mills, Goldbeck, Hartmann and Mason)
Aria, "Ernani involami," from "Ernani" .... Verdi
        (Mme de Lussan)
Music to the tragedy of "Struensee". .... Meyerbeer
        (First time in America)

There were two other novelties not mentioned on the program. For the first time in this country Mr. Thomas introduced the harp and the English horn into an orchestra,[1] convincing evidence of the attention he had given to orchestral needs and possibilities and of his attitude toward innovations.

As to the results of this daring venture, the testimonies are

---

[1]This statement, which appears in the second, or program volume of the work Mr. Upton edited for Mr. Thomas, at p. 51, has been questioned. It is supported by an annotation in Mr. Thomas's handwriting on the original program for the concert preserved in the Newberry Library, Chicago. One may remember that in 1862 the number of orchestral compositions commonly performed and requiring a harp was small.

various. The *Times and Messenger* the next Sunday, May 18, said that "in point of success and excellence, this concert was all that could be desired," and reserved comment on the audience, perhaps because this was in size disappointing. It appears that difficulty was had to make the event attractive. The correspondent of *Dwight's Journal of Music*, then the most influential musical periodical in America, said[1] that the concert was "a decided novelty, but I don't think it was a pecuniary success, for nearly everybody there were deadheads; indeed the deadhead system is carried to such an extent in this city that when I meet a person at a place of amusement I decide, until I have absolute proof to the contrary, that he belongs to the noble army of D. H.'s."[2] After a broad intimation that the general price of admission was nearer a quarter than a dollar, he went on to say that "the charming effect of the harp obbligato created some surprise" and queries as to why this instrument had been "unseen, unheard" at the Philharmonic concerts. The critic thought that the piano was "but an inharmonious substitute for it." He found the "Struensee" music to be the most important number on the program and very successful with the audience but "dreadfully heavy." "Wagner's 'Fliegende Holländer'—suggestive at least—was received as well as could be expected." "This concert was on the whole," he concluded, "one of the most interesting of the season, and spoke well for the aims and intentions of Mr. Thomas." But the New York *Tribune* did not like the Wagner number. "'Der Fliegende Holländer' was ingeniously destitute of melody," observed this astute commentator. "Ghastly rumpus was its main feature."[3] He refreshed himself with the "Struensee"

---

[1] Issue of May 31, 1862.

[2] May 14, 1862.

[3] I find another journal of the day that dipped into the arcana of criticism. It thought that the overture was "an unexpected success," because "most of the audience expected a dreary waste of dissonant harmony and were agreeably surprised to find not merely definite ideas and action but melody."

music, because therein "harmony and melody were not abol-
ished and there was reference to the beautiful."

So far, good. But there was one ominous note struck in one
criticism that had almost the premonition of fate, being mild
foretaste of the fault-finding about his programs with which
he was to become bitterly familiar throughout his career. One
newspaper said this:

The concert was absolutely a success and one which the young
conductor, Theodore Thomas, may congratulate himself upon. At the
same time it would be better appreciated in Vienna or Weimar or
Dresden than in New York.[1]

The artistic results, if not the money receipts, encouraged
Thomas in his belief that he had chosen the right way. Perhaps
it was with another sigh that he finally relinquished the career
of a violinist. "What this country needed most of all to make it
musical," he wrote of his new ambition, "was a good orchestra
and plenty of concerts within the reach of the people."[2] There
was nothing of the kind when he began. The Philharmonic that
year, its twentieth season, gave five concerts. Even if these
had been well done and well attended (and some testimony
insists that they were neither) the effect would have been negligible. For one pregnant reason: They were designed to be good
concerts and stopped there; they were not designed to break
open the closed door of public interest and get a foothold inside.

That made the difference, and marked the new man and his
era.

"I thought the time had come to form an orchestra for concert purposes," Thomas wrote.[3] "I therefore called a meeting
of the foremost musicians of New York, told them of my plans
to popularize instrumental music, and asked for their coöperation."

---

[1] Unidentified clipping in the Newberry Library.
[2] Autobiography, p. 50.
[3] Ibid, p. 51.

How much they gave of it does not appear, but one astonishing thing is certain. Their help was nothing in the way that now would be held first of all indispensable. Neither they nor anybody else contributed capital to this singular enterprise; all his capital lay in the restless and capable engine of his mind, now started ahead, and an enthusiasm and persistence that were most powerful in that they were proof against his own weaknesses.

The trying-out concert at Irving Hall was followed, as soon as might be, by others. He was a busy man now; with his peculiar nature he would have been wretched otherwise. On June 30, of that year, 1862, at Dodworth's Hall, that famous tent of a famous tribe, with William Mason, S. B. Mills, Bergner the 'cellist, and an amateur vocal quartette, he gave a concert for the benefit of the sick and wounded soldiers of the Union Army. With Mason, Mosenthal, Bergner, and Matzka, he continued to rehearse thrice weekly for the Mason-Thomas chamber concerts. On September 18, 1862, he opened a season of orchestral concerts at Irving Hall, boldly offering as a novelty Carl Philip Emanuel Bach's symphony in D Major, its first performance in America.[1] He seems for these concerts to have made a reduction in the announced admission price; perhaps also he felt strong enough to curtail "the noble army of deadheads." The New York *Tribune* said of the first performance:

Mr. Theodore Thomas is very ardent and liberal in giving good concerts. Not only has he a capital orchestra of sixty performers, but a harpist, pianist and vocalist for his fifty-cent performance.

On October 1, 1862, he appeared as violin soloist at a concert given by Gottschalk.[2] On November 1, 1862, the newspapers

---

[1] *Dwight's*, September 27, 1862.

[2] Louis Moreau Gottschalk (1829–1869), native of New Orleans, at one time the most popular of American pianists, composer of that mournful offering, "The Last Hope, a Religious Meditation," of which twenty-six editions and adaptations are preserved in the Library of Congress.

reported that the Brooklyn Philharmonic had appointed him to conduct its concerts.[1] December 2, he gave a concert at Irving Hall with Eugénie Barnetche. December 6, announcement was made of the eighth season of the Mason-Thomas Quartette of which he was leader and program maker and general manager. On March 22, 1863, he shared with Robert Goldbeck the work of conducting Goldbeck's symphony, "Victoria," a composition whereof the world seems now quite unaware.[2] On May 9, at his Irving Hall concert, he produced Berlioz's symphony, "Harold in Italy."[3] October 24, 1863, he began a series of matinées at Irving Hall. May 2, 1864, he conducted in Philadelphia the first performance of William H. Fry's opera "Esmeralda"; May 4, he was in Philadelphia again as director of the musical festival there. November 5, he was the soloist at the first concert that season of the Philharmonic, playing the Mendelssohn concerto.

Of this the New York *Times* for November 6, after calling the Society "this money-grubbing corporation" and saying "it is useless to grumble at the mention of its members or their greed for larger dividends," observes that "the second solo was performed by Mr. Theodore Thomas, a worthy and prominent member of the society, who, we are glad to find, is at length acknowledged to be able to play the fiddle. The piece was Mendelssohn concerto (opus 64 in E), and three rather long movements were interpreted with great power and precision. Mr. Thomas produces a fine tone, stops absolutely in tune and

---

[1]The Brooklyn Philharmonic was organized on a plan quite different from that of its New York namesake. The Brooklyn Society was composed of music lovers, usually men of means, that did not themselves take part in the performances but provided the money for them. A conductor was engaged at an annual salary and he furnished the players, including the soloists. As the Brooklyn audiences were so largely composed of persons skilled in music, Mr. Thomas began at once to play for them music of a much higher grade than he played at his other concerts. The difference shows his skill in program making, in which he had never a superior, and again reveals clearly his educational aim.

[2]*Dwight's*, March 28, 1863.

[3]*Ibid.*, May 16, 1863.

plays without any affectation of restraint. He was completely successful." November 13, he received from the Directors of the Society a formal letter thanking him for his performance.

Early in the season of 1864–1865, he came to one of the turning points of his life, for he announced a season of "symphony soirées" to be given at Irving Hall—by his own orchestra. Hitherto he had been scratching along with players engaged separately for each performance. He had now a band to some extent under his own control.

It was evident that he was forging ahead, he was justifying his choice, he was inducing people to listen to him, he was making inroads upon the field that had looked so forbidding. The public was growing into a receptive mood about the music he was furnishing. What was that music like, then? Here is the program for the first Irving Hall matinée, October 24, 1863:

Overture, "Prometheus" ....Beethoven
Overture "Oberon," for two pianos ....Weber
      (L. M. Gottschalk and Harry Sanderson)
Symphony in E flat, No. 3.........................Mozart
Cavatina "Qui la Voce" from "I Puritani"...........Bellini
      (Miss Lucy Simons)
Caprice "Illusions Perdues"   )
     "O ma Charmante"   } ....Gottschalk
     "Pastorella e Caveliere")
      (Mr. L. M. Gottschalk)
Selections from "Il Ballo in Maschera"..............Verdi
Polka, "Aurora Ball" ....Strauss
Waltz from "Faust"................................Gounod
      (First time in America)
"Oberländer"......................................Gungl
      (Mr. Thomas and Mr. Mollenhauer)
"Electric Polka" for two pianos....................Sanderson
      (Messrs. Gottschalk and Sanderson)
Quadrille, "Bijouterie" ....Strauss

The key of this is easily found now. He was aware of the demand for "giants and dwarfs" and at the same time working slowly away toward better things. He juggles a Mozart symphony in between a piano duet by celebrities and a vocal solo, an innocent little symphony, perhaps people would hardly notice that it was there. If they did and were incensed at the intrusion, here was a wealth afterward of proper things to make atonement—solos, two polkas, a quadrille! What more could one ask?

Not that he escapes condemnation. The astute press is not always deceived and often visits upon him the damnation reserved for all innovators. When on April 8, 1865, he plays for the first time in America, Bach's "Passacaglia" (Esser arrangement), the New York *Tribune* gives him an inferior sample of the comments he must face for a great part of his life.

"The dull part of the program," said the *Tribune*, "lay in the Passacaglia of Bach, a fair representation of the treadmill. A culprit may tread on it for a day without advancing a step. It simply goes round in the most obvious style, generally respectable and dull like a church warden, colorless and uninspired."

When he played Mozart's symphony for violin, viola, and orchestra, the *Tribune*, which was the foremost authority of the day, said that "one would prefer death to the repetition of this production"; and when he brought out Liszt's "Mazeppa" a weekly journal called the *Album* said it was "the uttermost trash ever given to a New York public."

He had other troubles with the press, one may surmise. On January 14, 1865, a beacon light of civilization called *Watson's Weekly Art Journal*, after reviewing Thomas's symphony soirée of January 7, makes this candid confession:

We did not purpose to notice these concerts for the reason that the conductors of the enterprise refuse to our columns the advertisements they give to other journals. . . . We notice these concerts because they deserve to be noticed and as a matter of justice whereas we should have withheld mention had we consulted our merely personal feelings.

The price of a casual advertisement is fortunately of small amount to us although it is true that every little helps.

Yet, he continues, this cunning schemer in the face of deserved rebuke, to slip over these symphonies and other classics, hated as in his heart he knows them to be. At the concert of October 31 there he goes again, starting with a Haydn symphony in E flat. Yes; but the next moment you notice that he follows this with an appeal to patriotism—"The Union," a paraphrase on national airs by Mr. Gottschalk, with the arranger himself at the piano. This takes the sting out. To be sure that all is well and the audience placated, the next number is Strauss's polka, "Aurora Ball," most popular, after which operatic selections (vocal), a piano duet, a waltz, and at the last, as something to add the effect at which he was really aiming, he played the "Tannhäuser" March.[1]

No public could long resist such a course of tutelage, resolutely and adroitly carried out.[2] At the third matinée a Mozart symphony, antidoted with pianists performing upon two pianos, with piano solos, vocal solos, a Strauss waltz, a Strauss quadrille —but still a symphony gone down, swallowed, endured, no casualties reported. At the next, Beethoven's Second. This is delicate treading; we are approaching the critical point of the engagement. We must maneuver a little: behold it inconspicuous there among an aria from the always popular "Il Ballo in Maschera," a Strauss polka, another aria, a quartette from "Rigoletto" (master stroke that—"Rigoletto"!), a Strauss waltz, and other propitiations. At the next concert, November 28, what does he do but repeat that Beethoven's Second, thus daring to fasten in their minds the themes he had intro-

[1]All these programs, some with annotations by Mr. Thomas, are preserved in the Newberry Library collection, Chicago.

[2]"We have elsewhere spoken of Gottlieb Graupner as the father of American orchestral music. This is certainly true in a chronological sense, but as regards the establishment of a high standard of execution, the introduction of a true epoch of interpretation, Theodore Thomas deserves that honorable title." Elson, p. 59.

duced the week before? Juggler! Prestidigitator! What show has ancient and respected prejudice against such tactics? Ten matinées this winter and each with a symphony all sugared up, disguised, even predigested. He will end by making them like it in spite of themselves, this man.

CHAPTER IV

Like the Siege of a Fortress

WHETHER he would have plunged ahead on this road if he had known what it was to cost him is something to speculate about. At least, behold here the mercy that gives us hopes but denies us previsions. He had in this year done a thing that, being without precedent in musical history, any wise man then or since would have told him was impossible, and achievements of this kind are never stimulative of caution. Without a cent of his own, with no supporting society, group, or even individual, wholly alone in a city whose interest in orchestral music was next to nothing, he had organized a grand orchestra, and from its earnings, whatever they might be, had financed it through a regular season. This, we may recall ponderingly, in the America of 1864, where a brass band, a piano and the Jones Family Bell Ringers represented to the average person the attainable peak of musical joy. The thing seems now like some form of madness; even in this day no grand orchestra supports itself, or can. He must have had an airy confidence in himself, this youth. "The Theodore Thomas Orchestra," launched on these impossible terms upon its first season of symphonic soirées at Irving Hall, December 3, 1864, was his own wild bold notion, sprung exotically, it appears, out of his craving for artistic excellence. In his view of the matter, from an orchestra that he did not control he could never get the results he wanted; he could never have a composition so played as to satisfy his conscience while it took captive the interest of the public. Say that ten times a year a player performed under his direction; a hundred times a year the same player would be playing under somebody else or nobody. Before Thomas could fine him down to reasonable worth he was off again and all the Thomasian instruction wasted.

But with this he took upon himself a heart-breaking load. He must be his own manager; he must steer with the nicest care. An unprofitable concert this week must be offset with one next week that yields cash in hand; must, or these sixty-odd men, waving their contracts, will be clamoring and writ-serving.

In these perilous straits he was greatly helped by a thing not usually deemed assistant to mankind. He clawed offshore by grace of a rank delusion. No one knew better than he the mental processes of the average American, and no one knew worse the point of view of the contemporaneous American man of wealth. About this his reasoning was perfectly plausible and perfectly fallacious. Because in Europe, all grand orchestras were supported by government as factors in public education, and without extraneous bulwarking could never exist, Theodore Thomas assumed that the rich men of America would do for the American public what the governments of Europe did for the European public. Besides, for himself, he never could see any good sense in gaining money merely to have it. Every mind has its weak spot; this was his. He could not grasp the idea of heaping up a fortune and then sitting upon the heap. So far as he could see, the only excuse for getting money was to use it for some rational purpose, and of all the objects for which money could be spent none was so rational as music. In America were great numbers of men that had become exceedingly wealthy. They owed something to the land where they had been enabled to do this, and as a means of liquidating that indebtedness, what so glorious, what so obvious, as to supply to the masses the ennobling and incalculable benefits of good music?

He was sure, then, that as soon as he had demonstrated the permanence and worth of his object, rich men would make haste to support it and so enable him to carry it to the adorable conditions he held needful to the true orchestral excellence. First, he wanted a band of musicians that performed virtually under his direction, being so well paid that they could concentrate every attention upon their orchestral duties. Second, he wanted a permanent home for them, a hall designed for orchestral concerts and so fitted for the best results.

These were desires to grow upon him. Perhaps the more he was disappointed about them the more they grew; the more they grew the more the want of them irked him daily.

The year was 1864 when he took up the heavy responsibilities of the Theodore Thomas Orchestra. It was also a year momentous in this record, because it was the year of his marriage and by the smile of heaven, not often turned his way, he had to wife an admirable helpmeet.

To this pertains a right pretty little story, the romance of the violin. Theodore Thomas was a well-favored youth; more than one woman had thought so. But he was all for his work and his ambition; women were outside of both. The bachelor style of living was good enough for him, said he, not knowing what his good fortune had in store. At Farmington, Connecticut, Miss Porter was then conducting her school for young women, the most famous institution of the kind in America. Her professor of music was Karl Klauser, another of the many unsung heroes of our artistic history,[1] devotee of good music and sedulously at work to spread it. Having heard the Mason-Thomas Quartette in New York, he induced Miss Porter to bring it to Farmington and give regular concerts at the school. Among the pupils was Minna L. Rhodes, from New York, member of a family with some place in the city's history; a girl of unusual mentality and character. She was both musical and observant. The first time the Quartette played at the school she noticed the remarkable tone and singular finish that pertained to the work of the first violin. This prompted

---

[1]Mason, *Memories of a Musical Life*, p. 29.

her to note what kind of person was making these unusual sounds. She saw a young man in whose face anyone might read honesty, worth, and purpose. After the concert, the pupils were introduced to the players. An acquaintance was thus formed and young Thomas found Miss Rhodes to be of the one class of womanhood that he admired. She had sincerity and intelligence. In his own phrase, he did not care for merely pretty women. The acquaintance was maintained after the pupil had left Miss Porter's academic roof. The next year the engagement was announced of Theodore Thomas and Minna L. Rhodes.[1]

She made him an ideal wife. For one thing, she was wholly sympathetic, and in the stormy years that followed, if ever a man needed sympathy, it was Theodore Thomas. She knew music, knew what her husband was trying to do in music, and made her first objective to smooth the way for him. In every crisis of his life was to appear the good woman, often rather strangely and never more happily than here. In an old New York newspaper I find an eloquent though somewhat unconventional tribute to the wonderful influence that now came into his career.

"She is an enthusiastic housekeeper," says this writer, "and boasts that her husband has never had a badly cooked meal since they were married. To which we might add that Mrs. Thomas is as good a mother as she is a wife, that she is a highly educated and cultured woman and that she never troubles her husband with jealousy or expensive costumes."[2]

Testimony is unanimous that they led a life of rare and almost incredible harmony and happiness. If Mrs. Thomas was a good housekeeper, her husband had domestic virtues of his own. One of them was that he never carried his troubles so far as his

---

[1] Another unusual man not long after found a wife at Miss Porter's school—Georges Clemenceau.

[2] *Mail and Express*, April 12, 1888.

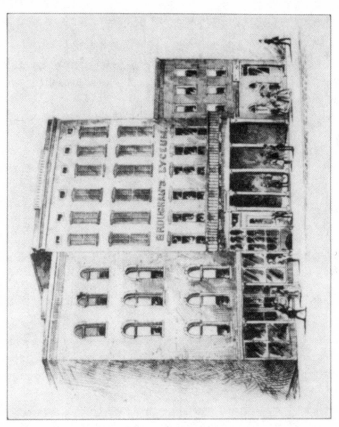

WALLACK'S THEATER

A typical New York playhouse
of that period

THE STADT THEATER

No. 37 Bowery. Thomas played in its
orchestra while still a boy

CASTLE GARDEN

Where Jenny Lind sang and Thomas first heard a symphony

fireside. The savage attacks that came to be made upon him
and his work were to his supersensitive nature like so many
poisoned daggers thrust into his flesh to rankle and torture long
after. But in his household no one ever knew from him why he
sat up all night.

The first season of the Theodore Thomas Orchestra at Irving
Hall, 1864–1865, drew enough money to pay the bills, but what
was more important, it made an obvious impression upon the
public. As before, this young man looked squarely in the eyes
and unafraid the fearful wild fowl of the symphony. At every
concert that season he toyed with the monster. Beethoven's
fangless F major, the Eighth, came first. After that he gave
them Schumann's Second, Raff's "Vaterland," Mozart's
symphony in D (called No. 1), Beethoven's Seventh. How did
he manage to make these go and draw crowds in spite of the
ill name of the thing? He sugared them as before, carefully
compounding the dose; one symphony to three vocal solos, two
piano solos, one light-waisted orchestral novelty, and one good
old stand-by that everybody could whistle. The Philharmonic,
meantime, continued to give its regular season, playing programs impeccable and uninspired as before, and leaving as
much for memory as dewdrops on the rock.[1] So far as one can see
now, these worthy men might have continued thus their occasional wonders to perform till all were purple in the face and
never have wakened the Castle. Yet here was the potent fact
that two orchestras now existed in a city that previously had
not supported one. How could that be? It was evident that the
younger was drawing upon a new element. The better programs
that he offered were one great attraction. He gave the people

[1]"The antiquated, old fogyish New York Philharmonic Society, long since distanced
by the Brooklyn Society in the matter of novelty, variety and general excellence, will
soon have another formidable, and I trust, successful rival in a series of 'Symphonic
Soirées' under the vigorous management and leadership of Theodore Thomas, whose
efforts in the cause of classical music have been so widely appreciated. The subscriptions
already paid in ensure its financial success and there can be no doubt as to its being a
most profitable and enjoyable enterprise." (*Dwight's*, December 10, 1864.)

what they wanted, plus much else. But the way he played these programs was another and still greater magnet. He knew how to seize upon the interesting thing and play it in an interesting manner, a manner that conquered the interest of the most reluctant.

People did not talk at his concerts.

The following summer he had his first little reverse.

Far out in the suburbs of those days, as far as One Hundred and Tenth Street, was an open-air amusement place called Belvidere Lion Park. Thomas and half of his orchestra were engaged to play three afternoons a week at this place. Perhaps what happened was not really a reverse; perhaps he was but testing out. He started with the regulation things, a march, a Rossini overture, a waltz, a polka, a potpourri, galop, quadrille, (not "Firemen's"!) and the like—Rossini, Auber, Strauss, Fahrbach. At each of the next three concerts he tried a symphony. There must surely have been an uproar, for at the fourth concert he switched back almost violently to the waltz, polka, and quadrille strata of human development. Mrs. Thomas surmises that the management objected.[1] In any event, he had found the difference between the audiences that came to Irving Hall and those that could be gathered of a summer night, and he never forgot the lesson.

The next season, 1865–1866, the Irving Hall soirées proceeded upon the sure lines he had felt out the previous year. He utilized every soloist that New York then adored, Parepa-Rosa, Fleury-Urban, Adelaide Phillips, Fanny Raymond, William Kreissman, Carl Wolfsohn, William Mason, S. B. Mills; with well-known names he trapped the unwary. They came to hear famous soloists; once inside, he spellbound them with a solo and loosed the symphony before they knew it.

With him this was the implacable gauge of failure or success.

---

[1] *Memoirs*, p. 23.

He knew it was not enough to play a symphony in public; to play it was nothing unless people heard it. He knew that no one really hears music that does not in one's own mind echo and repeat it as it unfolds and moves along. Wordsworth knew about the inward eye;[1] there is no less an inward ear, and its part in the real hearing of music is indispensable. The reason people did not like symphonies and classical music in general was because they could not manage this feat of repeating back, or thought they could not.

"But what is there so terrible about a symphony?" says Thomas.[2] "As a rule, the principal themes of which it is constructed are as simple melodies as any man ever whistled, a few notes like the song of a bird. Now as soon as one has conquered these two themes, he has in reality conquered the whole movement in which they occur, because so much of that movement is made from the material in those themes. What is necessary, therefore, is to enable people to conquer the themes. After that the rest comes of itself."

The difficulty that hedged around this simple feat was a phantom of the imagination. People, terrified by the name of symphony, would not stop to catch or notice the short melodious themes, but mentally fled in terror—*ventre à terre*, so to speak. Thomas set out to teach them this trick; to train them so they would no longer be symphony shy. From the mass of orchestral literature he chose compositions with unobjectionable names that contained whistle-able passages, passages that the inward ear would catch and the mind echo as it went along; passages similar to a symphonic theme, wherever such passages were to be found, in waltzes, polkas, overtures, suites, anything on earth that had this quality, provided also it had some dignity and musical merit otherwise. If he could get the people into the

---

[1] "The Daffodils," for instance.
[2] Interview in Chicago, 1903.

habit of picking out a tune and remembering it he could get them into the habit of picking out the key themes of a symphony and remembering them no less.

In his Irving Hall soirées he was perfectly willing to play a symphony that would shoot over the heads of nineteen in twenty of the audience if he could place next to it a Strauss waltz or a Rossini overture that had a passage parallel to, or suggestive of, the symphony's neglected theme. He believed that with this juxtaposition the theme would not long remain unperceived.

This was one secret of his masterly program making, in which he was admitted to be unequalled. Another was an indomitable sense of the congruous. The pieces he selected hung together; they cohabited in amity and without quarreling; the ear was not offended in one composition with a dominating note that clashed with the memory of the composition just preceding it. Of course, he was not always able to do this, but he always tried to do it, and I believe his general success in this aim was one reason why his audiences of that day went away satisfied and uplifted and eager to return.

As he went on, certain compositions became standard with him as useful to his ends. These he had no objection to repeating in the same season or even on the next program. In his series of "Popular Concerts," 1863, he played Strauss's "Aurora Ball" polka three times because it contained something that answered his purposes.

To the Belvidere Lion Park engagement succeeded the next summer a much better engagement at Terrace Garden, where he could have a larger orchestra and draw larger audiences. He remembered well what he had learned at the Lion; it was seldom necessary to give him two demonstrations on the same point. Having sounded the shoals of open-air audiences, year of grace 1866, he steered accordingly; polkas, waltzes, marches, overtures, and now and then, when they were off their guard, a movement from a symphony.[1] He was searching for keys to their interest, sympathy, and confidence; they must come to feel that any new, strange, fearsome looking musical novelty that he might put upon a program would probably prove harmless because he had put it there. To win this point he was willing to go fairly far. When he played Bosquet's "Linnet Polka" at Terrace Garden he had the piccolo players hidden in the trees whence they suddenly poured upon the astonished audience below a flood of bird-like melody. When he played the "Carnival of Venice" he had the tuba player hidden in the garden shrubbery—out of which the police chased him under the impression that he was a practical joker.[2]

One thing he would not do, to one thing he was stiff-necked as any old Friesland Lutheran. The selections he played might be as light as feathers, he would not play anything among them that did not have actual musical value. His programs may be scanned in vain for an exception. He was bent on making his audiences yield to him, not on surrendering to them. About this he had all his own way. The summer night concerts became a feature of New York life; for ten years he was to repeat them. His fame grew, and his power. In the winter the soirées continued as before; for the season of 1865–1866 he added Popular Concerts on Saturday afternoons; for the season of 1866–1867, Sacred Concerts on Sunday evenings. With all this, the Mason-Thomas Quartette, of which he was still manager, director, and program-maker, giving six concerts in New York and others out-of-town, as at Farmington and elsewhere—a busy man. He kept up the Brooklyn Philharmonic concerts, also, in which he had a kind of restful joy; he could play what he wanted to play there, and the hall was not wholly a trial to his better sense of acoustics. From 1862 to 1866 he

[1]These programs, to be found in the second volume of Mr. Upton's *Theodore Thomas, a Musical Autobiography*, demonstrate Thomas's purposes and methods. They show an almost even advance from the first to the last.

[2]Autobiography, p. 54.

shared the Brooklyn conducting with Theodore Eisfeld; after that he has it all to himself. At his second concert there, March 7, 1863, he conducts for the first time in his life Beethoven's Fifth Symphony; for the first time he shows to the public his conception of the fateful

On April 14, 1866, he has another joy supreme. He produces in Brooklyn for the first time Beethoven's Ninth, the great choral symphony, all his life the object of his peculiar devotion —for the first time![1]

On November 24 of this year, the second concert of his soirée series, he gives it again, with a quartette of eminent singers and the Mendelssohn Union furnishing the chorus. A great event; listen to the comment:

In the name of the highest interest of art, Mr. Thomas deserves our thanks for bringing out this symphony. With energy and industry he overcame the impediments that lie in the way of such a performance and the call he received at the end of the evening was certainly only a well-merited recognition.[2]

He is happy now in other ways. He has a home; the babies are coming; he plays on the floor with them; there is no man to whom home means more. By all accounts, he is a different being when he crosses the threshold there. Outside he is looked upon, not without awe, as taciturn, severe, exceedingly digni-fied, one that watches his words warily and his walk the same. When the front door of his house closes upon him he drops all that, acts like a rollicking youth, plays with the babies,

---

[1]Mr. Upton thought this to be the first American performance of the Ninth, but the Philharmonic gave it at a special concert as far back as May 20, 1846 (Ritter, pp. 280–281).

[2]*Dwight's*, December 8, 1866.

jumps over the chairs to make them laugh, tells funny stories
and acts them, and is the life of the household. Even when his
curiously daring ventures outside are hanging by eyelids, he
is the same "Pop" to the children.

Birthdays are great events in that abode; anybody's birthday, Mrs. Thomas's, Baby Franz's, the maid's. The celebration
usually begins in the morning and keeps up all day. He devises
it, the taciturn man with the stern face people are a little afraid
of. Not here; he makes the house to shake with gales of laughter
and with his own hands brings in the birthday cake. When he
goes out the next morning he pulls down that mask again,
gets behind it—needs it! For I can tell you one thing about this
man: He must keep a hold upon himself, and the mask helps
him.

In 1866, Steinway Hall was built and he could move away
from Irving, which he never liked. Steinway was not his ideal
for orchestral uses, but it was better than an old barn.

And now I think I had better record a little chapter of incidental record that will show what manner of man we are dealing
with and what odds, contentions, and battlings he must face in
his proselyting tour into heathendom. It was at the concert of
February 23, 1867, in the new Steinway Hall. He had programed
for that occasion the first performance in New York of Liszt's
"Mephisto Waltz," of which he had given the first performance
in America at a Brooklyn Philharmonic on December 8. It
had gone well in Brooklyn, but the New York audiences were
different. On that February evening, the people had come with
appetites whetted for the "Firemen's Quadrille," maybe;
maybe for the "Linnet Polka." Of this, the Abbé's idea of a
waltz, they disapproved early and with candor. Its unconventional strains had not proceeded far when the audience began
to hiss, howl, and whistle until the uproar compelled Thomas to
stop. When there was something like quiet, he started again,
and again the clamor broke out until he desisted. When this

had been repeated, Thomas turned to the audience, took his watch in his hand and waited until the howling had ceased. Then he said:

"I will give you five minutes to leave the hall. Then we shall play this waltz from the beginning to the end. Whoever wishes to listen without making a noise may do so. I ask all others to go out. I will carry out my purpose if I have to stand here until two o'clock in the morning. I have plenty of time."

The audience subsided, Thomas began at the beginning and played the whole waltz and there was no more disturbance.[1]

Despite these encounters in the No Man's Land of his campaigning, his life for the next two or three years goes well. He gains terrain for his fighting. In the summer of 1867 he ventures upon a fleeting trip abroad, goaded by the notion that he must see what other conductors are doing and sit in tuition at the feet of the great. With misgivings he goes, for, after all, compared with practitioners of statelier lands, what is he but an acolyte in this gracious art? As he goes, he keeps a little notebook diary, and enters in it a plain, good story.[2]

First to London, and he has not been there long before he begins to pluck up heart; he finds nothing better than he has done at home and much that is far worse. Thence to the Continent, Paris, Munich, Vienna, Dresden, Berlin, Hanover, hearing performances good and bad and saying so frankly. The opera at Paris he deemed "extraordinary—wonderful!" At Munich, Gungl's orchestra he thought inferior. "No comparison to mine," he wrote. Ella as a conductor in London he set down as "a monkey," Dr. Wylde as "very bad," and Rietz as the first he had met that really knew something. Tausig he hailed as "the ninth wonder of the world." Of Bott's conducting of Beethoven's Seventh he wrote: "A man of no talent and no conductor. We would not dare to play so in America."

---

[1] Frau Lilli Lehmann, *My Pathway Through Life*, p. 344.
[2] Mrs. Thomas, pp. 36–40, prints copious extracts from this diary.

In Vienna he studied Strauss with care, noted what he made of his dance tunes and brought back many for use in America. One thing he learned while he was in Europe. He was plainly astonished to find how well known he was there. European musicians had been watching with interest his venture in America; they had sought his programs and perceived that here was an original and ingenious force from which great things were to be expected. That he had played many of the newest compositions of the most famous European composers was well known everywhere and gave him unusual prestige. Whereas he had expected to have to introduce himself, he found himself known and welcomed with a cordiality that surprised as much as it gratified him. At Vienna the orchestra of the Conservatory played for his benefit; in Dresden Rietz went out of his way to show him attention; at Berlin Tausig played for him "everything imaginable," Thomas wrote, "and became very confidential." In Paris Berlioz presented him with his own copy of the Requiem Mass, cordially inscribed.[1] Beyond the one thing he learned was one thing he gained, which was the enduring friendship of all these men and many others; Hans von Bülow, for instance. Every art has its own speech, and every artist, though surrounded with friends and family, has his periods of desert loneliness unless he can talk to somebody in that speech. Conducting, one of the most intricate and difficult of the arts, has a language that only conductors can understand. Even to excellent musicians that are not conductors it may be worse than Greek. Thomas found in Von Bülow, then the most famous conductor in Europe, a fellow disciple that understood this tongue, and the two corresponded as long as Von Bülow lived. I will give a specimen of their conversation to show what this language really is, and afford a glimpse of the real labors of a conductor.

Thomas said that, in his judgment, the score of Beethoven's

---

[1] Mrs. Thomas, p. 37.

Ninth Symphony was wrong at the end of the $\frac{2}{3}$ measure in D in the Allegro ma non tanto (Finale). Von Bülow replied that Thomas was correct about this. "The C in the wood winds, as a melodious tone, is correct, therefore in the viola and contralto voices must be resolved. I agree thoroughly with your action in strengthening the canto fermo in the trumpets and horns in the $\frac{2}{3}$ tempo. Two years ago I added this in the orchestral parts here. In the finale of the Eighth Symphony, development of $\frac{2}{2}$, I had the two trumpets enter at the beginning of the theme in A major, to strengthen the feeble wood winds in the sustained tone E, and also at the fourth section at D major on A." And so on.[1] It is a world without end and with speech that sounds more like Winsch or Moldavian than anything we know. Shall I have this figure played on the bassoons or the horns? Shall I have the oboes enter at the beginning or the end of the forty-fourth bar of the D major section of the Scherzo? They are like the stars for number, these questions,[2] and most of them about atomies the layman never suspects to exist, but out of which is built the structure of his delight.

Back in New York from his musical pilgrimage, Thomas makes his way with another winter of many cunningly planned concerts; then, summer of 1868, he moves his orchestra for the season to a new garden, the Central Park, where a building has been constructed for it, so much has it become a feature of New York life.[3] The opening of this moved him to an unwonted exercise. His early ambition had been to be composer as well as violin virtuoso. Both hopes he had surrendered when he was lifted by fate into directorship. He now reverted to one of his youthful loves and composed for this auspicious occasion a march, "The Central Park Garden March," now lost to fame. It was said at the time to be lively and engaging, but

---

[1] Mrs. Thomas, pp. 42–44.
[2] In the classical symphonies they frequently arise because of corrupt or faulty scores.
[3] Fifty-ninth Street and Seventh Avenue, afterward a famous riding academy.

in after years the composer would hear nothing about it. One thing that must have stirred him was that this building at the Garden, erected especially for his orchestra—not much in architecture but still a building—was some little realization of his dream and pointed to the rest of it. After a building for the summer, a building for the winter; there would never be any permanence to the orchestra until it had a hall. With all this steady growth of interest in orchestral music and all this demonstrated success, the wise, unselfish rich men that were to come with this offering could not be far off. They had not yet knocked at the door, that was true; but one could see from the roof of Central Park Garden that they were on their way.

He managed the affair with skill and art. When he began the summer-night concerts, there was no place in New York where one could go, have light refreshments, and listen to really good music. He provided such a place. He made it attractive to the eye, first, and then otherwise alluring; principally by his programs, which must have been studied with anxious care to further his process of wedging. He made them into three parts, so that there might be long intervals in which folks could eat, drink, talk, and walk. It is odd to reflect that these things are and long have been familiar upon the continent of Europe but continue to be chiefly alien to America as to England. The Anglo-Saxon must take his music no less sadly than his other pleasures.

What did they hear at the Central Park Garden other than the march dedicated to its glory, that opening concert, May 25, 1868? It was a typical program; after the march, Wagner's "Rienzi" overture, Strauss's "Beautiful Blue Danube" waltz, a fantasia on Donizetti's "Daughter of the Regiment," overture to "Oberon," the Bach-Gounod "Ave Maria," a ballet scene from "Robert le Diable," Von Suppé's overture to the "Pique Dame," a Strauss polka and polka mazourka, a serenade for flute and French horn, a quadrille, "La Grande Duchesse,"

Offenbach. And was that all? No, indeed; slipped in there between the "Ave Maria" and the ballet scene was a bit of symphony, the Allegro Vivace movement from Mendelssohn's "Reformation."

At the next concert but one he does the same thing. Mendelssohn's "Wedding March" (it always catches the young people); Auber's "Masaniello" overture, dramatic, pulsating, easy to get; a Strauss waltz, played so that all listeners felt their feet twitching; a young woman to sing an interesting song; a fantasia, an overture, and then the scherzo from Mozart's Symphony in E flat, between Schumann's "Abendlied" and the "Linnet Polka." One hardly knew it was there; those that did not examine their programs too closely never suspected the trick of it.[1]

One hundred and eighty-seven Garden concerts in the two summers of 1866 and 1867—with programs thus devised.

In the winter the symphony concerts win slowly to favor, the Popular concerts draw increasing audiences, the Brooklyn Philharmonic concerts come near to satisfying his artistic desires. In the season of 1867–1868 the Mason-Thomas chamber concerts reached their highest point in quality of programs and of performance. "Mr. Thomas played superbly," says *Dwight's* critic, reviewing one of these. "We have become so accustomed to that gentleman's preëminence in anything he undertakes that we sometimes overlook the fact that he is one of our first violinists."[2] Also he has become a recognized feature of city life. At the New York Symphony concert of February 15, 1868, an unusually large audience is noticed, and the critic says that "it would really appear that people are beginning to appreciate Mr. Thomas's untiring efforts to afford them an opportunity of hearing and enjoying the very best music at a very moderate price."[3]

---

[1]Upton, Vol. II, p. 103.
[2]*Dwight's*, January 18, 1868.
[3]*Ibid.*, February 29, 1868.

On this occasion he gave them for the novelty he always sought, Von Bülow's ballade, "The Minstrel's Curse" (first time in America),[1] the "Coriolanus" overture, Spohr's violin concerto played by Carl Rosa, and—Beethoven's Seventh Symphony, the whole of it, and the people liked it, at last!

All this looked like the substantiality of success; in truth, it was nothing but the shell. The old trouble lurked under this goodly outside. He had no money. By enlarging his orchestra he had bettered its output but increased his expenses. The New York Symphony concerts for that season, 1867–1868, were given at a loss of $500[2] which he made good with the slender proceeds of the Garden concerts, coming out with all debts paid.

> "Oh, it is pitiful,
> In a whole city full,
> Taste there is none—

or at least not enough to enable Mr. Thomas to pay his expenses," wrote the critic of *Dwight's*.[3] With that season, also, ended the chamber concerts. They had been unprofitable from the beginning;[4] for all their unequalled artistic merit, so that the European musical world followed them with increasing respect, they had been unprofitable. That good man, William Mason, had quietly from his own pocket made up the deficit year after year.[5] The last concert in New York was on April 11, 1868. For thirteen years the combination had given regular performances, season after season, to come to this conclusion.

Thomas's own finances went meantime from bad to worse.[6] The venture of a grand orchestra, exclusively employed and financed from its own earnings, was too desperate. The sym-

---

[1] It had been a failure in Europe. Thomas seems to have changed it somewhat before he played it.

[2] *Dwight's*, November 21, 1868.

[3] *Ibid.*

[4] *Ibid.*, March 1, 1869.

[5] Autobiography, p. 39. They paid "the expenses of the hall and the doorkeeper."

[6] Mrs. Thomas, pp. 51–52.

phony season of 1868–1869 was only another chapter in the one story; admitted artistic success, increasing influence, and increasing deficit. The more the people acquired the taste he hoped for them, the more he must increase his expenses to meet that taste. As the summer went on, it was evident that the Garden concert receipts would not fill the gap left by the previous winter. He had no means of his own, no financial supporters, no rich friends, and no guarantee fund to fall back upon. All he had was a noble purpose and a large handful of contracts obliging him to pay so many salaries every week. He saw that he could no longer take the risk in a field he had worked to the utmost, and the one shred of hope left to him, if he was to keep his orchestra together, was to explore new regions.

There are as many sacrifices for the cause of art as for the cause of religion or of country, but the trouble is, the sacrifices for art, being mental or spiritual and not done with racks and firing-squads, are uncelebrated. Theodore Thomas, on many grounds, hated to leave New York. He had for it the unreasoning (or maybe unreasonable) affection that so many others of its old-time residents used to have. Besides, his home was there, his babies were there; his home meant everything in the world to him, next to his apostleship. He hated to travel; all his life he hated it. Still worse, to go away at that time was to leave his work when it was but begun; New York would now endure a symphony but did not passionately yearn for it. Yet with all these allurements pulling at him, he saw plainly there was no other way. He admitted that his symphony concerts and all the rest, even his beloved Brooklyn, must be abandoned for the next season, and early in November, 1869, with his orchestra, he took to the road.

New Haven, Hartford, Providence, heard him with delight and paid well to hear him, and at last he debouched upon Boston, the musical and artistic capital of the country. If he had doubts of his reception there they were brief. After one hearing,

Boston surrendered to him, brought out the laurel, and never thereafter wavered about him. Only, he found in the press criticisms a certain flavoring, not then exactly sour, but slightly disquieting, that he was destined to know too well afterward. The critics found fault with his programs[1]—because they were too modern! Too much Wagner, too much Liszt, not enough of the good old revered classical prophets, said the stern gospellers of this cult, looking with reproof upon bold heretics.

But the people, musicians and all, rejoiced in him and his programs alike, and brought him substantial tokens of their regard; he prospered (modestly) on the road. From a successful engagement in Boston he moved westward by Worcester, Springfield, Albany, Schenectady, Utica, Syracuse, Rochester, Buffalo, and so on to Chicago, then back by St. Louis, Cincinnati, and other cities to Philadelphia, and home. Everywhere the public had heard of him and crowded his concerts; he came back with money in his purse. Not much money; but even a little was a stranger to which he was prepared to give welcome. Furthermore, he came with the head of the orchestra, for that time, at least, above the dark waters. The next winter, 1870–1871, after the close of the Central Park Garden season, he traversed the same route, extending and varying it. Now he visited the cities that knew and loved him, and he went to others where the soil was virgin to his mission. He had hated to leave New York; in point of fact, it was the best thing he could have done. He was now spreading over the country the seed he had been sowing in but one city.

About this I hope to be not misunderstood. Theodore Thomas did not invent musical interest in America, wielding a magic wand or handing the cup of wizardry to transform people as Circe the Odysseans, only the other way. What he did was to manage to reach down to the latent and unexpressed interest

[1]*Dwight's*, November 6, 1869, and April 23, 1870.

and cause it to come up and be articulate. One way that he did this was through his artful program making, which I have sufficiently indicated and which he carried out wherever he went. The other was through his peculiar playing of the programs aft he had made them. As to which comes at the apt chronological juncture an illustration pertinent to all.

Hans Balatka,[1] one of the great and admirable souls whose work for art lives after them, was then making his desperate sortie to redeem Chicago. He had an orchestra there, the Chicago Philharmonic, by all accounts a good organization, and he a most excellent conductor. But of course, it was not exclusive, and we might well stop to see what difference that made. It was not exclusive; necessarily the members rehearsed with him two or three times a month and blew horns in a brass band or maybe coopered barrels the rest of the time. God knows it was hard enough to get seventy of them together, Chicago, 1868, without inquiring too closely about their other pursuits.

On the night of November 26, 1868, at Farwell Hall, Hans Balatka gave one of his excellent concerts,[2] at which he played Schumann's "Träumerei." The next night, November 27, Theodore Thomas gave a concert at Farwell Hall at which he, too, played Schumann's "Träumerei." So here were the two interpretations laid side by side, one might say, for the inspection of the Chicago public. Balatka played the piece with distinction, with grace, with charm, and according to the canon. But he played it straight through, and plainly, with the orchestra all at normal. Thomas played it with only the strings, leaving out the basses, and at the last with strings muted and all the marvelous effects of faëry that I have described. Of course, there was no just comparison. Balatka had and deserved the approval

---

[1]Born at Hoffnungsthal (prophetic name!), Moravia, March, 1828; came to America in 1849. There is appreciative reference to his good work in Otis's *The Chicago Symphony Orchestra*.

[2]Upton, *Musical Memories*, p. 266.

LOUIS ANTOINE JULIEN   CARL ZERRAHN

CARL BERGMANN   GEORG HENSCHEL

FOUR FAMOUS CONDUCTORS

Reprinted from Elson's "History of American Music"
and Howe's "The Boston Symphony"

Thomas at twenty-four

Mason at eighteen

THOMAS AND HIS FRIEND MASON

of a coldly correct musicianship; Thomas swept every hearer away into cloudland.[1]

"It was a revelation," said the *Tribune* next day. "Dance music played by such an orchestra is enticing enough to wake up a graveyard. We carry away with us alluring memories of that delicate dream work of Schumann's and the sound of the muted violins, and best of all, the Allegretto of the Eighth Symphony which Thomas selected for the encore to the 'Träumerei.'"

It is but too evident from this that here in Chicago again he is at his old tricks. "You like the 'Träumerei'?—listen to this," says he, and slips over a part of a symphony.

In Boston, the next autumn, 1870, he was able to play a two weeks' engagement. If the critics continued to lament his fondness for modern composers, they acknowledged unreservedly the substance of his services.

"But Mr. Thomas gave us real music also," said one, "so we need not fear. And had we room, we should do what we meant to do, try to express in full our sense of obligation for the admirable examples he has brought us of orchestral interpretation, and our conviction of the great good that such an orchestra, visiting all the musical centers and sub-centers of the land is doing, must do, in awakening a taste for music of the highest kind. It has justly been called 'missionary work.'"[2]

Travel was now become his business. New York, his home city, he saw only through the summer season, when he played at Central Park Garden. In the summer of 1869 he gave there 160 concerts; in 1870, 132; in 1871, 134. For his tour of that season, 1871–1872, he had enlarged his plans as well as his orchestra. He was to go into new territory; in all the regions where before he had planted he was now to water with new compositions. In Chicago he was to play two weeks at the Crosby Opera House. Every season, having no capital, he was

[1]See also Otis, p. 11.
[2]*Dwight's*, November 5, 1870.

obliged to incur a debt that he might finance the beginning of the tour. So close to the rocks he was at all times; he must borrow until the first concert receipts. This year he borrowed a little more, and set forth confidently, to walk into his first great disaster.

There was then living in Chicago at Twelfth Street and Michigan Avenue, another of those indefatigable champions of good music to whose unobtrusive efforts the country owes so much. Philo Adams Otis was his name; his father a pioneer in the days when Chicago was an Indian trading village, himself a pioneer in every good cause. On the morning of Monday, October 9, Mr. Otis started from his house to note the course of a fire that had broken out the night before. At State Street he came upon a line of men walking cityward and carrying musical instruments. Music being the business of his soul, he spoke to them.[1] It appeared that they were members of the Theodore Thomas Orchestra, just arrived. At the Twenty-second Street station of the Lake Shore & Michigan Southern Railroad they had been cast adrift with the information that their train would proceed no farther, and they were now walking down to the Opera House because they were to have a rehearsal there that morning. They did not walk far. Mrs. O'Leary's cow had done her justly celebrated work the night before and at the hour for rehearsal there was no Opera House and not much of a Chicago.

Mr. Thomas got his musicians together, commandeered a train and took them to Joliet, Illinois, to await events. And here he did a thing characteristic of that real man that he so carefully hid behind his mask of austerity. The contracts with his players contained the usual provision that, if performances should be prevented by accident, fire, flood, or that elastic intervention known legally as "the act of God," salaries were to cease likewise. Thomas, already in debt and cheated of the engagement with which he had expected to pay his creditors, refused to take advantage of this clause. The next engagement

[1]Otis, p. 13.

was to be at St. Louis, October 23. He kept his men at Joliet those two weeks and paid them as if they had been playing all the time. It was a generosity that ruined him. Chicago had been his largest hope on that tour. It failed him, and when the season was over he was penniless and in debt.[1] He was one of those uneasy souls to whom debt is a mad pursuing demon with horns and hooves. Anxiety plucked hard at him when he began anew the Central Park Garden series, May 14, 1873.

Yet he had accomplished that winter two things that, beyond any suspicion of his, were important in the history of American music and his own. He had clinched in Boston the hold of orchestral music and so started the movement that was to flower in the great Boston Symphony Orchestra; he had created the appetite, he had set the fashion. In one Boston engagement he had (plump in the faces of the critics) produced twenty-six orchestral compositions not before heard in America's musical capital but destined to a long acquaintance there. He had played, too, in a new way many old favorites, and opened to new hosts the Elysian fields.

That was one good thing. The other was that at Cincinnati he had started the plans for the Cincinnati musical festival of 1873, the first in the remarkable series of such events that has never ceased since and has been a center dynamo of musical inspiration for all the West.

This meant much for that mission of his and much for himself. He was so constituted that he must have work to keep him in mental and physical health.[2] In the worst of his troubled days if he had on hand some great project, he could shut himself into it and often defy his worries. The Cincinnati Festivals in after years were a boon to him. The preparation of the programs was an absorbing occupation, with healing in its wings. At the beginning he owed it to the timely appearance of the

[1] Mrs. Thomas, pp. 71–72; Autobiography, pp. 59–60.
[2] Mrs. Thomas, p. 72.

good woman. On this visit he had made the acquaintance at Cincinnati of Maria Longworth, then Mrs. Nichols, afterward Mrs. Bellamy Storer, an enthusiast about music and all other arts, and a restless, aspiring, commanding, and marvelously efficient being. It was in reality she that suggested the Festival, and Thomas, with her intelligent coöperation, made the plans and worked out the details. Without her help and her capital there would have been no such enterprise.[1]

And now he came back to the Central Park Garden, where the story of the programs is like the account of a prolonged siege skilfully conducted. He began, as we have seen, at about the level of the "Linnet Polka." By 1870 he had led his flock up to the symphony (occasionally) and they stood still and were unafraid of it.[2] In that queer little pocket notebook of his he worked out his programs far in advance and made quaint curt comments as he went along. The book for 1870 has this notation: "At last the summer programs show a respectable character and we are rid of the cornet! Occasionally a whole symphony is given." It is the Te Deum of his triumph.

The citadel he had approached with mines and trenches and lines of circumvallation. The programs show. At the first concert that year he had occupied his first trench, which in those years was won with the "Tell" overture. This was a work perfectly fitted to his designs; it was easily mastered, there were things in it a man could whistle, it was lively and varied, it expressed something human. It might be light and superficial, but it went with a bang, and what was much more important, it had hooks in it to seize and hold the imagination. This was exactly what he wished to do about symphonies, and he saw that a man that had taken to heart the "Tell" overture was not far from the kingdom of heaven whose four square walls bound the symphonic streets of gold.

---

[1]Mrs. Thomas, p. 73.
[2]Upton, Vol. II, pp. 115–116.

Ten nights later, May 19, he played the "Tell" again and that night accompanied it with the third movement of Beethoven's Eighth. That is, having won a trench he proceeded to consolidate his position and then stole out and captured another, showing good tactics. An educator is like a general: he must be wary. A week later he slips in two movements (the cunning schemer!) from Schumann's D minor, the No. 4. Next week he puts in one movement from Schubert's Unfinished and two movements from Schumann's First, the larghetto and scherzo. A little later he springs two movements from Schubert's C major. All these carefully masked behind many Strauss waltzes, polkas, behind arias and solos, but also behind Beethoven overtures and other things always rising in quality.[1] It is a great fight; he is winning it. It is much to be "rid of the cornet," by which he means that it is no longer necessary to have brass bands and horn soloists night after night to lure people into the Thomas clutches. They come of themselves. "Well, go thy ways, old lad, for thou shalt ha' it," symphony and all. On August 18, he plays Mozart's in D and the thing is done. Soon after he can play Beethoven's Sixth; and the Garden constituency (much more representative and difficult to win than any highbrow audience gathered of a winter night in Fourteenth Street) likes it and thinks the picture of the storm is great.

He was mindful of the fact that while many persons came regularly to these summer concerts, his following was, after all, somewhat shifting; he must provide for newcomers as well as old. As he went on, he leaned more and more upon a certain range of compositions as handy introducers to the symphonic taste and mood, the "Tell" overture, Liszt's Second Rhapsody, certain Strauss waltzes, particularly the "Blue Danube," Weber's "Invitation to the Dance," and to a less degree the

[1] "But it was also noticeable that the evenings devoted to the severer class of music, old or new, in the Garden Concerts at New York were the most fully attended." (Grove's *Dictionary of Music*, p. 195, Vol. 5, Edition of 1910.)

"Coriolanus" overture, useful because of its repetition of one theme until even the least musical could get it. Of 125 specimen programs played at the Central Park Garden, the "Tell" overture appears on fifteen. At the same time, no man could have been more zealous in hunting out novelties of worth. It was at these concerts that Wagner's "Kaiser March,"[1] "Huldigung's March,"[2] and many other compositions now standard favorites had their first hearing in America.

"The only difficulty," wrote one commentator, "seemed to be to prevent the crowd from being too great, for Mr. Thomas's personal popularity is such that doubling the usual price of admission seemed to increase rather than diminish the attendance."[3]

One night at these concerts he was in collision with the encore fiend, with results attractive to the philosophical. The belief, still lingering, that in demanding an encore the public is conferring a favor on the performer, was then universal. The reverse of this shield is still chiefly unexhibited. Take an orchestra, for instance. A composition that an audience demands again may have left the orchestra too tired to play at all. It may have left such an impression as the conductor is unwilling to disturb by an inferior repetition. There may be other good reasons why, for the sake of the audience itself, an encore is highly undesirable.[4] It appears from the records of that day that Thomas gave encores sometimes and sometimes he declined them. On this occasion the audience demanded a repetition of the "Huldigung's March" immediately after the orchestra had played Liszt's "Fest Klange." Thomas felt that the players were too tired to do themselves justice and sought to escape by many genuflexions.

[1] June 22, 1871.
[2] September 8, 1871. See Upton, Vol. II.
[3] *Dwight's*, June 29, 1872.
[4] Thomas has explained all this in his remarks on "The Encore Habit," which are part of the Introduction he wrote to the printed volume of his programs; an adequate and reasonable explanation, to be found at p. 2.

The audience refused to be satisfied with these and continued to demonstrate. Whereupon Thomas calmly left his stand, took a seat among the players, and allowed the noise-makers to proceed until they were weary.[1] It was a bold thing to do and an injudicious. It adorned him with a title that he had hardly earned and that therefore stuck to him the rest of his life, more or less. To a part of the public he was now Thomas the Autocrat. Nothing could be simpler. Sometimes he gave encores, sometimes he did not. Hence, autocrat. Yet one might possibly reflect that an orchestra is not an electric piano; it is not turned on and off with a handle. A grand orchestra, if it is anything, is as much a spiritual as a material projection. A perfect performance requires not only the utmost concentration and spiritual exaltation among the players but a peculiar rapport between players and leader. To any conductor that is also an artist a defective performance is a species of torture, while to the audience it is in effect an injury. It was for their own advantage that Thomas negatived the will of the plaudit mongers. Nevertheless, there was the ostensible fact. Sometimes he gave encores and sometimes he gave them not. Hence, whim, caprice, and the autocrat.

It was he also that exercised conspicuously a mollifying effect upon such bad manners in the audience as we have before noted. He made people stop talking by the expedient of remaining with his hands in the air until he had won silence. He had other methods equally effective and still more fertile in additions to his autocratic renown. One night, at the Central Park Garden, he was playing a movement from a Beethoven symphony, a work to him like the altar of the covenant, when a young man that sat with his girl near the front wrecked the harmonics by repeated attempts to light a match and so fire his cigar. The matches were of the old and explosive style and every time they snapped the nerves of the sensitive Thomas

[1] *Dwight's*, June 29, 1872.

were wrung like a man on the rack. At last he could stand it no more and dropped his arms. The orchestra stopped in the middle of a cadenza. Thomas turned around and fixed his blue, blazing eyes on the offender.

"Go on, young man," he said with the ironic politeness that signaled the worst to those who knew him, "Go on and light your cigar. Don't mind us—we can wait."[1]

To Carl Bergmann, New York had owed its first introduction to Wagner; at the Philharmonic concerts he played Wagner when it was as much as his artistic life was worth. Theodore Thomas, following this worthy pioneer, made Wagner popular, made him an idol, ended by making him, in the curious way we are to see, a power to unhorse himself.

"When Wagner was little more than a name in America," says W. S. B. Mathews, "Thomas began to give copious extracts from his works. It was as long ago as 1870 that he introduced the 'Ride of the Valkyries,' by Wagner. This strange piece made a great impression. Not long after he was able to add the 'Magic Fire Scene,' from the same opera, and 'Siegfried's Funeral March.'[2] The sources from which he obtained these and other Wagnerian excerpts soon became to the whole musical world of America and Europe a curious and baffling puzzle, long debated. It was well known that Wagner, with the utmost care,[3] guarded his compositions, refusing to allow any of them to go to America under the belief that America would lose for him his European copyright. In the face of this absolute prohibition, Theodore Thomas continued to bring out Wagnerian novelty after novelty. How did he get them? Mrs. Thomas prints[4] a letter from Hans von Bülow, written in

---

[1]Upton, *Reminiscence and Appreciation*, p. 133.

[2]*A Hundred Years of Music in America*, pp. 421–422. Prof. Mathews was writing from memory and antedated the first actual performance of "The Ride of the Valkryies" by two years.

[3]Mathews, p. 422.

[4]Mrs. Thomas, pp. 78–79.

August, 1872, in reply to one from Thomas asking Von Bülow's intercession with Wagner on this point. Von Bülow says it is useless; Wagner obstinately refuses to allow even German conductors to see these coveted works. Still Thomas continues to get them. Mrs. Thomas, who does not herself know how he got them, thinks the secret will remain hidden.[1] Prof. Mathews thinks he knows it.

"It is generally believed," he says, "that Thomas received his copies of these pieces from Liszt, who had them copied without Wagner's knowledge, believing that in no other way could he more rapidly advance the great composer's recognition." And again he says: "The 'Bacchanale' from Wagner's 'Tannhäuser' [the piece Thomas most desired to secure through Von Bülow], Mr. Thomas obtained from Paris and played it several years before it was heard in Europe outside the French Opera House, for which Wagner originally wrote it."[1]

On September 17, 1872, he had created enough of a passion for Wagner to give an exclusively Wagnerian program when he played the "Kaiser March," the Vorspiel to "Lohengrin," Vorspiel to the "Meistersinger," Vorspiel and finale from "Tristan und Isolde," and for the first time in America the "Ride of the Valkyries" and the ballet music from "Rienzi." In recognition of this event, Wagnerians in New York gave a banquet to the orchestra and its leader and formed that night the Wagner Verein, Theodore Thomas, president.

It raised $10,000 for Wagner's Baireuth enterprise.[2]

_____

[1] Mrs. Thomas, p. 79.

[2] "Wagner for a long time despaired of the visible execution of his ideas. At last the celebrated pianist, Tausig, suggested an appeal to the admirers of the new music throughout the world for means to carry out the composer's great ideas—viz., to perform the 'Niebelungen' at a theater to be erected for the purpose, and by a select company, in the manner of a national festival, and before an audience entirely removed from the atmosphere of vulgar theatrical shows. After many delays, Wagner's hopes were attained, and in the summer of 1876 a gathering of the principal celebrities of Europe was present to criticize the fully perfected fruit of the composer's theories and genius." (Ferris, *Great Musical Composers*, p. 144.)

CHAPTER V
Wagner Comes in and Goes out

ALL these years the sower was scattering seed across the country, but, except for the summer night's planting, none in New York, which he had first undertaken to redeem. This disquieted him: he was desperately fond of New York. For three years the symphony concerts had been intermitted, and other persons than Thomas had lamented the loss of them. In August, 1872, he had unexpected evidence of this effect. A group of eminent men of New York, Whitelaw Reid, Henry de Coppet, and others, united in a petition to him to resume his winter work in the city and give to New York some of the pleasure he was now giving to so many other cities. They did not offer him a hall in which he could do this, nor a guarantee fund to uphold him. They only asked him to come and play and take the risk.[1] It is safe to say that in these days no conductor would dream of such an adventure, and this man was already harassed by debts and without money or the means to get it. He must have puzzled long over the problem, for he did not answer the letter until September 18, when he sent an acceptance.

He had now involved himself in some of the most remarkable saltatory feats ever known to traveling amusement combinations. As there was no permanent home in New York and the orchestra could be kept alive only by its out-of-town engagements, he was obliged to rush up and down the country like some form of maniac, carrying the whole band with him. In

---

[1]Mrs. Thomas, p. 82; Autobiography, pp. 61–62.

that winter, 1872–1873, he played six engagements in New York, and between them covered the whole of his regular route and more. He would work out West as far as Chicago, St. Louis, or Cincinnati and then shoot back to play in New York and Brooklyn. Then he would play the New England cities, make another leap back to New York and be on his way to Chicago, Milwaukee, and Kalamazoo, whence again a wild flight to the metropolis.[1] For a man that hated traveling, this will be admitted to be a kind of crucifying. Four times that winter he got as far West as Chicago, and six months he had of these journeyings without respite from September 26 in Albany to March 30 in New York.

He was one that was all for home and the fireside; to these he was become no more than an occasional visitor. He liked good things to eat and drink;[2] he was condemned to live upon the petrified steak and amorphous potatoes then and long afterward the standard dietary at the interior American hotel. He liked an uninterrupted series of advancing programs played week upon week in one place where he could note effects; now was he a wandering comet of music, shining upon one-night stands that knew him little and his canons less.

In his curious make-up there was not enough stoic to leave him callous to hardship and injury, but enough to keep him silent about them. He never complained about his traveling troubles, although they must have been at times heartbreaking. He would finish an evening concert at 10:30, let us say. For reasons I shall presently unfold, he must then have something to eat. By the time this duty was performed, midnight would be long passed. He might get to bed at 1 o'clock. By 5 a bellboy would be pounding at his door. There was a train to Goshen at 5:45 and the troupe must board it to make the next engagement. Sometimes the seven-times accursed train left at 5 or 4:40, or

[1]Mrs. Thomas, p. 85.
[2]Upton, *Reminiscence and Appreciation*, p. 252.

other barbarous, unseemly hour. No matter; he must hop up, snatch a cup of coffee (strong enough to lift the house, it was, incidentally),[1] and start for the train. After which, he must try to impart to his players all the strange spiritual and psychological inspirations out of which great performances were made.

For the better part of six months this was the life he led. There was also something else, and worse, to torture him. I have spoken of his horror of bad halls, places where the effects he wanted were impossible. If they were of this order in the large cities, imagine them in the small! He played in churches where there were echoes and in pavilions where every finer strain was lost among the rafters, and at the end, but for his religion and his training at his mother's knee, he would have been ready to die amid cursings and the gnashing of teeth.

I said he liked good things to eat and drink, but he drank and ate in extreme moderation. He drank wine and sometimes beer. Of wines he was a connoisseur; he knew all the famous vintages of the world, but a glass or two out of a bottle was enough for him; he tasted the sunlight and flowers in it as he tasted melody in music and with much the same æstheticism.

His life he regulated with the utmost rigor; a fact that with his constitution of iron explains the labors he was able to undergo. He was all for the straight walk in all things; with the rest he would have no smut. About the time we are now speaking of, a friend was one day in his office transacting business, which being concluded the visitor started to tell a story. In a moment or two the nature of it was disclosed; it was going to be salacious. Thomas stopped him.

"You must not tell stories like that to me," said he.

"Why not?" asked the friend, a little nettled. He was not used to be reproved by his men associates.

"Because in the first place I don't like them," said Thomas, "and in the second place they are not for me to hear. Suppose

---

[1] Mrs. Thomas, p. 251, and again at p. 253.

you tell me this story and to-night when I am about to conduct some work of beauty and purity I catch sight of your face in the audience. Do you not see that involuntarily my mental state is distorted from the idea of purity I ought to have, and it will not be possible for me to give to that composition the interpretation of perfect purity that it demands?"[1]

Fanatic, or fossil, I suppose he would be called by a later and wiser day; at least he exercised upon himself the incessant watchful scrutiny of a devotee doing orisons. A great reader, always with a book in his hand when not at work upon his performances, he made it an absolute rule to avoid not alone everything impure but everything rubbishy; would not read light novels, sensational newspaper stories, or other literary offal. Mrs. Thomas quotes him as saying:

I avoid trashy stuff. Otherwise, when I come before the public to interpret master works, and my soul should be inspired with noble and impressive emotions, these evil thoughts run around in my head like squirrels, and spoil it all.

A musician must keep his heart pure and his mind clean if he wishes to elevate instead of debasing his art.

And here we have the difference between the classic and the modern schools of composers. These old giants said their prayers when they wished to write an immortal work.[2]

Early in his experience as a conductor he had formed the habit of eating but little before the battle of a concert, holding with wise public speakers and wise actors that as his task was psychological and spiritual his mind and spirit were best and freest when he was farthest from any state of physical repletion. This is the reason why he must have supper after the concert; the strain being over, the physical man reasserted himself. When he was about to conduct a great work, like Beethoven's Ninth or a Händel oratorio, for that day he saw nobody, did not come to

[1]Communicated by one of his surviving friends. Conf. Mrs. Thomas, p. 16.
[2]Mrs. Thomas, *ibid.*

the family table, and partook of only the slightest food sent to his room where he had imprisoned himself to meditate and to prepare his soul for the ordeal.[1] An impression once persisted in some minds that the conducting of an orchestra was, after all, rather simple: wave your arms and make signals and so to the end. As a matter of fact, it is one of the most complicated, difficult, intorted, and bedeviled occupations known to man. No matter how many times Thomas might have conducted a Beethoven symphony, for instance, whenever it recurred upon one of his programs he gave to it as much intensive study and thought as if he had not before seen it.[2] He went over in his mind all the difficult phrases and worked himself into the mood required as a skilful pilot works a ship into its marks. Then he went to the stand, impressed his feeling upon the players and came home happy—or depressed, as the case might be.

But in the beaten way of narrative again, he got through that season, 1872–1873, alive by the grace of his abnormal physique, but without money in his purse. Seventeen times he returned to appear in New York and Brooklyn, but meantime he had journeyed four times to Chicago and given eighty-five concerts outside of New York. Three engagements he had played in Boston, two in Cincinnati, two in St. Louis. He had resumed, to his joy, the conductorship of the Brooklyn Philharmonic; he had completed the conquest of Philadelphia. In Boston the critics still grumbled a little about his too modern programs, but they acknowledged ungrudgingly the master spirit and skilled hand that prepared those feasts. "That it is the most perfect orchestra on this side of the Atlantic, in all respects except in numbers," wrote one, "is clear enough, and has been clear for several years—indeed from the time that it began its annual circuit through the music-loving towns and cities East and West." He went on to recite the advantages

---

[1] Mrs. Thomas, p. 414.

[2] Otis; Upton, *Reminiscence and Appreciation*, p. 348.

this band possessed in playing so much under one leader, and then added:

Not every one, nor one in a thousand, probably, could wield them with the power and the intelligence and subtle faculty of Mr. Thomas. He is rarely gifted for the master spirit of an orchestra; in a singularly cool and quiet way, he has his forces perfectly in hand. We only marvel sometimes at his taste,

and so sounds again the sad wail over Wagner and Liszt and Berlioz whom, despite so much advice from his betters, this person insists upon playing.[1]

At the end of the season he has his revenge, this incorrigible one. He makes for two weeks a combination with Rubenstein, the popular pianist, and Wieniawski, the hardly less popular violinist. To hear these famous men the people rush headlong, filling each hall to capacity. Having thus secured them in a corral from which there is no escape the villain Thomas proceeds to make them listen to a new and higher grade of classical music and they cannot help themselves. It was at the close of this tour that Rubenstein, writing to William Steinway, said he had found in America "the greatest and finest orchestra in the wide world." He had been in Munich, Brussels, Amsterdam, London, Paris, Vienna, Berlin, all the great European art centers, but had found nothing like this. But one orchestra, in his judgment, could play as well, the old Imperial of Paris, composed of trained musicians that were engaged for life and rehearsed a number twenty times before they gave it; but even these had no Theodore Thomas to conduct them.[2]

When at last he is done with traveling for that season, does he rest? As much as the trade wind. At once he plunged into a week's Musical Festival at Steinway Hall, New York, with a chorus brought especially from Boston and the best solo singers

---

[1]*Dwight's*, December 14, 1872.
[2]Upton, *Reminiscence and Appreciation*, p. 239.

in America; an event in New York's musical history. Without intermission followed the Cincinnati Festival that he had planned with Mrs. Nichols. The vocal soloists were Annie Louise Cary, Myron W. Whitney, Nelson Varley, Mrs. H. M. Smith. There was a chorus that sang "The Heavens Are Telling," from Haydn's "Creation"; a Choral from "Tannhäuser"; "Welcome, Mighty King," from Händel's "Saul"; other pieces, and public school children that sang "The Star-Spangled Banner." Seven programs; the orchestral numbers being chosen (of course) to further Mr. Thomas's ulterior aim. As he knew a great crowd would be drawn from all parts of the West and contain many to whom the grand orchestra would be a novelty, he made a liberal sprinkling of light works among the things he wanted them to carry home. Three Strauss waltzes and a Strauss polka, Auber's overture to "Fra Diavolo," the inevitable "Tell" overture, and the "Träumerei," but he also played Schumann's Second Symphony, Beethoven's Ninth, a movement from Beethoven's Eighth, and two movements from Schubert's C major.[1]

The veritable grandeur and splendor of this achievement, to which the West, or the East either, in 1873 has known no fellow, strikes deep into the popular mind; not alone in Cincinnati, but throughout all the interior. It is talked of in hundreds of communities represented in that vast throng in the old Exposition Building; it continues to be talked of. It has disseminated music into remote regions as the heart sends blood to the finger tips.

From Cincinnati back without loss of time to the Central Park Garden. This season he is happier than ever; he has led his indifferent, casual, summer-night public to the point where he can give one night in each week a whole symphony, and his public likes it and begins to understand it. Happier, again, because certain rich men seem to be entertaining a purpose to

[1] All these programs can be found in Upton, Vol. II, pp. 156–182.

THE GERMANIA ORCHESTRA

Carl Zerrahn at the left; Carl Bergmann in the center. Reprinted from Elson's "History of American Music"

INTERIOR OF TRIPLER HALL

Afterward Booth's Theater. It was here that Thomas for the first time appeared
as soloist in a New York concert

build him an orchestral home, the realization of his dream. He always said they would, and now he is so sure of them that he draws up a complete plan for such a building. Seating capacity ordinarily 2,500, but so arranged that for festivals it can be increased to 5,000; the right proportions and shape of the hall so as to secure the best sound results; the slope of the floor, the finish of walls and ceiling—all in wood, for the sake of the sound. Summer-night concerts, winter symphony series, an orchestra engaged permanently, 70 for the summer-night concerts, 100 for the winter symphony seasons. For the winter, five months; twelve evening symphony concerts, twelve symphony matinées, twenty-four Sunday evening concerts for the masses, twenty-four concerts, one every week, for young people, and then out-of-town engagements every other week. For the summer, a concert every evening, a matinée every Saturday afternoon. Any rest for conductor and men? Assuredly; two weeks, in which he may be conducting a festival in Cincinnati.[1]

Everything was thought out in this plan, provided for, detailed; even the beer tables for the summer nights. He saw the structure arising; he knew what it would look like. What a central station for the musical education of America! He must have been supremely happy when he was projecting this bounty for generous and altruistic wealth. He would not have been happy at all if he had known the dreary years that would pass before he should see any of it realized.

He wanted a chorus, too, in this great establishment; a chorus highly trained, so he could do the Ninth Symphony as it ought to be done, and a school; a school in which ensemble playing should be taught with other branches of music so as to assure America a future supply of orchestra players and be rid of this necessity to send abroad for everybody. All music was to be taught there, harmony, counterpoint, composition. And (wise and thoughtful man!) he conceived that there should be a school

[1]Mrs. Thomas, pp. 96–98.

orchestra pupils should learn to conduct—one that should play the compositions of pupils and so give budding genius a chance.

It was the ripe fruit of all the thinking he had done about music in America. Much of the dream was to come true, but not then. The company or society or committee of rich men that Thomas had always envisioned failed him and faded away. He was left facing the same old situation, almost incessant traveling, one-night stands, the horrors of the country hotel, harassing debts, the grim struggle to live, this loss to be balanced by to-morrow's gain, and the rest. What hurt his pride was something else. So much confidence he had placed in the advances of these Mæcenases, he had announced to the orchestra and to the public that after the spring of 1874 he would not make another tour of the country, since the orchestra was to have a permanent home in New York. The next season, 1874–1875, found him again upon the circuit.

For the sting of this disappointment, there was consolation in the second Cincinnati music festival, May, 1875. That there was to be a second was in itself proof that he had sown wisely and well; that for this second he could distinctly raise the quality of the music he offered was another balm to his soul.[1] No more Strauss polkas, no more waltzes, but music of an enduring merit, enduring interest, Beethoven's Seventh, great chorals and solos from the oratorios, great songs by great singers, Wagner, Mendelssohn, Schubert, tremendous things, sufficiently relieved with lighter compositions, the "Tell" overture, the Second Rhapsody; but for the most part, grave, serious, enduring things. The second festival is even more successful than the first had been. The third is immediately arranged for.

"It is to the high honor of the Festival Committee and of

---

[1] "The whole country is beginning to taste the fruit that Theodore Thomas has been so long cultivating." (New York *Tribune*, May 20, 1875.)

"Thomas's orchestra is gaining fame abroad. Liszt, Raff, and Wagner express a desire to have their works performed by this society, and Raff has recently composed for Thomas a suite in five numbers for solo violin and grand orchestra." (*Brainard's Musical World*, February, 1874.)

Theodore Thomas," wrote the special correspondent of the New York *Tribune*, "that he did choose works like the 'Song of Triumph,' the Bach 'Magnificat,' which are as yet far above the apprehension of the public. The festival broke up in the midst of an indescribable scene of enthusiasm, singers and audience all hurrahing together, and loud shouts for Thomas rising above the din."[1]

He was reputed to be the coolest and most self-possessed conductor that ever raised a baton, and many a person that saw him for the first time had an impression (for the moment) that he must be uninspiring. At this second Cincinnati festival a newspaper correspondent that secured a good place from which to watch the imperturbable Thomas had another story to tell about him like this:

Those that are accustomed to see him conduct his own famous orchestra and note the calm composure and grace of his leadership ought to see him on his war-horse when he leads a vast chorus in addition. He is, indeed, a master of the situation through all excitement, violent in gesture, imperious, impetuous, striking with his baton, beating out with both arms, stamping his feet like a big drum, even shouting out the word of command—he seems to center in himself the passion and the energy of the chorus. He fixes the eyes of all the singers on himself, and carries them with him in the rush of his rapture. . . . All the singers say how excited he makes them; he is a born leader.[2]

But things were not really going as well with him as superficies indicated. In more ways than one he was beginning to reap the results of too much prominence. In Boston a daily newspaper, because he would not abandon his plan about programs, accused him of mercenary objects. "There is no question of Mr. Thomas," said this authority. "His efforts are for money and ambition, and he is, as a shrewd entrepreneur, abundantly

[1] *Tribune*, May 20, 1875.
[2] Baltimore *Bulletin*, May 16, 1875.

able to settle all these matters with his patrons."[1] When the Cincinnati Festival Committee in its prospectus said that the community owed to him "its appreciation and love of what is purest and best in music," some newspapers derisively remarked that lovers of classical music existed in America before Theodore Thomas was born.[2]

This would be unimportant if Thomas were not so sensitive to every unfair attack and if it were not symptomatic of a growing trouble. He came back now from his Cincinnati success to the summer-night concerts and a new disaster. His very success was tending to his undoing. For these twelve years he had been teaching the people of New York to understand and to enjoy orchestral music. For ten years his summer-night concerts at Central Park Garden had been a feature of New York life. New York had taken most kindly to the innovation of a concert garden with a little good beer and a great deal of good music. The crowds had been growing, year after year, in size and enthusiasm. The result was to have been expected. A host of imitators sprang up. Summer-night concerts in garden spots were opened all about the city. At most of them the music was of the boshiest kind, but they were gardens, they had beer, and the great point about them was that they were in the neighborhood and accessible; one no longer had to travel by horse car (and belike ferry) the weary leagues that lay between one's home and Central Park Garden. Intraurban communication in those days was a fearful and wonderful thing. A dweller in Brooklyn that went at night to a New York theater had best take his evening meal along with him and make a picnic on the street car. The new concert gardens obviated much of that trouble. Nearly every man could find one somewhere near his home, and the difference in the quality of the music was not enough to his mind to justify him in sitting up most of the night.

---

[1] *Tribune*, May 20, 1875.
[2] Boston *Advertiser*, December, 1874.

The result of all of which was that the Thomas summer season of 1875 was the worst in point of receipts[1] he had ever played in New York, although in the excellence of the programs offered it was the best. The joy of those that attended was unbounded, the criticisms were most laudatory, even the critics highest of brow admitted a splendid achievement, and the owners of the enterprise decided to close it for lack of receipts. This was the last summer that Thomas played at Central Park. He went away defeated in purse and crowned with an extraordinary victory. He had created in his city a movement for music that nothing could stop and for which his rewards were a spiritual satisfaction and a load of debt.

All this time he was financing his enterprise alone. Incredible as it may seem that in all that great city there should not be enough public spirit among its wealthy men and women to give him authentic help, yet that was the fact. Nothing is clearer now than that this man was performing for the community a work of education and public service beyond all estimate, and he had to go to it alone. To keep his orchestra together he was now obliged to travel all summer as well as most of the winter. In one way, and that pertaining to his mission, this had an advantage: it compelled him to enlarge his circuits and visit new fields. Otherwise it was only an additional torture. What oppressed him most was that with all his traveling and his incessant labors he sank farther and farther into debt, and this despite the most rigid personal economies and sacrifices. The outlook seemed all but hopeless, when in 1876 the American Centennial year opened. In good time he was cheered by an appointment to be musical director of the ceremonies, and an offer to play with his orchestra in Philadelphia while the Centennial Exposition should last. He never suspected that his evil

---

[1]It appears from *Dwight's*, September 18, 1875, that these troubles were multiplied by the lessee of the Garden, or someone else, who disappeared, leaving large bills for Thomas to pay.

fate concealed behind these goodly things two blows heavier than any that had so far fallen upon him.

The arrangement was that he was to give nightly concerts at a hall provided in an inconvenient region of Philadelphia. Thomas was wise and shrewd about many things, but if he had been able to manage his business adroitly while he was heart and soul intent upon spreading musical knowledge and obtaining orchestral perfection, he would have been the phenomenon of the ages. The arrangement about these Philadelphia concerts was ill considered.[1] The persons that engaged him guaranteed nothing; it was he that assumed all the risk. This he thought was nothing, because of the occasion. Being himself full of the spirit of the Centennial he thought the great crowds that were coming to the exposition would throng the concert hall at night. The physical facts against him were too ponderous. Philadelphia stretched over all outdoors. There was no center for the crowds nor anything approaching one. The exposition visitors were scattered at night over an immense area and stayed in their hotels and boarding houses. I believe theaters and other evening amusement places had at first the same experience.[2] The evening orchestra concerts were sparsely attended and the only tangible result of the engagement was the sure promise of more debt.

This was bad enough, but in Thomas's mind not comparable to the other catastrophe that overtook him.

As director of music for the Centennial exercises he thought to make the occasion memorable by producing a new work especially written for it by the composer that he held of all living composers most in reverence. Virtually, he had intro-

---

[1] Autobiography, pp. 66–68. Thomas calls the Philadelphia engagement a "dismal failure." If he had had more ego he might have found a measure of success in it.

[2] "All the musical enterprises connected with the Centennial proved to be financial failures, except the Centennial Musical Festival of ten days beginning September 20, which was under the leadership of Thomas." (*Brainard's Musical World*, November, 1876.)

duced Richard Wagner to America, he had played for the first
time in America nearly all the Wagnerian repertoire, he had
formed and was president of the Wagner Verein, he had received from Wagner letters of effusive thanks. He was sure that
the composer that had written the "Kaiser March" and the
"Huldigung's March" would write now a march far surpassing
even these great creations; for if he had been so moved by events
of a merely monarchical and reactionary character, what would
be the effect upon him of a great celebration of a people's
freedom? Thomas opened negotations for a Centennial March
to be played as the overture to the ceremonies at Philadelphia,
May 10, and after some hesitation, which might, perhaps,
have made Thomas wary, Wagner agreed to undertake the
work.

The first chill came with the news of the conditions imposed.
The price was to be $5,000, which for the times and the nature
of the piece was staggering. It afterward appeared that Wagner
knew it was exorbitant and was merely taking advantage of the
situation to secure an unreasonably large fee; for the time was
now so late that no negotiations could be opened with another
composer. Wagner seemed to know also that he was laying
himself open to criticism, for in his letter he defended the price
he was asking by referring to the amount Verdi had received
for his latest opera.[1] But what stung worse than the extortion
was the manner of it. Wagner stipulated that the $5,000 must
be deposited in the hands of his banker before he would deliver
the manuscript. He was dealing with a nation on a great festival
of national and historic importance, and he acted as if he were
dealing with a gang of sharpers.

Still worse remains behind in this story. Wagner in his letter
entered voluntarily and unreservedly into an agreement that
the Woman's Committee of the Exposition (in whose behalf
Thomas was acting) should control the publication of the march

[1]Mrs. Thomas, p. 112.

in America and that he would not publish it in Europe until six months after the first performance in Philadelphia. This agreement he violated. The piece was published for his benefit before the march was performed in Philadelphia.

To balance these humiliations, Thomas looked eagerly for the arrival of the score, feeling that such a composer, having such a theme, would create a masterpiece, a marvel, a thing to make the world's joy. At last, the banker having functioned and Wagner having fingered his $5,000, the precious parcel came. Thomas tore open the wrappers, and behold, a piece of musical tripe, a bunch of junk, a collection of musical bosh! The thing was utterly unworthy—unworthy of the occasion for which it was written, of the man that wrote it, and of the nation from which it emanated.

Mr. Thomas labored indefatigably to better it. Punk it was and punk it remained, and it was with a sore heart that he raised his baton to play it on that May morning, 1876.

The blow went home and sank deep. It seemed to have power to hurt in every way that a sensitive man can suffer spiritual pain. In the first place, it tore up the favorite Thomas creed of the inevitable kinship of ethics and art. His firm conviction was that artists were, or ought to be, above the playing of tricks and the doing of things dishonorable. An artist was untrue to his art if he stepped an inch from the way of honesty. In Wagner the musician Thomas had believed he read Wagner the man. The disillusion was another twinge. His strong national pride was hurt because he saw plainly that Wagner had viewed not only the occasion but the country with contempt. Anything was good enough for Americans. A final and gratuitous smart was the thought that he had been the means of putting upon the program of a great and solemn national festival a composition beneath the dignity of the day and its significance. This was an unjustifiable view because on all sides the choice of Wagner had been applauded as the best that could be made;

but a man of Thomas's conscience takes upon himself burdens of blame to which he has no title. He never forgave Wagner. It is odd to record that he continued to play Wagnerian music as much as before, made transcriptions from Wagner's compositions and carved his name on his list of greatest composers; but all intercourse ceased between the two men. The wound rankled all the rest of Thomas's life. Twenty-eight years after, happening once to mention it to him, I was astonished to find that it was still painful.

Meantime, he was sorely tried in other ways. The failure of his Philadelphia engagement brought final ruin upon his head. The sheriff came and seized all his belongings. He had next to nothing aside from his library of music and his instruments. The library he had been laboriously collecting all his life; it was his pride and consolation. The sheriff took it all; likewise his baton, music stand, every musical instrument that he owned; even his very inkstand, leaving him the shirt on his back and the shoes on his feet. The manuscript of the unlucky Wagner Centennial March went with the rest; thereby, it is likely, causing Theodore Thomas no superimposed anguish.

Fourteen years had passed since he had decided to give up his career as a virtuoso and take on the task of making America musical, and so far as he was concerned, the only tangible result was wreck.[1]

In this desolation, he was urged by his friends to take refuge in the bankruptcy court, which would clear away his difficulties. For exactly such cases the bankruptcy law had been made, that honest men, overtaken by misfortune, might have a chance to begin again. We may perceive that at first he did not fully

---

[1] "No one will blame Mr. Thomas for being a little out of humor. In the first place, he was engaged to give concerts in Philadelphia, but the hall provided for him was totally unfit to be used as a concert hall by such an orchestra as Thomas's, and when he at last, through many other and petty annoyances, was compelled to give up his engagement in the City of Brotherly Love, it was too late to begin his concerts at Central Park Garden. And so it came that the famous Thomas Orchestra had for a time to be disbanded." (Editorial in *Brainard's Musical World*, October, 1876.)

understand the substance of this proceeding. After long urging he consented, the papers were prepared, the pen was put into his hand to sign them. It seems to have dawned upon him then that bankruptcy meant his creditors would never be paid. The soul within him revolted. He threw down the pen and refused to sign, shouldered the load, and went out without an engagement, an opening anywhere, or business, but determined in his rugged way that he would pay those debts.[1]

When the sheriff descended upon him, the Theodore Thomas Orchestra, of course, had been disbanded. For some weeks he was drifted about, resolved to make a way out of the mess and proceed with his chosen work, but without a promise of the least opportunity. In the depths of his misery, the eternal feminine reappeared in his story. In Philadelphia was one, "of her gentle sex the seeming paragon," Mrs. E. D. Gillespie, his unselfish friend, the unselfish friend of all things good and fine, chairman of the Woman's Commission of the Centennial Exposition. She was laboring all this time to bring light into his darkness. At last she managed an engagement for him to give a series of orchestral concerts at the Philadelphia Academy of Music, that historic hall that has housed so many noble enterprises. On this chance, which seemed in no way too robust, he called together his scattered band and started once more up hill. And now observe how chanceful a path he trod, for this time the concerts went prosperously, the hall was well filled, money was made if no purses were stuffed, and at the end of six weeks this sorely tried man found himself able to make another winter tour and find a basis for his hopes.

Where were the rich men of America that were to appear *ex machina* and save and glorify art?

We have news here of but one, and he not really rich. Dr.

---

[1]Autobiography, p. 67; Mrs. Thomas, p. 19; Upton, *Reminiscence and Appreciation*, p. 193. Mrs. Thomas prints an extract from a letter of Thomas's poignantly recalling his miseries in those days.

Franz Zinzer of New York hears about the sheriff's sale of the seized property, quietly slips over to Philadelphia, and for the sum of $1,400 buys library, scores, instruments, baton, inkstand. Two years later he presents the whole to Mrs. Thomas, without conditions, except that if she lends any of the works to her husband he must take good care of them!

All that season, 1876–1877, was spent in the travel that his soul loathed, one-night stands, tearing like mad to and fro across the country, seeing his family at long intervals, a figure more familiar to railroad brakemen than to his own son. When the ordeal was over, he longed to resume his work in the summer-night concerts in New York, but there was no place and no opportunity. Just at the moment when he was again headed for wrecking, the other good angel of his career shone upon him, maybe a trifle bedraggled as to robe and damaged as to harp, but angel nevertheless. His destiny was shaped by good women and Chicago; one having rescued him at Philadelphia, the other snatched him now from the next impending reef and changed all the subsequent steerage of his course. The city of Chicago would like to have Theodore Thomas and his orchestra spend the summer there, giving nightly concerts, such as he had given in New York. Well, where in Chicago? Heaven help us all—in the old Exposition Building, a huge thing of iron and glass, two city blocks in length, stretched along the lake front, the mammoth cave of all great buildings, the last place on earth for an orchestra's uses, colossal as the pyramids and empty as a drum!

Any port in a storm. It was Chicago or disband. Thomas chose Chicago, but when he thought of the Exposition Building it must have been with a sinking heart.

CHAPTER VI

A Tempting Offer

NO OTHER city of men seems to have been so much the butt of captious girdings and carpings as the city of Chicago. A literature of small wits long ago fixed for it a place of contempt as of one given to large vaunting but small achievement in all ways better than the dollar hunt. Because there was much packing house there could be little civilization, concluded the scornful East, being strong on logic. Yet the truth is that in enthusiasm for the gentle and refining arts, in idealism, in all that is meant by that easy phrase, public spirit, in a perfectly sincere devotion to good causes, Chicago far outshines New York or Philadelphia or any other Eastern city, and in all America is unequaled save by other communities in the West. If such a statement be challenged, one need no more than refer to the manner in which Chicago from 1897 to 1927 sedulously and tastefully adorned itself, and then to its sterling record of devotion to music.

It had always been reasonably musical, Chicago; it had been one of the first cities in America to guess what Thomas was aiming at and to give him effective support. If the Chicago Fire had precipitated his first ruin, the rehabilitated Chicago came now to his help in his time of greatest difficulty, as it was destined to do again in his long and troubled career.

Old Chicagoans will not need to be reminded of this Exposition Building that stood so long on the lake front, starting at Adams Street and ending at Madison, huge, not ungraceful, and strong in historical reminiscences. Chicago erected it, outdoing itself, as a kind of challenge to the world after the fire.

"You say I am crushed, I will show you," was the purport. For years great conventions and an annual and creditable industrial exhibit were held there. Garfield was nominated under its roof in 1880; both Blaine and Cleveland were nominated there in 1884. It could accommodate 50,000 people. By the side of it ran railroad tracks, trunk lines and suburban, where all day and all night the trains went thundering; close by was a switch yard with whistlings, bell ringings, and screechings. Thomas was to occupy one end of this illimitable waste with an orchestra of seventy men.

The thing seemed merely preposterous; above all for him, with his abnormal sensitiveness to every untoward sound condition and that fanaticism of his about perfection. To this day it seems mysterious that he should have agreed to any such proposal. Even when we have admitted his desperate estate, his fraternal affection for his orchestra and desire to keep it together, when we have added to these the work he had set out to do, that great thing of spreading the taste for good music, explanation seems to go lame. I can suppose only that he knew his Chicago and that he felt he had no choice, he must get on with his life work; if not in New York, then in Chicago; or Oshkosh, or Baraboo. Not being of the surrendering kind, he would hang on so long as there was a place in America that would give him a hearing.

So now he did a perfectly characteristic thing; with the peculiar readiness of his many-sided mind, he planned to make the best of what he could get. The first maddening problem was about sound. How could seventy men be heard in that huge cavern? He had recourse to his studies in acoustics and all alone devised and made a sounding board that commanded the wondering attention of all acoustic engineers and experts and is still standard in technical works on this subject. It was a vast contrivance of wood erected at a certain angle immediately back of the players. With potted trees and shrubs he marked off the concert space from the rest of the gigantic building, and so effectually that one never noticed the gloomy void beyond. With other plants and shrubs he made a garden, cool and sweet and attractive.

The sounding board worked incredibly well;[1] in that great building one could actually get as good effects as in any ordinarily sized hall.

Some years afterward architects in the East sought to copy his idea in this device but found difficulties.

"The Thomas sounding board does not seem to work well for us," said one of them.

"Of course not," responded Thomas. "They have overlooked a vital point. There must be an open space of eighteen inches at the bottom and my angle has not been observed."[2]

In the gardened area farthest from the band were tables where one could have beer and light refreshments. For those that came only to hear music were seats nearer and without tables.

It is no fiction that he knew his Chicago well; he had been there so often and noted so accurately its developing musical taste, year after year. Here, as everywhere else, he made his programs with study and research to fit at once the situation he encountered and the grand aim that controlled him. Whether he succeeded I can show from one illustration.

He had for manager in those days George B. Carpenter, a good man[3] in faith and practice, ingenious no less than sympathetic. He suggested early in the season that to record the reality of the public interest and at the same time encourage it, there should be sometimes programs selected wholly by public request. He did not know what he was laying upon Thomas's shoulders. Requests, to be considered, must be

---

[1]*Dictionary of Architecture*, article on "Sounding Boards."
[2]Conf. Mrs. Thomas, pp. 124–125.
[3]Otis, pp. 15–17.

limited to compositions the orchestra had already played in the current season; but even within these bounds (and others) the demands came in such windrows it was almost impossible for one man to sort and properly to consider them. So then if we wish to know what Chicago thought of these efforts, here is the first Request Program, played July 15, 1877.[1]

Overture, "Tannhäuser"	Wagner
Allegretto, Eighth Symphony	Beethoven
Largo	Händel
"Rhapsodie Hongroise, No. 2"	Liszt
Overture, "William Tell"	Rossini
"Träumerei"	Schumann
"Fastasie Caprice"	Vieuxtemps
"Funeral March of a Marionette"	Gounod
Waltz, "Weiner Bonbons"	Strauss
"Amaryllis"	Ghys
Overture, "Zampa"	Herold

This, placed by the side of programs he played in the early days of the Central Park Garden, say eleven years before, is the sure measure of his work. Beyond all question, he was leading the whole country after him; he had lifted it out of the stage of giants and dwarfs, of the "Firefly Polka" and the "Skinners' Quickstep." When he started in New York, May 13, 1862, he did not dare to have more than two orchestral numbers on his program and appealed to the public with vocal and instrumental soloists. It would have been so (or worse) in the Chicago of that day; but now he was addressing a public of a different thought. He could make for it programs exclusively of orchestral music and that of a fairly high grade. Chicago responded with a kind of holy joy; hard times, strikes, and all. Presently the concerts became a popular feature of Chicago life. Next, some of the business men began to notice that here was an asset. Scattered through the Northwest were thousands of persons of a genuine

---

[1]Printed by Upton, Vol. II, p. 198.

love for music and a considerable knowledge of it. The Thomas concerts began to give them a reason to visit Chicago. In this inconspicuous and unforeseen way was laid the foundation of Chicago as a musical center. The orchestra laid it, at the old Expositir Building; laid the foundation of what might be called now a leading industry of the city.

The Request Programs became a regular feature of his work, that season and afterward. It must be admitted that those of 1877 make a good showing for Chicago, Windy City of the Packing House. Within two years I have known many a European orchestra of renown to play programs less advanced; and if the Chicago requesters did vote a Strauss waltz into their festival, and the "Zampa" overture, there was the fact that enough of them of their own free will had voted for the Eighth Symphony. Mr. Thomas did not interfere with the choosing except so far as was required by the rules of the game. The majority had its way; even when the necessary incongruity of the numbers that this brought about caused him agony of spirit, even when it dislocated the fine art of congruous program making that meant so much to him. The majority had voted; there was no appeal.

I suppose there never was a musician with fewer prejudices or fads about music. Anything that was good was good, no matter where it came from. Art never had any nationality for him. In all other ways, he was an ardent American; in the way of art, America must stand with the rest. He was eager to see composition encouraged here, but repeatedly he said he would not play any piece merely because it was American; merit must be the only standard. It was a matter of conscience. Personally, he greatly relished the French composers of his own time but he would not unduly exploit their work. While he was playing in Chicago this summer he gave a curious illustration of the catholicity of his tastes and the size of the musical fields he had explored, by making up one program exclusively

M. CONKLIN,
OF
DODWORTH'S BAND,

Begs leave to announce to his friends and the public that his

BENEFIT CONCERT

will take place at the

APOLLO SALOON,

ON MONDAY EVENING,
APRIL 26th,

when he will be assisted by the following eminent talent, who have most kindly volunteered their valuable services:

DODWORTH FAMILY;
MASTER THEODORE THOMAS,

probably the most extraordinary Violinist in the world, of his age;

DODWORTH'S BAND;
MASTER MARSH,

the Infant Drummer; and

MR. DANIEL DAVIES.

PROGRAMME.
PART I.

1 Introduction, from Lucrezia Borgia; Dodworth's Parading Band .... Donizetti
2 Serenade, "Star of Love," Dodworth's Serenade Band .... Wallace
3 Concerto Militaire, Solo Violin, Master T. Thomas .... C. Lipinski
4 Glendon Polka, Dodworth's Parading Band .... A. Dodworth
5 Cavatina, "Still so gently," from Sonnambula's Choir Corps .... Bellini
6 Infant Drummer's extraordinary performance

PART II.

7 Grand Quartette, from Di Bravo's Falisco; Dodworth's Serenade Band .... Rossini
8 Violin Solo, Carnival of Venice, Master T. Thomas .... H. Ernst
9 Serenade, from Don Pasquale, Dodworth's Serenade Band .... Donizetti
10 Cavatina, "Son Vergin Vezzosa," from I Puritani, Cornet Solo, Mr. Allen Dodworth .... Bellini
11 Quadrille, "Grace Songsters," Dodworth's Quadrille Band .... H. B. Dodworth
12 Trio, from Norma, "A de quel," Messrs. Allen, Harry B. and Charles R. Dodworth .... Bellini
13 Trip to Richmond, Dodworth's Quadrille Band .... H. B. Dodworth
14 Aria, by the Martial Corps, M. Conklin and D. Davies

Concert to commence at 8 o'clock.
Tickets 50 cents each.

THE OLD-STYLE PROGRAM
The occasion was one of Thomas's first public appearances

HANS BALATKA
An early apostle of good music in America

from the works of Scandinavian composers, another exclusively of French, a third exclusively of Italian.

Fortune never came with both hands full for this man; there was always something wrong. This summer, although Chicago took him to its heart, never to let him thence, he had a plenitude of troubles, first and last. One was the great railroad strike that at the height of his season broke in to fill people with alarm, keep them in their houses, and blur his success. For a time, one end of the Exposition Building was occupied by the Thomas Orchestra, discoursing celestial harmonies, and the other by detachments of troops, furbishing arms. Another affliction was the recurrence of attacks of depression and discouragement of which only a few of his friends were ever aware.

One evening, while Chicago was like an armed camp, George P. Upton entered the Exposition Building at the concert end. It was long before the concert hour, and the place was deserted except for the figure of one man that sat bowed over a table in an attitude of deep dejection. Upton drew near and saw to his astonishment that it was Theodore Thomas. Says Mr. Upton:

He looked up and beckoned to me. I sat down by him. He said:
"I guess I am a little blue to-night. I have been thinking, as I sat here, that I have been swinging the baton now for fifteen years, and I do not see that the people are any farther ahead than when I began. And, as far as my pocket is concerned, I am not as well off. But," and he brought that powerful fist of his down upon the table, "I am going to keep on, if it takes another fifteen years."[1]

He was the more open to such despondent overcomings when he was away from home and therefore deprived of the stimulus that lay in the duty of keeping the always carefree face. It was customary with him, when traversing what Mrs. Thomas calls "The Thomas Highway"[2]—that tiresome route of so

[1]Upton, *Reminiscence and Appreciation*, p. 217.
[2]Mrs. Thomas, pp. 52–53.

many thousand miles that he tracked until he knew every whistling post—it was customary with him to be thus assailed after a concert. Perhaps the hall had been unusually bad, perhaps the orchestra had been too tired to respond, perhaps his own utter exhaustion was responsible. In any event, he would go away half crushed to earth with a sense of failure and so to the hotel, swearing that he would give over the traveling and live at home if he had to turn salesman. A little supper, a glass of wine, and a cigar would bring him safe to his moorings. The next morning he would leap from his bed after a few hours' sleep and dash to the station with the step of an athlete. The megrims were gone and forgotten.[1]

But about Chicago, 1877. He stayed there that summer and played fifty concerts.

To one of them on an August night came a young man from Marquette, Michigan, who was slated by the gods to be a great and beneficent influence in Theodore Thomas's life; a young business man, come to Chicago on a business errand. The railroad strike was at its worst stage, all business was thought to be in peril, this young man had come on an errand to save his own. He was worried and perturbed, doubtful when he left home if he could reach Chicago, doubtful in Chicago if he could return home. The night was very hot. He wandered out for fresh air and came upon the Exposition Building. From it instead of shots and battle cries issued the divinest music.[2] He went in, and presently he had forgotten all about the strike, the state of business, his troubles of to-morrow, and was floated out into a world he had never dreamed of. The next night he was there again. So long as he remained in Chicago he was every night at the concerts, he carried the memories of them back to Marquette, they ran in his head, they would not leave

---

[1] Testimony of a former manager for Thomas. See also Thomas's letters, printed by Mrs. Thomas at pp. 250, 253, 303.

[2] *Outlook Magazine*, February, 1910.

him, and some years afterward they flowered into motions that
had enduring effects upon the life of Chicago and all the West.

His name was Charles Norman Fay. Remember it, for you
will encounter him again in this narrative.

Chicago had more than one way to show its approval. Toward the end of the season Thomas was pleasantly surprised to
have one day a letter signed by hundreds of Chicago citizens
expressing the pleasure and profit they had received from the
concerts and asking that a night be set apart in which they
could testify to the gratitude and good will they felt toward
him. They came, they testified, and sent him away warmed as
to his heart and empty as to his purse. The sum total of the
summer's work was the old story. Artistically, a great success;
financially, no merchantable tokens. And there were the debts.

"In some things all, in all things none are crossed," sang
stout old Father Southwell a night after he had been tortured.
It was so here. Thomas went back to New York unshaken but
penniless, to come upon a bit of rare good fortune.

What, all this time, had that stately but somewhat un-
weatherly craft, the ancient Philharmonic, been doing in these
troubled seas? It is curious evidence of the greater wisdom of
the Thomas methods that, while he had been advancing steadily
toward a larger clientèle, the good old Philharmonic, giving its
regulation five concerts a year, had almost dropped beneath
the horizon. This was particularly bad for it, because, being
a coöperative enterprise, its members looked for dividends at
the end of the season, and as Thomas rose in popularity and
success the Philharmonic receipts fell off. For the season of
1870–1871 they had totalled $15,085 which meant a dividend
of $203 a share. The next year they went a little above this
and the dividend reached $216. Thereafter came a steady
decline.

All this while Carl Bergmann had continued to be the sole
conductor. Of late he had begun to lose his hold alike upon his

art, his public, and himself. It is an unpleasant story of a good man's decline; let us get through with it. He and Thomas, although for a time fellow members of the Mason-Thomas Quartette, had not been good friends. Thomas made the programs and was eager for certain new things that Bergmann opposed, maybe from whim, maybe from jealousy.[1] After a time, Bergmann dropped out, and his place was taken by Frederick Bergner, one of the greatest 'cellists of his day. Bergmann, sincere musician and a pioneer to be honored, had his character lesions. As the Thomas star ascended, he felt his own declining and seems to have taken to drink. His income from Philharmonic being small and as a teacher smaller still, Thomas took pity on him and offered to share with him the leadership of the Thomas Orchestra, with a salary. Bergmann accepted the offer, but on the morning of the first rehearsal failed to appear or to send an excuse for his absence; a fact that to the discerning will be enough.[2]

He was still the titular conductor of the Philharmonic for the season of 1875–1876, but the public, which seldom fails to sense that something is wrong even when it can put no name upon the trouble, would have none of him. The receipts for that season sank to the lethal total of $1,641, for five concerts; $328 a concert. The players' dividends went down to $30 for a season's work, rehearsals and all. For the fourth concert Bergmann was incapable and George Matzka must lead. On March 24, 1876, the society felt it could endure him no longer and requested his resignation.[3] Matzka led the final concert that year. It was a sad eclipse of a brilliant mind.

Once, about this time, Theodore Thomas, entering a restaurant, came upon poor Bergmann, his old-time leader, old-time companion and fellow artist, maudlin, and a crowd of merry-

---

[1]Mason, *Memories of a Musical Life*, p. 198.
[2]*Autobiography*, p. 37.
[3]Krehbiel, p. 70.

makers tormenting him. The high temper that was always latent and ordinarily chained up in Thomas broke loose. Squaring his powerful arms and clenching his fists he advanced upon the crowd and drove it right and left.

"Respect the Bergmann that was if you have no respect for the Bergmann that is!" he shouted, and took the unfortunate man home.[1]

Dr. Leopold Damrosch, coming to America in 1871, had conducted successfully the Arion and other singing societies, and then the German Opera. For the season of 1876–1877 the Philharmonic Society elected him to the vacant conductorship. The results were not happy. Dr. Damrosch was a great conductor, but the public would not respond to his efforts, and the receipts for that season were ghastly. The five concerts reaped a total of $841, or $168 a concert, and the dividends were but $18 each, which I think is the lowest figure in the Society's history. It meant that the orchestra was playing to virtually empty seats.[2]

Meantime, if Thomas was making no money for himself, he was drawing great crowds and winning much applause. The significant fact stands out in the records that the most prosperous years of the Philharmonic were from 1869 when Thomas, having begun to travel the country, had left New York, down to 1873, when he returned. While the favorite was away there was no other music but the Philharmonic; when the favorite returned the Philharmonic could go hang.

In these conditions, Dr. Damrosch having failed to win popular approval, the venerable craft might give up the fight and vanish, or it might surrender to the only man that apparently could make it go. Negotiations, begun as far back as Bergmann's collapse, dragged over a long period. Philharmonic ambassadors wished Thomas to disband his own orchestra and discontinue his concerts. The suggestion offended him; he was deeply at-

---

[1] Upton, *Musical Memories*, p. 185.
[2] Upton, *Reminiscence and Appreciation*, p. 151.

tached to the men that had played with him so long and gone through so many vicissitudes for a common object. The treaty-makers withdrew and both sides went their ways. But this year the case of the Philharmonic was desperate. Without conditions, the Society offered the conductorship to Theodore Thomas, and without conditions he accepted it.

The honor was great and the advantages were greater. The Philharmonic assured him an income; small, but an income; and in those days of debt he was glad of a dollar. It also gave him prestige and a great opportunity. The next season of the Philharmonic the receipts shot up from $841 to $6,402 and the dividends from $18 to $82. He not only saved America's foremost musical organization from the rocks but steered it to a popular success.

But the feat had its drawbacks. He had now two orchestras on his hands in a city that could ill support one. "We smell evil in this dualistic activity," wrote the man in *Dwight's*, who had an ill-divining soul, but this time with reason. Thomas sought to meet the situation by making the concerts of his own orchestra at Steinway Hall of a popular and introductory character and those of the Philharmonic at the Academy of Music more classical and advanced. It was the indicated course of wisdom.

Always afterward he was a little sensitive about the assertion, often made at that time and later repeated, that the Philharmonic was forced by his rivalry to elect him conductor.[1] There was no great harm in the story, for the rivalry was not of his making. It existed chiefly in the public mind, and if Dr. Damrosch had been able to charm the general ear, Thomas would never have succeeded to his place. But all his life Theodore Thomas was beset by supersensitiveness about the printed word. Excellent in philosophy about many things, for this he had none. He could never grasp the idea, plain to others, that a criticism is nothing but one man's opinion and therefore of the nature

---

[1]Autobiography, p. 73.

of bagatelle, whether favorable or unfavorable. The fundamental absurdity of the whole system of newspaper criticism never
occurred to him. He tried to avoid the reading of all newspapers
except the one that came regularly with his breakfast. He had
overlooked the Thoughtful Friend. This pest, who hangs upon
the skirts of every man of prominence, was rife in that day also
and never failed to send to Thomas carefully marked copies of
newspapers that contained articles assailing him. Sometimes
true to form, Thoughtful Friend enclosed them in a letter with
facetious comments. He never knew the pain he caused.
Thoughtful Friend had ever a limited imagination.

One day, when in the midst of a campaign of misrepresentation, lies, and abuse, Thomas came into his office where there was
the other kind of friend.

"What did you do last night?" asked this perceptive soul,
noticing Thomas's haunted and weary look.

"Sat up all night and read Shakespeare," said Thomas.[1]

He could not sleep when he was under malicious attack.
To him every cruel thrust was rack and thumbscrew. He was
to be well acquainted with such nights before he was through.

The Philharmonic incident had still more fateful consequences.
I have never yet encountered a soul-searching inquiry as to the
operations of the popular mind about orchestra conductors, but
one would seem to be needed. Why people like a man one year
and do not like him the next, why they like some men at all,
why a conductor should become a popular hero merely because
he transforms the second movement of Beethoven's Seventh into
a jig, why in so many minds there can be no moderate liking or
disliking of a conductor, just what is the substance of the spell
that some conductors seem able to cast over a putrid performance, are mysteries yet to be explored but rich in promise to the

---

[1]He was an ardent Shakespearean all his days. "Every soul ought to be able to sub-
merge itself in a soul greater than itself," he said once, referring to his devotion to
the dramatist. "It is rest and refuge."

questioning soul. One will yet remain, more fascinating than the others.

It is the violence and unreason of the Orchestral War.

The seeds of one were now planted in these events and the growth was to be hardy, surviving more than forty years. Dr. Damrosch, a great conductor, was of the happiest and most attractive address. He had made many friends in New York, some of power and influence. These felt that he had been unfairly treated by the Philharmonic. The catastrophic failure of his year of leadership they attributed to causes beyond his control; a strong Damrosch faction grew up in New York. The more it waxed the more bitter it became against the man that, according to its assertion, had ousted the good Doctor by rivalry. "Dr. Damrosch, the ex-conductor of the Philharmonic band, entertains the idea of organizing a new orchestra," wrote one sad-souled correspondent of *Dwight's*, "and it would be highly interesting if New York suddenly could boast of three large orchestral societies."

There was more than a possibility in the foreboding. Within a few years the thing came to pass; three orchestras in a city that with difficulty had maintained one. For the time being it was averted by what seemed to some persons the unpardonable folly of the principal figure in these maneuvers. Theodore Thomas decided to leave New York and make his home elsewhere.

To explain. This man Thomas, part dreamer, part practical man of affairs, had for sixteen years cherished a vast and glittering vision. It was the idea of a musical America, understanding, loving, and following the greatest works of musical art, and this to be reached by two instrumentalities: orchestras permanently endowed, permanently housed, and great schools that were to spread the glad tidings of musical joy everywhere for the coming generations.

There was now suddenly presented to him a plan by which

both sides of this beautiful dream were promised, and although it seems now to have been a plan largely chimerical if not impossible, he was so dazzled through much dreaming that he was carried away by the mere beckoning image of it.

Ever since the great Thomas festival of 1873 had been succeeded by the greater Thomas festival of 1875, the city of Cincinnati had taken to itself (not without some strutting and preening, maybe) a place in American music hardly second to that of Boston itself. An understandable fervor of enthusiasm had decreed these festivals to be a permanent feature of the city's life. Public spirit, rising to the occasion, erected one of the greatest and best auditoriums in this or any other country, the famous Cincinnati Music Hall, a structure magnificent in design and nearly faultless in accouterments. This was now nearing completion. To inaugurate it Thomas gave there the third festival, beginning May 14, 1878. He must have felt some of the pride of an architect when he looked upon that great and worthy temple, for men said that this was his work.[1]

From Cincinnati he went back to New York to face the dreariest outlook that had yet beset him. He must keep his orchestra together, he must get on with his work. Chicago for the time was impossible, the Central Park hall was done for, he played that summer of 1878 in Gilmore's Garden, the great, unsightly cavern that stood at Twenty-sixth Street and Madison Avenue before the days of the more famous Madison Square structure. It does not appear that the concerts were particularly successful or that they helped to better his situation. Besides his debts, which haunted him continually, he was harassed by the problem about his orchestra. The difficulties of maintaining it through the winter months were oppressive; manage as he would there must be some appearance of rivalry between his organization and the Philharmonic; he must seem to the public, or a part of it, as more or less competing against himself. Then these

---

[1]His statue now stands in its main foyer.

winter concerts, although showing the increasing musical interest of the metropolis, did not yield enough money to meet expenses, and he must continue to travel to live. It was a hand-to-mouth existence at best and beset with ceaseless anxieties. For instance, he could by no means count upon the out-of-town audiences. If he encountered one small audience he must make up the loss at the next town. Three small audiences in succession might ruin him, and the size of the audience was dependent upon too many things outside of his control; weather, floods, strikes, and riots were to be counted with. The arrangement was as in previous years. He played in New York one night and in one-night stands for five. His children were growing up and he saw little of them. So far as he could see, there was no hope that his situation would improve, and he looked upon himself as the Wandering Jew of music, condemned to travel up and down the earth.

It was his fate also, being a dreamer, to go beset with mirages, and that which opened before him now had in it a disillusion so savagely cruel that human ingenuity could not have equaled it for the malignity of circumstance.

One day in July, when he was leading this dull and unprofitable season at Gilmore's, he was electrified to receive from Colonel George Ward Nichols, a wealthy man of Cincinnati, husband of Maria Longworth Nichols, a letter announcing that a great national school of music was to be established in Cincinnati, with Theodore Thomas as its head and director.

The thing he had dreamed of.

"Are you not tired of carrying the weight of that orchestra?" said the letter. "Will you not accept the opportunity of firmly fixing yourself for life in a position which you can, if you choose, make distinguished and successful?"

It was like asking a starving man if he would not like something to eat. The weariness of the load of the orchestra was beyond all words. Of a sudden a power had appeared to take the load from his back. He responded with joy, there was brief correspondence, and then came a formal invitation, signed by twenty-two wealthy men of Cincinnati, underwriting the Cincinnati School of Music and bidding Mr. Thomas to become its head. In it were these paragraphs:

It is proposed to establish an institution for musical education upon the scale of the most important of those of a similar character in Europe; to employ the highest class of professors, to organize a full orchestra with a school for orchestra and chorus, and to give concerts.

In this invitation we recognize your special fitness for a trust so important, and believe that if you accept you will be taking another step forward in the noble work of musical education to which your life has been so successfully devoted.

If they had been mind readers, these men, they could not have more perfectly touched Thomas upon the reflex of his thinkings and ardent desires. Here were the phantom rich men come at last and bearing in their hands the actual thing he had planned long before in New York; the permanent orchestral home, the school, the ensemble training, the chorus, everything complete, everything dignified and worthy. He must have been swung clean from his holdings, for he forgot all his caution and worldly wisdom. He never stopped to inquire what were the purposes and ideals of these men; he signed the contract on the spot.[1]

On one side the allure seemed fairly real. He could save his beloved orchestra; he could take it to Cincinnati, where its finances would be looked after by the school; he could go on teaching music and lifting its ideals; he could travel just enough to spread his instruction, but travel at ease and without worry; and he could pay off the last of those debts. The contract provided a salary of $10,000 a year, and he knew he could make enough more by outside engagements to win clear from his creditors.

------

[1] Upton, *Reminiscence and Appreciation*, pp. 177–185; Mrs. Thomas, pp. 144–176; Grove's *Dictionary*.

Intimate friends warned and protested, enemies jeered and flouted; the public wondered and a part of it objected. An acrimonious debate sprang up as to whether New York had or had not treated him with ingratitude, whether he was or was not being driven to a community of a warmer heart. Little those things concerned him. Every prospect seemed fair in his eyes. In his letter of acceptance he said:

This is a step in the right direction and Cincinnati is the right place to begin. We want a concentration of professional talent and mechanical training, such as we have in other branches of education, and a musical atmosphere. The formation of a college such as you propose realizes one of my fondest hopes, and I shall work hard to make it superior in all branches of musical education.

The faculty must consist of professors eminent in their departments of instruction. With the assistance of a complete orchestra we shall have the professional talent that can teach the use of all orchestral instruments. I am ready to begin all this work at once, and advise that the college be opened during the coming autumn.

Within a few days I shall forward to the Board of Directors a preliminary plan of the course of instruction to be adopted.[1]

The certificate of incorporation of the College, or University of Music, as some of the correspondence called it, declared that its object was "to encourage and cultivate a taste for music and establish a college for instruction in it." The capital stock was $50,000; George Ward Nichols was the president; Reuben R. Springer, John Shillito, Jacob Burret, and Peter R. Neff were the other directors.

The prospectus was perfectly lovely. Everything that heart of Thomas could desire was there: instruction in every branch of music, permanent orchestra, frequent symphony concerts, a quartette for chamber music, training in ensemble playing, encouragement in composing, singing, chorus training; everything. Some of the newspapers at home scoffed at the whole

[1]August 20, 1878. Printed in full by Mrs. Thomas, p. 149.

thing. Let them scoff! John C. Freund in the *Music Trade Review* said bluntly that Theodore Thomas was not the man to be placed in such a position. *Dwight's*, which followed him in all his motions and was his potential Boswell, more than intimated the same belief. Part of the lay press broke into clamors. The Chicago *Tribune* took up the issue and accused New York of treating shabbily the greatest conductor and promoter of music it had ever had. The *Advertiser* and other journals in Boston were inconsolable. "By the blindness of New York," said the *Advertiser*, "Boston loses the delightful series of concerts that for several years has refreshed and instructed its ears." The *Music Trade Review* was ready with the retort discourteous:

And why has not Boston, with her "world-famed" musical culture, secured long ago the services of Theodore Thomas? Last season, a great deal of money was sunk in symphony concerts in Boston and Mr. Thomas had to make up the loss. Even if Theodore Thomas had remained in New York we hardly think that the Hub would have enjoyed next winter "the delightful series of concerts which for several years past have refreshed and instructed her ears."[1]

Too late a movement was started to provide in New York the simple facilities Thomas had so long desired and thus to retain him. Colonel George Ward Nichols was interviewed on this point by the Cincinnati *Commercial*.

"Was money raised to keep Thomas in New York?"
"Yes, and a large sum, over $30,000 would have been subscribed had it not become known that the effort was useless."
"How about the orchestra? Does Thomas bring new men?"
"Yes, he will bring several musicians who will be professors in the college and play in the orchestra. These men are the very highest in the profession; there are none better in Europe."

---

[1]*Music Trade Review*, issue of September 3, 1878.

The contract was for five years. Hard-headed business men, those that drew it up. They slipped into it a Shylockian provision that Thomas was to assemble and train the orchestra outside of his college duties, provide it at his own expense with all its music, go on tour with it and pay one fifth of his earnings from it into the college treasury. Thomas did not care. It is likely that if the contract had bound him to fetch a hair off the great Cham's beard he would have signed it. His dream was about to be realized and what were terms compared with that?

He brought to a close the melancholy season at Gilmore's, not without acrid comment from the disaffected press, the trouble being as of old the nature of his programs.

"On Saturday, September 28," writes one of these critics, "the season of summer-night concerts at Gilmore's Garden reached the end. The hopes that the management had entertained for the last night were hardly fulfilled. The Garden did not show the crowds that formerly used to frequent the place during the closing weeks. Even the news of Theodore Thomas's early departure for the West did not stir up the public to any enthusiasm. People protested against the high-toned music at the place by their conspicuous absence, and the season at the Garden cannot be counted among the managerial triumphs."[1]

After one year of popular leadership, the Philharmonic was now left without a conductor. An election was called and Adolph Neuendorff, more celebrated as composer than as leader, was chosen to the place, receiving forty-six votes to twenty-nine for Leopold Damrosch. Much more than the superficial significance attached to the balloting. Thomas was to hear again from that day's plebiscite. The *Music Trade Review* wrote of it:[2]

Nobody can say that Dr. Damrosch is not a musician of the highest ability, of great talents and remarkable intellectual powers. When he conducted the concerts of the Philharmonic Society the dividends

[1]*Music Trade Review*, October 3, 1878.
[2]*Ibid.*

of the members fell down to a trifle, which was quadrupled when Thomas took the baton in hand. As in political life, so among artists, it is too often to be found that the minority that has been defeated is ready to abuse the successful candidate of the assembly, even after the election.

On September 30, the Thomas family, bag and baggage, left the old home where it had lived so long, and started for Cincinnati. In the mind of Theodore Thomas, he was done with New York, fond as he was of it. He had before him at last the work he had always wished most to do. With what one of the newspapers called "his unbounded energy and fire of youth," he wanted to begin it.

If the family looked back through the windows that morning they saw the rooms filled with the flowers of farewell people had sent there the last remaining days.

His debts were to be paid, his school established, and his worst problems solved, thought the good easy man. Men's fates run in grooves and his did not lead that way.

CHAPTER VII

Turned Back at Cincinnati

THE first week in October, 1878, the Cincinnati College of Music began with a great throng of pupils. No enterprise of the kind could have hoisted sail under better auspices. Thomas was a matchless organizer. His chart in full had been adopted by the directors and was now precisely followed. Each department had at its head a specialist of note and well able to teach. The West was on fire for music; the matriculates came from as far as the Missouri to enroll under such tutelage; there was hardly room for them. All the musical world, here and abroad, had eyes upon the experiment; no one had ever tried to do so much with so many famous instructors.

The first few months in Cincinnati were probably the happiest period of Thomas's artistic life. He was working full tilt ahead, which was always his peculiar passion, and he was paying those debts. Of work he seems to have had enough for three men. He directed the college, engaged the teachers, mapped out the courses, and himself taught classes. He personally marshaled the chorus and taught it. He organized a string quartette and played the violin in it. He gave a regular season of twenty-four public concerts with the orchestra. He took charge of the preliminary work for the festival of 1880, which was to be given under the auspices of the college, and started upon rehearsals for it. Once a month he went to Brooklyn and conducted its Philharmonic. His contract called for a six weeks' vacation. Instead of taking it, he gave summer-night concerts in Cincinnati, to the first of which 4,000 persons came. He had never been apostolic in so many directions.

THOMAS AT TWENTY-TWO

Reprinted by permission from Mrs. Thomas's "Memoirs of
Theodore Thomas"

OLD STEINWAY HALL AND THE ACADEMY OF MUSIC

The orchestra department of the school he constructed on his own lines to secure the utmost of technical skill with an understanding of the principles and purposes of musical art. A peculiar feature was that orchestra students were obliged to begin with vocalization. Their first studies were in the chorus classes and they did not touch an instrument until they had learned to sing. When that was accomplished they began upon violin or clarinet, taking also harmony, counterpoint, and technique. He even put in a department of composition. He had separate schools for the piano, organ, score playing and conducting, for elocution, concert-room deportment, and dramatic expression. In twelve months he had a chorus of 300 trained voices, and a second symphony orchestra composed of the students of this school. The artistic success of the enterprise was carried as if by assault. It is likely that at the time there did not exist in the world another school of music better equipped or giving a more competent instruction, and equally to be believed that few music schools anywhere had larger or more enthusiastic student bodies.[1]

If it should be asked what kind of a schoolmaster Theodore Thomas made, it appears that he was strict, firm, authoritative, unmerciful to fakers and idlers, and electrical to all that went to the place with honest desire to work. The tradition of him that lingered long after was of a person of abnormal energy, infinite patience with detail, and no patience at all with the horse-players. One day he caught some of the young women of the chorus performing church choir tricks of levity and fooling. He sent them about their business with remarks that must have caused their ears to tingle. If they were seeking amusement, there was nothing to detain them at the Cincinnati College of Music. He had a gift of sarcasm that bit like acid and he used it pitilessly upon the insincere. It appears, on the other hand,

---

[1]Upton, *Reminiscence and Appreciation*, pp. 179–181; Mrs. Thomas, pp. 158–168; Autobiography, pp. 80–81.

that to students that were really trying even when they were a little slow or dull he was so kind and tolerant in a rugged paternal way that they adored him.

All the musical world listened to the news of these activities and applauded. For a time the croakers and prophets of evil were overwhelmed. Instead of not being the man for such a task, Theodore Thomas was proving that of all men he was the best equipped for it.[1] Before the end of that school year rumors began to reach New York that all was not well with the Cincinnati College of Music. With the beginning of the next semester these took definite shape to the effect that the musical director was dissatisfied with his position and had insisted upon certain changes. Soon followed palatable stories of dissensions and rows in the institution, and in March, 1880, a year and a half after his engagement, Thomas suddenly threw up his contract and returned to New York.

"The Thomas temper," said Wisdom, and winked. It does not now appear that temper had anything to do with the trouble, except to add picturesque language to the final flare-up. What had happened to Theodore Thomas was a strange contingency. The commercialism that he had sought to restrain and ameliorate in America had turned upon him and gored him in a way no finite being could have foreseen. As thus:

He had not operated long as the head of the Cincinnati College of Music before he began to wonder whether he and the president of the Board of Directors talked the same language. Colonel George Ward Nichols was an able business man, excellently trained, eminently successful, who could not conceive of an investment except in terms of business. That is, you

---

[1] "Among the many discriminating friends whom Mr. Thomas made as an orchestral director, there were not a few who hesitated to form or express an opinion as to his fitness for the directorship of an educational institution. If all doubts in that regard have not yet been dispelled they bid fair even to vanish altogether." (*Dwight's*, February 15, 1879.)

TURNED BACK AT CINCINNATI   127

invested your money to get a return upon it, and not otherwise. If you started a College of Music and issued stock to float it, of course that stock must return dividends; not in sentiment but in bankable cash. Otherwise, why invest? The Cincinnati College of Music being a business enterprise, exactly like any other, existed to earn and to declare dividends. Now to Theodore Thomas the idea of making money out of music was exactly like the idea of making money by the sale of women's virtue. He would as soon have thought of keeping a bagnio. Naturally, it was not long before these diametrically opposed ideas began to signal a collision. Colonel Nichols, being a first-class business man and president of the Board of Directors, went about the institution restricting expenditures, suggesting economies, and correcting lesions—business. Mr. Thomas, being under the dominion of a great eductional purpose, went about the institution enlarging expenditures and ordering an opposite medicament for lesions. Soon the two authorities found themselves giving contradictory instructions, and the faculty began to wonder whose instructions had the right of way.

The most ardent of his admirers have never contended that Theodore Thomas was essentially a lamb. With some others, not his admirers, and not well acquainted with him, he had the reputation, much beyond any deserving, of being a bear. In my observation, virtually every man that has had a difficult executive post has had something of this repute. There may be men of soft and insinuating manners that can also direct great projects and great organizations, but they are rare in this sad world. It is recorded that the Angel Gabriel, being charged with a managerial mission here on earth, lost his temper at it, and most men similarly situated have sympathized with him. It seems to be a fact in natural history that the lamb, excellently designed for table purposes, shows but imperfectly in leadership. The strain of imposing one will upon another produces in most mortals made of dust certain sequelæ, eruptive or mordant. Experienced politicians and able opportunists learn early to conceal these things; men of a franker constitution exhibit them on the spot and so have done with the matter, meantime getting the name of autocrat, tyrant, or bear. Theodore Thomas, if I knew anything about him, was not testy nor unreasonable nor temperamental.[1] He had shown in his long life of so many mutations that he could obey orders as readily as give them, but he believed that if he was the captain of anything he was captain, and like Skipper Nares, held one captain to be enough for any ship he ever saw. For many years he had governed his orchestra with no one to dispute him. The experience he now encountered of a divided authority abraded him. He could not adjust himself to it.

The first clash came over a point of fundamental policy. Colonel Nichols was in favor of taking anybody that came with good money in hand; why stickle about his brains so long as he had acceptable funds? The money of the musical was no better than the money of the dumb. Thomas believed that since some persons were born into the world congenitally incapable of music, there should be an examination to avoid wasting time. Colonel Nichols believed that persons coming with current coin should be allowed to enroll for any period they were willing to pay for, capable or incapable. Thomas believed that as hundreds of half-baked youth were in the habit of thinking on Monday that they would like a musical career and on Saturday that they would rather run a fishboat, only such pupils should be admitted as were willing to sign up for a year.

When Thomas was organizing a chorus in the college, men and women, he issued to the candidates a circular of admirable instructions and wound it up with this double-shotted paragraph:

[1] "I can be led with a silk thread," said Thomas, grimly, "but I can't be hauled with a ship's cable. In all matters except one—art—I am willing to give up my way, but there I am a tyrant." (Mrs. Thomas, p. 169.)

There is another subject about which I must speak very plainly. We invite to this choir only those that are in earnest, that wish to become skilled singers, and that will meet our effort to teach with corresponding effort to learn, and will attend the appointed hours for study and the concerts. A private student in the College that loses a lesson is the chief sufferer, but the neglect of the members of the Choir injures that symmetry that is made by the perfect balance of the parts. Furthermore, it is not desirable that singers should join the Choir for a brief period only. The plan of instruction embraces a term of two or three years.

THEODORE THOMAS.
Musical Director.

Colonel Nichols regarded this circular as subversive of the best business principles.

Wishing to accommodate pupils that came with good hard cash to stay but a short time, he held that the school year should be divided into short terms. Thomas, with mind upon artistic results and not balance sheets, wanted a school year of two long terms.

Early in the second year, the controversy had reached such a stage that teachers began to resign because they did not know whom to obey, Nichols or Thomas. The unlucky Thomas held on, still hoping to find a way out of the doldrums. Stories of the impasse began to be telegraphed about the country and to do the College harm. At last, on February 27, 1880, Thomas thought he could stand no more, and wrote a letter to the Board of Directors that leveled at their heads an ultimatum.

On two points: First, the school year was to consist of two long terms; second, he was not to be interfered with in the direction of the instruction given at the College. "I am willing to assume this responsibility," he said, "but I must insist upon being intrusted with the exclusive direction of the school in all its departments," underscoring for Nichols' benefit the "exclusive." Everything relating to the finances he **was willing** to leave to the Board and the Board alone. But he looked upon his position as that of a president of a college and the Board as the college's trustees.

"Under these conditions," he concluded, "with a curriculum established, and discipline maintained, I have confidence in the prospect of building up a great musical college. Under any other conditions I consider further effort in that behalf futile. ...I shall be glad to receive your answer by, say, next Tuesday."

The Board was composed of business men that were not accustomed to being addressed in this way by their employees. They replied, asking Thomas to explain in more detail his understanding of the duties and authority of a president of a university to its Board of Trustees. Thomas responded in a spirit of impatience. He said:

I cannot in justice to myself consent to continue longer responsible for a school, the direction of which is not confided to me, and am therefore entitled to know without delay what will be done. I simply insist on being in fact what I am now only in name, viz., Director of Music of this College. That office I am entitled to under my contract, and I decline to act any longer as assistant or associate director.

The business men on the Board seem to have been unable to deal with the situation thus created. Instead of giving Mr. Thomas an answer of yes or no, they constructed an essay on their excellent intentions and favored him with it. They could hardly have hit upon anything more effectual to enrage him. He thought they were practising evasion, which in his view was a higher power of lying. Face to face with men or crises, was his way. It is not to be pretended that he was particularly tolerant about other opinions on this point. He sat down at once and fired at the Board this shell of dynamite:

Cincinnati, March 4, 1880.
To the BOARD OF DIRECTORS OF THE CINCINNATI COLLEGE OF MUSIC,
GENTLEMEN:
I am in receipt of the letter of your Committee, dated the 2nd instant. I regard it as a misrepresentation of my position, and an

evasion of the real issue. That position and issue you certainly cannot misunderstand, in view of the communications, written and verbal, which I have had with your Committee and the President of your Board.

I therefore deem all further negotiations useless, and respectfully request you to relieve me from my duties on October 1st, or as soon thereafter as will enable you to secure my successor.

Yours truly,
THEODORE THOMAS.

With what impact this arrived we may surmise from the swift action of the Board to accept his resignation at once instead of on October 1. It must have been a warm meeting that took this step.[1] Thomas did not care. He was sick of the job and anxious to be clear of it. Rather curiously, the student body was all on his side in the controversy, and regarded his going as the death blow of the College. The citizens seem to have been with the students; so were the Directors of the Cincinnati Musical Festival, a body distinct from the College Board. These gave Thomas every evidence of warmest support. The next Festival was due in a few weeks and after he had left the College he devoted himself unremittingly to Festival plans, the greatest he had ever entertained.

Thus he came back to New York, utterly defeated in his great hope, cast once more against the blankest uncertainty, poorer in prestige, no richer in pocket than when he had stood out the Gilmore's Garden season, two years before. In other ways, his state was still worse, for now he was no longer sure of having his orchestra, and for a time uncertain about engagements. The debts excessively irked and depressed him; he had no more than begun to pay them off in Cincinnati. They grew to be an obsession with him; whenever the front door bell rang he fancied the

---

[1] September 19, 1885, the New York *Tribune* published a three-column article by H. E. Krehbiel, written after a visit to Cincinnati, in which he reviewed and summarized the story of Thomas's connection with the College of Music. As Mr. Krehbiel could never be accused of partiality toward Thomas, and as he was a trained and deliberating journalist, I have, in the main, followed his narrative of this episode.

sheriff had rung it.[1] The memory of the disappointment at Cincinnati must have been grievous upon a sensitive man. Yet if he had no effrontery and not enough philosophy to bear unmoved these flying shafts of misfortune, he had at times something almost as good: he had a facility in losing himself in work, and when his troubles grew heavy upon him, he betook himself to his Festival programs.

They began May 18 with his own adaptation of Bach's cantata, "Ein Feste Burg," and Annie Louise Cary and Italo Campanini were among those that sang in it. Next came Mozart's "Jupiter" symphony and Händel's "Jubilate." All the numbers on all the programs showed advance upon the foregoing Festivals. Slowly the country was following in his wake, much as an old-fashioned three-master used to follow a tug up to the pier.

It was at a rehearsal for this Festival that he had his famous encounter with Campanini. The great Italian had a terrible habit of singing at the audience even when he was in a duo or a scene. This offended Thomas, who was all for the ensemble and the effect. At last he plainly rebuked the offender. Campanini bridled up with resentment and was on the point of leaving the show. By the next morning he thought better of the correction, and in a manly way admitted his error. He said at the next rehearsal:

"Perhaps you are right about that."

"If I had not been right," said Thomas, "I should never have spoken to you about it."

He was now chosen to his old position at the head of the New York Philharmonic, a genial turn of fate that gave him great content. It seemed to him that, as he was to resume active leadership in the metropolis, he ought to inform himself of what the European bands were doing, and he slipped abroad for the next two months. Dr. Damrosch had launched his New York

[1]Mrs. Thomas, p. 121.

Symphony Society three years before; there was now a sharp rivalry between it and the Philharmonic.[1]

Europe had relatively little more to offer him in 1880 than it had blessed him with in 1866. He traveled widely, he heard many concerts and operas in London, Leipzig, Berlin, and other places. He went to Weimar and met Liszt who showed him great courtesy. But while he had many pleasant experiences in the musical centers, he found little that enlarged his own equipment. He was obliged to admit that the general standard of excellence was disappointing. This was markedly the case in London, but true also in a less degree in Germany. Yet he had a certain harvest of good things. In London he received a new impression about Händel, and declared that at last he had learned the proper way to perform him. "I think it would be desirable to have a Händel cult in all countries," he wrote simply.

In Berlin he went to see and hear Joachim, so many years the darling violinist of Germany, and gleaned from him some new views about the playing of three of Schumann's quartettes. There, too, he heard "Tristan und Isolde," and recorded that he was "disappointed," adding the singular comment, "I do not believe this music will ever be popular," never foreseeing his own work in making it popular.

In London they took him up into a high mountain and showed him all the kingdom of British music. At a word, all would be his—directorship of the London Philharmonic, of the Covent Garden Opera, of any other musical endeavor he might wish to captain, large salary, lifelong position, large honors, and a missionary field that in needs was second to none. He waved them all off. For was London New York? Or fit to

---

[1] "Trouble came into Theodore Thomas's life through the advent of other conductors from abroad; first, Dr. Leopold Damrosch. There was not really room as yet in New York for another big orchestra, but Dr. Damrosch and his friends started the Symphony Society. Much friction and unpleasantness and financial embarrassment were the result." (Finck, *My Adventures in the Golden Age of Music*, p. 176.)

compare with it? He had noted in his way of sharp commentary the habit of English audiences of rapturously applauding wretched performances.[1] It is possible that besides patriotic impulses he felt he would be little at home in such a place. Instead he packed his baggage and went home, apparently content on landing, for he talked to the reporters in a strain of unwonted optimism.

Among the curiosities of the blows that his fate dealt him was a certain tardiness in vindication. Two years after he had left Cincinnati, the hurt being all healed up and forgotten, the course he had taken at such a personal sacrifice was proved to the world to have been just and right. Reuben R. Springer, the wealthy philanthropist, undertook to endow the Cincinnati College of Music, but only on condition that the policy insisted upon by Theodore Thomas should become the institution's fundamental law.[2] All purpose or even chance of making money from the operations of the college was expressly eliminated by the terms of this gift, and dissatisfied stockholders, if any, were informed they could have their subscriptions redeemed.

But meanwhile, here is Thomas back again in New York and engrossed in the old struggle. It seemed to him clear that the Philharmonic now offered the best opportunity for his peculiar ministrations.[3] In his letter accepting the conductorship he had written that he purposed thereafter to identify himself with the Society and would give no symphony concerts of his own that might interfere with the Philharmonic series. He added that as he was to live in New York again he could accept the leadership without any guarantee, but he thought that in the circumstances he might ask for twenty shares instead of the ten he had formerly held. He figured that twenty shares would bring him an annual income of $2,500, and as his salary from the Brooklyn

---

[1]Mrs. Thomas, p. 190. It is a quotation from an interview.
[2]Mathews, p. 502.
[3]Autobiography, p. 86.

Philharmonic was at that figure, he should have from the two engagements a total income of $5,000, which, although but one half of his Cincinnati salary, he regarded as good. It illuminates the man as he really was to learn that when by and because of his own efforts he had made the Philharmonic so popular that the dividends went up to $100, $150, and $200 a share instead of the $18 or $20 they formerly paid, he refused to accept the additional sums that were justly his and turned back to the Society everything in excess of the $2,500 a year he had originally asked for.[1]

The venerable institution owed him much more than the money he declined to accept from it. In the season of 1877–1878, when he took the baton that had fallen from the hand of Dr. Damrosch, he had so galvanized the Philharmonic into public favor that the total receipts were multiplied eightfold in a single year. When he went to Cincinnati and Neuendorff took charge, they declined from $6,402 to $1,493. As this would never do, the following season, 1879–1880, Thomas was besought to come on from Cincinnati six times and lead the Philharmonic, which he did and brought the receipts back to $8,714. Then he was made the regular conductor and the first season, 1880–1881, the receipts were $10,730 and the dividends $132. He did more than to rescue the society from wreck. He made it the foremost musical organization in America and gave it both popularity and a standard from which it has never since departed.

What I have tried to assert about the unusual breadth and facile power of this mind is no biographical illusion. For example, in an age of specialization no man is expected to be at once a great conductor of choruses and a great conductor of orchestras. The two functions are separate in music as are engineering and architecture in building. He seems to have been conspicuous among the modern instances of easy command over both offices. While at Cincinnati he had taken up choral

[1]Krehbiel, p. 75.

work, at first as part of his duties, being the head of a college in which it was taught, then as a thing in which he found an absorbing interest. Before long he was pursuing the study and theory of it as an art to be loved for its own sake, and, as usual with him, he hit out ideas about it. He dug into all the science of voice production, mastered the technique as if he were to teach it, and thenceforward included it in his tuitional mission. Now he went over to Brooklyn and organized a chorus there, 200 voices, which he trained himself. Soon afterward he started one in New York, and began to use both in concerts with the orchestra, particularly in the Ninth Symphony, for which he had a kind of passion.

The fame of his Cincinnati Festivals had long before reached New York, and for the Festival of 1880 a party of New York music lovers made the pilgrimage. They came back filled with joy and the spirit of emulation. New York, the metropolis, was not to be eclipsed by Cincinnati of the woolly West. The New York Music Festival Association was organized, with George William Curtis at the head. Music festivals were a fashion of the time. In 1881 Dr. Damrosch managed one that current comment did not wholly approve. The Thomas camp heard with jubilation that its idol was to rival this effort. May, 1882, was the time set for it. The biennial Festival at Cincinnati was due the next week; Chicago was clamoring for one the week after. Thomas conceived that the three offered a chance of an unusual event, the greatest singers of the day to be brought from abroad, the orchestra to be augmented, and each city to supply its own chorus, elaborately trained. Local choruses had an immense possibility of local effect; 500 persons, spreading direct personal interest into 500 homes.[1] With the plans for these gigantic undertakings he was all-absorbed when Yale Uni-

---

[1] "Nothing so awakens an interest in music as helping to make it." (Theodore Thomas in an article in *Scribner's Magazine*, March, 1881, entitled "Musical Possibilities in America.")

versity conferred on him the honor of the degree of Doctor of Music. A bit of character color lies on the fact that he did not use the title then nor thereafter and never so much as referred to it.[1]

Any mention of the New York Musical Festival of 1882 brings up the story of the Damrosch-Thomas orchestral feud, which is no pleasant chapter in the history of music in New York, but inevitable in this chronicle. When Dr. Damrosch was defeated for the conductorship of the Philharmonic after the disastrous season of 1876–1877, his friends, who included many men of wealth and influence, gathered around him and helped him to launch his own orchestra under the name of the New York Symphony Society. From 1877 on, this organization and the New York Philharmonic under Thomas contended for the support of the New York public. In all such contests one thing immediately ensues. The followers become vastly more concerned than the principals. In the American people the sporting instinct is ineradicable and extends easily even within the adytum of art, where it might be thought a rank intruder. Anything in the nature of a combat warms the Anglo-Saxon blood when cold to aught else. In a short time the orchestral war was on full tilt, the adherents of each faction clamoring and arguing in the street. Relative merits or demerits of the two leaders, at first the subject of the high debate, came to be wholly obscured. Social, financial, racial, and, finally, great political influences were involved in the struggle.[2] Left to themselves, Theodore Thomas and Leopold Damrosch might have conducted each his own orchestra on alternate days or side by side, and never made faces at each other; but the volunteers enlisted back of each would never be contented except with a row. A

[1] Upton, *Reminiscence and Appreciation*, pp. 246–248. The next year Hamilton College bestowed the same degree upon him. He had long been an elected member of the Italian Society of Artists, the Verein Beethoven Haus and other foreign societies.

[2] *Musical Courier*, February 25, and March 4, 1891. Among the famous names of the time brought into these stories were those of James G. Blaine and Andrew Carnegie.

blind partisanship, of course, produces not the best mood in which to listen to heavenly harmonies, but it fell now upon a certain part of the musical public, the race issue playing its own always deplorable part. The race issue—and a psychology of mystery about the orchestra that remains inexplicable. Exactly why one cannot hear a piece of music without piling upon the head of the conductor all attainable laurels of joy or signs of shame I know not. Dr. Damrosch was a good conductor; Theodore Thomas was a good conductor. Instead of thanking God for sending two good conductors at the same time, here we were, ready to exchange blows over a question that could never be settled in that way or any other, and settled or unsettled was all frivol to any real interest of mankind.

In this contest of Laputan speculations, individual traits of character that otherwise would have been trivial assumed for the amusement of other generations an abnormal importance. Away from the conductor's stand, it is clear that Dr. Damrosch had all the advantage. He had the social graces; Thomas had none. Dr. Damrosch threw around his conversation the charm of an Old-World polish; Thomas's speech was yea and nay. Among his players, Dr. Damrosch was known as "the School-master," because so much of his rehearsal time was taken up with his learned and polite discourses; Thomas attacked a re-hearsal with the grim resolution of a German drill sergeant, said not much, worked a great deal. Dr. Damrosch was in some quarters a social favorite; Thomas saw few persons and those mostly connected with his purpose. The visible results reflected these differences. Dr. Damrosch's clientèle was the wealthier and more influential; Thomas played to the larger audiences.

Competition between the two camps was not always seemly. When Brahm's First Symphony came out there was a strife to obtain it for the first American performance. Thomas won and announced it for a coming concert. Dr. Damrosch and his orchestra were to give a concert a few days earlier. Of a sudden the advertisements proclaimed that at this concert would be performed for the first time in America Brahms's First Symphony. In some way the Damrosch forces had cut in ahead of the Thomas battalion. As to the manner of this quick dash, two versions were current. The agent for Brahms, with whom Thomas had his contract, was Schirmer, the music dealer. One story said that a woman friend of Dr. Damrosch, an eminent woman of aristocratic connections, went to Schirmer and bought the score of him and gave it to Damrosch. The other version had it that a woman went to Schirmer, asked to be allowed to take the score to study it overnight, and carried it to Dr. Damrosch's house, where a large force of copyists sat all night to reproduce the parts before it must be returned in the morning. Whichever account may be correct, the success of the Damrosch forces exasperated the other side (more than it ever disturbed Thomas, I know), and from that time the war was intensified.

The two orchestras played the symphony, one a few days after the other. The cynical may note that the New York press, which had been fairly unresponsive to efforts to awaken the city from its musical trance, rose with enthusiasm at the sign of a directly challenged combat. Much space was given to descriptions of the playings under the two conductors. One reporter counted the beats and evolved the momentous fact that in the Scherzo, Dr. Damrosch proceeded at eighty-five beats to the minute and Theodore Thomas at only sixty-four. Dr. Damrosch, having made this record, was plainly the winner, by twenty-one beats.

Soon after, the hostile camps had other things to stimulate dissension. The Thomas Musical Festival was coming on. This was no copyrighted Thomasian idea; musical festivals were an old story before 1873, and in point of mere size, certainly, Patrick Sarsfield Gilmore had set a mark for them with orchestras, bands, choruses, anvils, guns, and church bells, that is not likely to be exceeded unless the world goes quite mad. Nevertheless, the success of the festivals at Cincinnati had linked to such enterprises the Thomas name. When Dr. Damrosch announced a great Festival, the summer of 1881, some of the Thomas following said that the maneuver was hostile ai. ' would be met in kind.

The rivalry, which, I must observe again with emphasis, was always felt much more among the rank and file than by the leaders, was watched without enthusiasm by some of the judicious. I find Oscar Weil writing about it[1] in a tone of aloofness that offers a sharp contrast to most of the utterances of his day. He is commenting upon the Damrosch Festival, which was regarded by him and some others as "too much of a big thing," and he says:

It was impossible not to hear within one's self the constant suggestion, "Musical Hippodrome," and to wonder, if there were no rivalry of conductorship and struggle for notoriety and position in our midst, we should ever have been invited to expend so much labor, money, and "gush" on such an utterly unmusical performance of fine compositions. We think not. The gist of the whole affair is probably to be found right here. We have two conductors with rival claims to precedence; each has his following. With no public—ours least of all, for many reasons—would mere professional excellence suffice to establish their relative positions; it has to be done through the magnitude of their conceptions, magnitude in this case (where the one writes but little, the other not at all) finding its expression mostly in the number of people they can get together for a performance, and the bigness or newness of the compositions they can put upon their programs. What more is to be done in the Festival announced for next year by Mr. Thomas—announced too with most unseemly haste and more than questionable taste, just before the announcement of Dr. Damrosch's—we cannot imagine.

To this the response from the other camp was that, as a matter of historical fact, the Thomas Festival grew out of the Cincin-

[1] *Dwight's*, June 18, 1881.

THEODORE THOMAS ABOUT 1877

ANTON SEIDL
The great conductor of the New York Philharmonic

nati Festival of 1880 and was not originally designed, as the enemy said, in the way of a ripost.

But without going further into these contentions, while the rival camps exchanged insults and jeers the principal figure on the Philharmonic side seems to have moved to his work intent upon more inspiring matters. He was now in his element, at his best and happiest. Cincinnati and the sting of it were forgotten, the debts were disappearing, and he had under his hand the thing he loved better than aught else. He had a great enterprise encumbered with a mass of details and all depending upon him.

His equipment of a mind that loved equally to conceive great projects and to fill in their interstices, had now full play. In making his orchestra programs weeks ahead he saw the outline of the effect he wished to produce, and then dotted every "i," crossed every "t," spelled every name correctly, put in every punctuation mark exactly right.[1] It was never necessary (or possible) to edit anything he prepared for publication. Lucky indeed was he if the printer was half so accurate. For an artist he was incredibly methodical. He carried in his vest pocket the little narrow notebook. In this he entered every day the things he was to attend to before nightfall—"arrange for chairs," "extra lighting," "decoration man," "see Zollner about tenors," "write Tomlins about Chicago chorus," "Beckel about basses"—twenty such entries might comprise the sketch for a single day. As fast as he disposed of an item he crossed it off.

Without some such system he never could have discharged the immense amount of work he had taken upon himself; even with it he would have failed if he had not had both this tireless frame and this competence over items. He seemed to overlook nothing. When he gave a concert with a chorus every member

---

[1] The originals of his programs show an almost old-maidish precision, down to the least pen stroke.

of the chorus knew exactly where he or she was to stand and how, and when the chorus moved upon the stage, or moved off, it went like a perfectly trained troop of soldiers. Suppose the soloists, after the manner of their kind and time, never to have learned how best to make entrance or exit, or how to acknowledge a recall; they learned now. Thomas taught them. In the orchestra he had the place of every performer's chair fixed to an inch; he himself designed the decorations back of them so as to obtain the best sound effects from the material used. If in another city he must leave the main task of training a chorus to a local leader in whom he had confidence, like the admirable Tomlins[1] of Chicago, still he must himself make flying visits thither, rout out that chorus, give it three hours of his inspirational finishing, and flit back to New York in time to conduct a Philharmonic, New York or Brooklyn.

Some years stand out brightly in annals that need such relieving. This 1881 was among them. Happy in the evolution of his festivals, happy in some recognition, however belated and halt of his objects, and now happy in another thing. Chicago, where he was always so much at home, wanted him back for more summer concerts at the Exposition Building; he could take up his work there. Victory in defeat he was always achieving, and now came one other unshadowed triumph in the ripening of the first and best fruitage of his sedulous seed sowing. The Boston Symphony Orchestra was formed, the spacious result of the demand he had fostered and the public taste he had led.[2] His continual coming had not wearied Boston but stimulated it

---

[1] For Tomlins, see Otis, *passim*, but particularly at p. 101.

[2] "Theodore Thomas made the Boston Symphony Orchestra possible," said Major Higginson.

"The Thomas concerts have contributed to musical development in Boston. They have sharpened musical perceptions. They have created a new audience and a new interest for orchestral music in hundreds dead to it before. They have greatly raised the standards in excellence and execution. They have made the public demand more and our own conductors and musicians try more. The effect is seen in the improvement year after year of our home orchestra." (*Memorial History of Boston*, Vol. IV, p. 448, edition of 1889.)

to wish an orchestra of its own. Maybe Major Higginson, who so generously assumed alone the deficit of this beneficent enterprise, was founding better than he knew. In the forty-six years of the honored career of the Boston Symphony Orchestra, it has added to the spiritual life and joys of hundreds of thousands of people and contributed to American music a persisting influence toward the noblest ideals. Few of those coming under its spell have reflected upon the man that laid its foundations and whose work so immeasurably transcends his fame.

For whatever spiritual satisfaction he had in this new proof of his mission, he had to pay in a material loss, which seems to be the rule about such things. As the Boston field was now abundantly filled, there was no longer any need for him to go there. In the old days of his gloom, New England, including Boston, had been solace and material stay. In a year or two the Boston Symphony Orchestra began to travel the near-by routes. This still further reduced the Thomas territory. Unless he would consent to enter upon a competition that he regarded as odious, the whole of New England, once his own, must now be given over to the Boston organization. He was building up music in America and as surely developing his own rivals.

Throughout this memorable year he was preparing for another service to the musical cause, of a different kind, not less in value. He had long known, as other musicians had known, that the concert pitch of all the orchestras in America, his own no less, was too high. It was a thing that no one was to blame for, a universal condition that in his judgment deprived the orchestra of some of its rightful accuracy, power, and effect. He made up his mind when, for the second time, he took the direction of the Philharmonic, that so far as that organization was concerned he would, within the next two years, bring its pitch to accuracy. Therefore, he gave all his players notice that at the end of that time the pitch of the orchestra would be lowered nine sixteenths of a tone, and all were instructed to prepare for the change, securing new instruments, if necessary, or altering the old.[1]

When the time came, after this ample warning, the revolution went into effect in a moment and without a hitch. But what Thomas could hardly have foreseen was that virtually at the same time he had effected the same change in every musical instrument in America. All the best instrumental soloists played with him. To keep any connection with him they were compelled to amend their pitch. When they appeared elsewhere they carried the new pitch with them. When now a noted soloist appeared with the Boston Symphony, for instance, to play in harmony with him all the instruments in the Boston Symphony had to be lowered. In a space of time almost incredibly short, pianos, organs, violas and harps, psalteries, timbrels and sackbuts, came down with a rush, and the whole of America was making music on a pitch nine sixteenths lower than before, merely because one man perceived that this should be done and had the courage and persistence to force its doing.

The new pitch had more advantages than pleasing the fastidious ear of Theodore Thomas. It was scientifically correct. Twenty-five years before, the French government had created a commission of musicians and scientists to discover the true basis of pitch. The new Thomas pitch virtually coincided with the findings of this learned body. I do not know that Mr. Thomas knew of this report. As nearly as I can discover, he was brought to believe the change was unavoidable by his studies[2] in vocal music at the time of the ill-fated venture in Cincinnati; good out of evil. The natural gaps between the singer and the orchestra were brought home to him then, and with emphasis. Another point that appealed to him was that with the new pitch

---

[1]Autobiography, p. 91; Mrs. Thomas, pp. 215–216. It appears that some of the musical instrument makers were furious and attempted to stop the reform because it interfered with profits. Krehbiel's comments in the New York *Tribune* are interesting.

[2]The tuning fork with which he made his investigations is to be preserved in the Congressional Library at Washington as a relic in the history of music.

he could play classical music as he wished to play it. He could render exactly all the ornaments and elaborations of the original, usually omitted in modern representation. He not only could but he did. From that time forth he faithfully reproduced every feature with which the old boys had adorned their manuscripts. For years he was the only conductor in the United States that did this, and I think the only conductor in the world, though I had better avoid the saying of this and thereby escape the wrath to come.[1]

The three musical festivals of May, 1882, New York, Cincinnati, and Chicago, are among the decisive musical battles of America. Nothing like them had ever been known; I am not sure that they have since been surpassed. The influence they exerted upon public culture was so great, so profound, and so far-reaching that it could not be adequately estimated then and cannot be now. The one thing that is clear, looking over the history of American music, is that the effects of these massive and powerful performances may still be traced. There were seven programs in each city; not repetitions, either. In each city the local chorus had to be trained, but the orchestra and the soloists were the same. The orchestra numbered 300 players, the chorus 3,000 singers. For the New York Festival the Thomas choirs of New York and Brooklyn furnished 1,200 voices that he himself had trained and the remaining 1,800 were assembled from Boston, Philadelphia, Worcester (always a stronghold of music), Baltimore, and Reading, Pennsylvania. The Cincinnati chorus also was not difficult to manage, for the repeated sowing of seed in that fertile field was now yielding an abundant crop. Chicago was the crux of the problem, and the labors Thomas expended upon it seem now puzzling and impossible.

Between the Cincinnati Festival and Chicago there was only

---

[1]However, I have for the statement the high authority of Bernhard Ziehn. (See Upton, *Reminiscence and Appreciation*, p. 229.)

a week of grace. As soon as he laid down the baton in Cincinnati he started for Chicago and began the rehearsals there, mornings, afternoons, and nights. He did everything himself. He planned the stage, designed the decorations, drew the diagrams, hired the players, secured the soloists, inspired the local committees, smoothed out the difficulties, salved temperaments, listened to complaints, adjusted rows, arose with the lark, went to bed long past midnight, poured out an inexhaustible tide of energy and gave seven performances that swept seven audiences from their feet. There is no end of testimony to this effect in the press of that day. People came from hundreds of cities and towns, West, Northwest, Southwest; came to be charmed and to go home with new ideas about music and an inspiration to further it in their own communities. Not idly, either, and not merely with good wishes. The origin of more than one great orchestra in the West can be traced back to the Chicago-Thomas Festival of 1882.

The sowing and the reaping.

But I have run somewhat ahead of my story. The New York Festival blossomed in the Armory of the Seventh Regiment, which would hold more than seven thousand persons and was filled at every performance. The careful Thomas had decorated the bare barn so that the first impression one had in entering was of a calm and serene beauty. Mme Materna from Baireuth was one of the soloists; Mme Gerster, Annie Louise Cary, Myron W. Whitney, George Henschel, Campanini were others. There was a great organ. The last number on the first program was Händel's "Utrecht Jubilate," and when the 300 players of the orchestra, the perfectly trained chorus, the organ, Miss Cary, and Mr. Henschel poured out the great solemn strains of this powerful work the effect was so tremendous that people were strangely moved. Nothing of that kind had ever been heard in New York; few persons, even among musicians, had conceived of such effects as possible. It was a revelation; it disclosed a new world.

Looking over the seven programs now they seem to have been wittily planned and observant of a good balance. Strictly orchestral numbers were somewhat subordinated to the vocal, thereby conforming to popular preference. The symphonies performed were Mozart's C major, Schubert's C major, Beethoven's Fifth (in a Beethoven program), and the seldom-performed Symphony to Dante's "Divina Commedia," by Liszt. The Beethoven program had but one other number, the Missa Solemnis in D major, in which the chorus and organ again triumphed. On the "Classical Program" appeared the overture and first scene of Gluck's "Iphigenia in Aulis." There was a Wagner program composed of scenes from "The Ring" and a Händel program when the whole of "Israel in Egypt" was given.

In contrast with the heavy simplicity of this occasion was the next program, which was all of Italian music, reaching to eleven numbers from Corelli to Verdi and Bazzini. The last number of the last evening was the chorus from the third act of the "Meistersinger," always a favorite with Thomas and performed in a way that gave the fitting finale to the most impressive musical event New York had ever known.

One characteristic comment from the great mass of newspaper testimony to the wonders of this festival I cannot refrain from quoting:

Of course, a great deal of the majesty of last evening's performance was due to the visiting organizations, the famous Händel and Haydn of Boston, always so sure and so well trained, and the admirable societies from Philadelphia and Baltimore. But the basis of it all was our own force (New York and Boston), and the whole body took their beautiful style and their animation from Thomas. It did not need this festival to prove that he is not less great as a leader of choruses than as a master of the orchestra, but the fact is now brought home to thousands who have been slow to realize it. To the best of our belief there has never been chorus singing in New York to approach the splendor of what he has given us this week.

First and last, all of his equipment seems to have had use this week, even to his might of arm and latent power of menace in his eyes.

One afternoon he approached the stage or rear entrance of the hall a full hour, as was his habit, in advance of the time for the concert, and found a policeman guarding the path. It was an era when the manners of New York policemen were generally deemed to fall short of the best drawing-room polish.

"I'm Theodore Thomas," whispered the leader, smiling cheerfully as he attempted to edge past. Law and Order interposed an immovable promontory.

"Oh, youse is Theodore Thomas, eh?" says Authority. "Well, if youse was Harry Howard, Jim Fiske, and Billy the Kid all in one, youse couldn't be gettin' in here."

"But I'm the conductor of this afternoon's concert," said Thomas, furling his smile, "and it's necessary for me to go in."

"Conductor, is it?" observed Brass Buttons. "Well, the car barns is at Forty-third Street and Sixt' Avenoo, and it's there youse'll be gallopin' next," and moved not an inch.

Thomas considered. He had much to do before the concert, and time was precious. He turned his blue eyes in the manner of a hypnotist upon the legal blockade before him and advanced slowly. A reporter that knew him ran in to help but was too late. Before he could say a word, Thomas had thrown his arms around the astonished policeman, lifted him into the air, cast him out of the way and vanished through the door.[1]

On the final evening, 8,500 persons crowded into the hall. When the last note of the closing chorus had been sung, the

---

[1]*Everybody's Magazine*, August, 1904.

audience refused to depart, but stood and continued to thunder and cheer for Thomas until he had many times returned to the stage to acknowledge the tribute. It is worth noting that the receipts from the seven performances were $19,000, a record for New York and a phenomenon in that day, the more when one considers the low prices of admission. There was a deficit, provided for by the guarantee fund subscribed before the Festival was undertaken. Deficits Thomas expected in the day's work, and was seldom disappointed. His estimate was that the education and musical advancement secured to the public by such an event were cheap at the price, whatever that might be. By scrimping the choruses and accessories he could have brought the series within the box-office receipts, whereupon it is likely that a syndicate would have taken up musical festivals as a business. He was not always wise, but he remembered Central Park Garden and was content. As for the guarantors, they did not complain; they seemed as content as he.

When it was all over, the Festival Association sent him a letter, illuminated, and signed by all the members, a letter of congratulation on the memorable success of the enterprise and of thanks for the "untiring energy, patience, skill, and devotion" of the leader that had made its success. It was an unusual letter; I think George William Curtis wrote it; in the singular felicity of its phrasing combined with a tone of conviction and sincerity of feeling, it sounds like Curtis, so happy and so lucent. Theodore Thomas might have thought when he read that letter that he had achieved his goal, won his purpose, planted the roots of good music in America, and so retired to watch the plants grow. Not he; for a singular reason. Do you know what pursued him all his life as the furies pursued Orestes? The notion that so far he had fallen short of his desire, but by the mercy of God he would crowd on and overtake it. He could see many things; he could not see that the results of his labors were in any way considerable.

With the letter went something else, worth noting. It was a rarely beautiful baton for a conductor, ivory, richly inlaid with gold, and on the handle was engraved this:

CHAPTER VIII
The Full Tide of Success

THE next few years were among the brightest of his life. Being so strongly vitalized, work was the law of his being. The season of 1882–1883 proved enough to satisfy even his abnormal desires. Besides his other captaincies, he had been elected to the leadership of the New York Liederkranz, that old and highly honored society that has done so much to uphold high musical standards in the metropolis. He had the New York Philharmonic, the Brooklyn Philharmonic, his own orchestra,[1] the New York and Brooklyn choral societies, with all the rehearsals and labors that these involved. He continued the regular orchestral seasons in New York and Brooklyn, he gave a series of popular concerts at Steinway Hall, a regular season in Jersey City, another in Orange, New Jersey, another in Philadelphia, a special series in New York with Raphael Joseffy as soloist, and then the concerts of the Liederkranz. What is this man made of? In one week, early in the season, before his real work was well started, he had eleven rehearsals and three concerts.[2] The little notebook shows a record of almost febrile activity. He could rehearse an orchestra all morning, a chorus

---

[1] "But I have no hesitation in saying that M. Colonne's orchestra is surpassed in fineness and fulness of tone, as also in force and delicacy of expression, by the American orchestra of 150 players conducted by Mr. Theodore Thomas. . . . I simply say that the orchestra conducted by Mr. Theodore Thomas is the best I am acquainted with, and its high merit is due in a great measure to the permanence of the body. Its members work together habitually and constantly; they take rehearsals as part of their regular work; and they look to their occupation as players in the Theodore Thomas orchestra as their sole source of income." (Colonel J. H. Mapleson's *Memoirs*, Vol. II, p. 53. A little later he speaks of the democratic equality observed in Thomas's orchestra as one of the reasons for its success.)

[2] Mrs. Thomas, p. 242.

all afternoon, lead a concert at night and be up with the sun the next morning ready to rehearse again. Rehearsing, particularly chorus rehearsing, is hard work; the sheer exhaustion of physical vitality involved in meeting, combating, and mastering the wills of so many other human beings and bringing to one smooth surface of harmony so many jarring voices, is worse than toiling at an oar or beating out horseshoes.

It appears that he was now happy, having the gratification of so many full-speeded activities and one other beneficence of fortune.

The debts were paid at last.

He could hear the door bell ring without the vision of the sheriff that he used to conjure for himself; largely out of nothing. Many a man has gone through life weighed upon by a greater load and laughed at it and his creditors alike. Thomas was of the order that would fret at the owing of a nickel five-cent piece. But in this year he gathered the last of a remarkable collection of receipts in full from all those creditors he might have eluded in 1876 by the back door of bankruptcy, standing ever ajar. His feet were clear of debt and his soul of self-reproach.[1]

He had no vacation this year: I do not know that he ever had any real resting time, rest being a mental process, not physical, and this being a mind that evidently revolves always upon some considered purpose. No sooner was the regular season over in New York than forth he started upon a transcontinental concert tour that reached to San Francisco by one route and back by another. It was in a way the greatest thing he had yet undertaken,[2] for he had arranged musical festivals not in three cities, as in the previous year, but in twelve; great musical events with choruses and elaborate programs of his own devising. I

[1]Mrs. Thomas, p. 121.
[2]*Musical Herald*, July, 1882.

have some purpose in noting now with emphasis the cities in which by this time such things were possible. Baltimore, Pittsburgh, Louisville, Memphis, St. Louis, Kansas City, St. Paul, Minneapolis, San Francisco, Salt Lake City, Denver, and Omaha, made the list; we shall have occasion to come to these again. Seventy-four concerts all told, in thirty cities, for besides the twelve festivals he visited eighteen other places with single performances. Seventy-four concerts in a tour that began April 26 and ended July 7, and involved fourteen thousand miles of travel. America had not before known a musical enterprise of such purposes and dimensions.

One fact about it even he might have noted as a portent. In former days when he traveled it was on so much of a commercial basis that he must carefully calculate his receipts and expenditures lest he be stranded on the way. Therefore he must limit his troupe to the number that the box-office takings would be likely to justify. But on this tour, for the first time, he was relieved of all such cares. In each place the fact was cheerfully assumed that the expenses would exceed the income and the deficit was provided for by local subscriptions. It was that curious factor in American life, the wholly unselfish public spirit at its strangely intermittent, often irrational, but usually benign work. The barbarian West arose and demonstrated a passion for culture that rather shamed the complacent New Yorker. All kinds, all creeds, all nationalities, dropping everything else in a common effort for music; here is the trait the Gungls, Trollopes, Dickenses, and all the other detractors have overlooked. In another country, could this be done without some form of government subvention? It was done here and with efficiency; we need not suppose of casual origin. One man, planning everything, took through his hands all the endless threads of detail; from New York, far in advance, he nominated the coöperators, stirred them to enlist and train the choruses, gave them the programs, inspired them to rehearse and then to re-rehearse, carried on a vast and burdensome correspondence with thirty localities, and had everything so provided that, when the time came, the performance slid through as on well-oiled ways. It seems impossible; it happened as I tell you; the records show it. One man did all this at a time when he was carrying on nine series of concerts in and around his own city. A man capable of so great an achievement could hardly be otherwise than a power upon his times and those to follow.

This phenomenal tour once concluded, he plunged into another summer-night series in Chicago. Next came a short season in Milwaukee, and then the whole family went to Europe for a tripping visit before the reopening of the season, 1883–1884, in New York. While he was in Munich, looking about, as always, for musical novelties, there was introduced to him a young man unknown to fame, who confided to him that he had written a symphony. Thomas was to leave Munich the next day and was now pressed for time, but a symphony was a symphony; he would rather miss his steamship passage than lose the chance of one of those supreme works of celestial art.

"Let's see your symphony," says he. The young man owns that he has only the first movement ready and produces that. Thomas was one of the few conductors of his time who could really read an orchestral score at sight; I mean, who could by running over the different parts with his eye, accurately construct in his mind the sound of the whole. He examined the young man's score and was greatly taken with it.

"If the other movements are up to this," he said, "I will produce it in America this season."

He had to wait a year before the young man had the whole work ready, but when that time came he gave to the world the first performance of the first symphony of Richard Strauss and had, ever after, the composer for an ardent friend and admirer.

Not without reason; in after years it was Thomas that introduced Strauss to America and made him popular here.

This season went by like its predecessor, a time of almost incessant labor, for all the engagements of the previous year, Philharmonic, Liederkranz, choruses, and near-by concerts were on his hands, and he had also undertaken to extend his musical ministry by adding a series of concerts for young people and another for what were called "workingmen." At the end he had another great countrywide concert tour, beginning at Boston, April 22, and, after a long circuit through the West, closing at Montreal, June 28. It was so largely devoted to Wagnerian music that it was called a Wagnerian progress, although works by other composers were interspersed. He had brought over the great Wagnerian soloists from Baireuth—Scaria, Winkelmann, and Mme Materna, with whom he joined a list of other great names, including Emma Juch. His principal festival cities this time were New York, Boston, Chicago, Cincinnati, and Montreal. In New York he had the Händel and Haydn choir from Boston; in Boston he had his pet choruses from New York and Brooklyn. The Wagner programs consisted of scenes from the operas. At Boston, for instance, on one night, he gave the Vorspiel and the Love duo and finale from the second act of "Tristan und Isolde," and then, after the intermission, the whole of the third act of the "Meistersinger." On other nights he gave scenes from all the operas of the "Ring" and then parts of "Lohengrin" and "The Flying Dutchman."

The Cincinnati Festival had certain thorns for him and one in particular that long adhered to sting and bother. Choral work this time was not up to his standard. In the years of his absence the chorus, for unavoidable reasons, had lost its usual verve. Some of the newspapers, still resenting the College of Music's fiasco, had from the beginning diligently scarified the old wound about the programs. These now leaped with joy to magnify the chorus's defects. In Thomas's opinion they thus greatly increased the original trouble. "Knowing the effect these adverse press notices had upon the chorus," he says, "I used to ask after a performance, 'How is the press?' The answer was always, 'The same.' Owing to this cause, as I have said, the chorus lacked confidence and the slightest untoward event during a performance would create confusion."[1]

One night, after the concert, Thomas and a member of the orchestra were sitting in the office of Music Hall when a young man breezed in, announced himself as a reporter, and began to ask questions.

"Wait a minute," said Thomas. "What journal do you represent?"

The young man named the newspaper that had been most virulent about the programs.

"I have nothing to say," said Thomas, and pulled his frostiest front.

The young man smiled ironically, inched the closer, and continued his machine-gun fire of questions.

"I tell you I have nothing to say," snapped Thomas again. "Now get out!"

The young man did not go but, still smiling, continued to talk. Wrath, long smouldering, burst forth. Thomas sprang to his feet, put forth his great strength and shot the visitor like a ball from the room.[2]

Strong is the guild spirit in most of us that work for a living. From that time the story ran that Theodore Thomas's hand was against newspaper men and many a newspaper man's hand was voluntarily but efficiently against Theodore Thomas.

For a nature so sensitive to have, on the other hand, a latent asset of self-mastery is an odd contradiction, but it was his. The same man disturbed by an incivility or a slander the rest

---

[1]Autobiography, pp. 83–84.

[2]Contributed by the member of the orchestra that was present.

THOMAS ABOUT 1890

"HE LIFTED HIS BATON AND HIS LEFT HAND"
Thomas starting a concert. A drawing made from life for the
Chicago Symphony Orchestra

of us would ignore or return in kind was, in the face of an emergency, so cool of blood and ready of resource that all his fellows marveled at him. On this tour he conducted at Minneapolis the second of his great festivals there. The auditorium, as I remember it, was a temporary wooden structure erected on or near the University grounds. The time was the mои ьh of June, usually in that latitude a season of storm and squall. One afternoon a children's chorus, several hundred strong, was on the stage, while Scaria, the great Wagnerian, was singing. A black storm was coming up, though no one in the house noticed it. Of a sudden, without the least warning, the lightning let go and struck a corner of the roof, setting it on fire.

In the deafening crash a wild panic arose. Scaria, white with terror, leaped backward and started to run. Thomas, beating the time imperturbably, called to the orchestra to go on. As Scaria dashed past, Thomas shot out his left hand to stop him. The hand alighted upon Scaria's right ear and stayed there. Thus holding the singer with one hand he continued to beat with the other, shooting sharp commands around him. The children were screaming in fright and the audience rushing for the exits. Thomas, never ceasing his beat, kept the musicians playing and stilled the tumult among the singers.

"Now go on with your solo," he said to Scaria, and to the stage manager, "Get these children off the stage." He was afraid something might happen to them. While the orchestra continued to play the children were quietly withdrawn. It looked like a part of the performance. Then the audience recovered its wits and Scaria his tones. The torrents of rain extinguished the fire in the roof.

This tour, like that of the previous year, was eminently satisfactory in an artistic way, and when it was over Mr. Thomas with his family again went to Europe. For the first time in many years, he intermitted his work in Chicago. He was now nearly fifty and enjoyed what was for him the novelty of an unfrowning prospect. He owed nobody, he was firmly established in New York with many projects on hand and an always increasing hold upon public attention. He went abroad, but not to Esens. It is one of the curious facts in his career that he seems never to have had the least interest in his birthplace. He did not know even the most important things that had happened there. Years afterward he wrote to George Upton that the records of his birth and family were in the town church and never knew to the end of his life of the fire that had destroyed those records and come near to destroying the church itself.[1]

The new year, 1885, dawned happily on him, for on that day he had what seemed to him the sure promise of the fulfillment of the dream that had haunted him so long he had come to regard it as a penalty and not a hope. What he wanted above all things else here below was what he called a permanent orchestra. Well, but was not the Philharmonic permanent? It had existed from antiquity, it was now far stronger than ever; if anything human seemed likely to endure, here one could find it. Not according to the Thomasian doctrine. What he meant was an orchestra with a home, a building of its own, an abiding place whence it should not be elbowed every week by vaudeville, say, or even opera. As to his thinking, an orchestra was not an orchestra unless it played always under the one leadership, so permanency was not permanency unless it carried with it a roof. This bow of hope now rose upon him in an unexpected letter from the Mayor of New York, William R. Grace, and 3,000 other citizens, asking him to undertake to guide an enterprise, for which (it was asserted) ample financial support had been pledged, to give regular orchestral concerts in the manner that such entertainments were provided in the cities of Europe, and asking him to outline a plan by which this might be done.

He leaped upon the proposal with the cheer of a wanderer that finds an oasis in the desert. There was nothing said in the

---

[1]Conf. Autobiography, p. 19.

letter about a home or permanence, but with facility Thomas read into it the purpose of his heart; being in those years adept at such clairvoyance. He responded with a long letter in which he gave the required outline, and it may be believed that if New York had then adopted his suggestions it would have become in the next twenty years the greatest musical center of the world. It did not adopt them; the permanent orchestra faded back into the mist of dreams, and the 3,000 citizens that had signed the letter of January 1, seemed easily to forget this, perhaps with other virtuous resolutions of that day.

The festival tour of the spring of 1885 began at Portland, Maine, and went through to San Francisco and back, being followed by a summer-night series in Chicago.

For once in his life the face that fortune turned on him seemed to have nothing but smiles. I doubt if a happier man dwelt that year in New York. He was busy in his art, the evidences of his influence upon the musical taste of America, proclaimed by everybody else, were undeniable even in his own vision; he still grasped some shreds of hope about permanency, and he had the New York Philharmonic, the pride of his life. I think he never had so much satisfaction in any other achievement. When he took the command the Philharmonic was at almost the last sad gasp. Now men saw its revival. Before his day, its five yearly concerts were attended by a few dispirited citizens that seemed to come from a sense of duty and remain in the way of martyrdom. Now its weekly concerts were so popular that at the beginning of each season all the seats in the house were sold to season-ticket holders.

The results of his labors were translatable into the choicest symbols of the American language. As observe: It was for the season of 1879–1880 that he succeeded Adolph Neuendorff as conductor. This is the story of the magic he exerted upon the Society's receipts and dividends:[1]

---

[1] Upton, *Reminiscence and Appreciation*, p. 151.

SEASON	RECEIPTS	DIVIDENDS
1878–1879	$1,493	$ 25
1879–1880	8,714	123
1880–1881	10,730	132
1881–1882	12,913	154
1882–1883	15,933	195
1883–1884	16,022	195
1884–1885	17,914	223

In five seasons he more than doubled his own high-water mark, which in turn exceeded tenfold the record when Dr. Damrosch was conductor. This seems to fix sufficiently high his place in the affections of the public—at that time.

It was the more remarkable because the dog star of the orchestral war was all this time raging.[1] Strange are the mutations of the popular taste and mind! How long ago was it that Theodore Thomas was ruined, penniless, and a kind of careering outcast as the result of his efforts to make one real orchestra live in New York? Five or six years. And now there are three orchestras all receiving from the public marketable tokens of appreciation and from the press no end of attention because there is supposed to be a fight. How many years did he go unregarded up and down looking for a rich man that would help the cause of musical art and getting nothing but cold frowns and a notable assortment of debts? Nearly twenty. And now at a touch the rich men come with tribute to support somebody else's organization. Reading the art history of America, there appears no great wonder that artists are sometimes cynics; what seems strange is that they are ever anything else.

If he still lacked that suitable hall for his band, the other steps of the throne of grace he trod with swelling acclaim. As most of the players in the Philharmonic were members of his

---

[1] "Who will take Dr. Damrosch's place is the only matter for deliberation, but that an efficient leader will be found there is hardly a doubt. The unhappy feeling that exists between Mr. Theodore Thomas's and Dr. Damrosch's adherents will prevent a call being made upon Thomas." (*Musical Herald*, March, 1885.)

own orchestra he had them under his sole control and could achieve with them some of the effects he desired. He was as popular throughout the music world of America as in New York. His name had conjuring power. If he desired to give a festival in any remote place, Eastport to San Diego, he had but to mention the fact and the funds were subscribed, the choruses enlisted, the training begun. Supposing him to stop long enough to reflect upon the days of the "Firefly Polka," he must have been astonished at the change. It was another kind of America that he was working with now. I have never known a man less given to self-worship; but he could not have made such a comparison without some realization of his own part in bringing about the change.

Everything looked well for him. He had bought an estate in Fairhaven, a quiet seashore town of Massachusetts, and every summer he moved his family there and spent with them what time he could spare from his work. He had means now to give his children the best possible education. He began to hope that he might have the means to leave them not penniless at the end.

And then, from this pleasing summit and goodly prospect, he was cast of a sudden into the depths of defeat and disaster. There is no armor against fate, sighs the old Elizabethan. No, nor defense of wit, either. Partly by his own bad judgment, partly by reason of that overwhelming faith of his about rich men and art, partly by the Napoleonic doom of teaching rivals how to beat him, but mostly because of circumstances that nobody could have foreseen or prevented, down he went.

CHAPTER IX

Grand Opera in American

IF THE name of any woman not a professional musician stands out in the history of American music, I should think it might be the name of Jeannette M. Thurber.

This worthy, sincere soul, really interested in music as an art, had long desired to be of some great, practical use to the advancing cause, and about this time believed she had found the thing most needed. Her husband had made a modest fortune in the wholesale grocery way and was sympathetic about her purposes. She had a social position, she had a boundless and fairly discreet energy. She now went about among rich acquaintances talking up her pet project, and seems to have been agreeably astonished to find how warmly (in some quarters) it was received.

One thing she did not know that only experience could have shown. It is always easy to get persons of wealth to endorse with kind words a conspicuous and well-sponsored movement in art, but difficult to induce them to back it with long purses. What she planned was an American School of Opera and American Opera Company. To float this she got up a formidable list of incorporators that owned or represented about one half of the wealth of the nation. Andrew Carnegie was president, August Belmont, Levi P. Morton, Henry Seligman, Brayton Ives, H. J. Jewett, Deacon White, and other wealth-haloed names adorned the list that circulated in Wall Street. Thence it traveled clear across the country, and took in N. K. Fairbank of Chicago, representing the great packing-house interests; George

M. Pullman, sleeping cars; W. D. Washburn of Minneapolis, the flour-mill interests; Charles Crocker of San Francisco, the Pacific railroads; John W. Mackay, mines.[1] Yes, it is safe to say that half of the nation's wealth was represented in that remarkable list. At last the halcyon days had come; America's captains of industry had awakened to their æsthetic duties, they were about to insert the golden levers and uplift art. The American Opera Company was to be endowed in a way that would signalize an epoch, and by universal verdict only one man could be considered as its commander in chief. He was Theodore Thomas.

So they approached him with this proposal and he accepted it. Despite the warnings of clearer-sighted friends, despite the lesson he had received at Cincinnati, he accepted it; and easily. He believed with all his heart in the fable about the millionaire and art. God knows why he should have believed it, except for the reason that he wished it to be true, or perhaps because all his days he had prophesied of it. You may wonder at the prophet that has confidence in his own predictions, but you can hardly blame him. Besides, this was to be a school of opera. A school was that other thing he had long desired; first, a permanent orchestral home; second, a school of music. At Cincinnati he had thought he was to have it; the disappointment only whetted his desire. And again, this was to be an American opera company, and there was never a sturdier patriot. American singers would no longer have to go abroad and change their names to win a chance to do serious work in grand opera; we were to have the best grand opera at home. After this, again, foreigners would have less occasion to make the jeers at America about which Thomas was always sensitive. We should have as good operatic art as any country going.

So, without assuring himself of the actualities of the financial

---

[1] Mrs. Thomas prints the whole astonishing list at p. 285.

support, he took the conductorship of the venture. To do this, he gave up that direct line of his advance in which he had been so deeply interested; he gave up whatever chance of good might still lie in the vague but alluring generalities of that letter of 3,000 New Yorkers; and he gave up much of his income. If he had only known it, he was giving up more than that. He was surrendering over his place in the city for which he had labored so long with such a singular devotion; and he was giving up his peace of mind for years to come.

But he went ahead. The American Opera Company was formed. Thomas formed it. He made it one of the most remarkable organizations that had been known in music. He prepared new and wonderful productions of all the operas to be given, new scenery, new effects, new accessories. He selected and trained the choruses with a purpose to make them different from any other opera choruses that ever had sung. He added his own orchestra, so diligently perfected through so many years. He designed, he planned, he rehearsed and revised; and he assembled the largest ballet ever seen in America.

He made new orchestrations for many of the operas.

More, he insisted that all the operas sung by an American opera company must be sung in the American language. If no translation existed, he had one made. All these labors are still on record; his scores are preserved in the Newberry Library, Chicago; go there and examine them, if you think any of this is overdrawn. You will find, for example, the full score of Gounod's "Faust" as used by the American Opera Company, his own orchestration on the lower part of the page, the text in German and French above, and just above that his own version, made in excellent metrical speech, done singably, with open vowels and all, and written line by line upon the score in his own hand with a blue lead pencil.

He must have labored like a horse in a treadmill, night and day. The yea and nay habit had its uses now; he could never have gotten through with his colossal job without his facility in quick decisions and the rapid discharge of business.[1] The first performance was scheduled for January 4, 1886, at the old Academy of Music, rejuvenated in honor of such a notable occasion. It went without a hitch, a fact that caused universal comment and amazement. The scenery, all specially painted by famous artists, was wonderfully good and beautiful, all the accessories were adequate, the chorus covered itself with glory, the soloists sang adorably. Critics, commentators, sceptics, joined the public in one swelling hymn of laudation. Operas had not been so produced in the memory of living man. What struck everyone was the flawless perfection of the details and their relation to the harmony of the whole. The picturing, for instance, was not more impressive than the art of the drilled and finished chorus.

This was the employment in which Thomas exulted and excelled.

There were twenty-nine solo artists in the company, all chosen by him, and it was eloquent of one of his fundamental faiths that of these, twenty were Americans. Emma Juch, Myron W. Whitney, who was one of the best bass singers ever heard on any stage, Mme Hastreiter of Louisville, Mme L'Allemond of Syracuse, were among these distinguished performers.

The repertoire for that season embraced twelve operas, and it must be admitted now that the range was remarkable and the taste that directed the choosing catholic. This is the list·

"Orpheus and Eurydice" . . . . Gluck[1]
"The Merry Wives of Windsor" . . . . Nicolai
"Lohengrin" . . . . Wagner
"The Flying Dutchman" . . . . Wagner
"Faust" . . . . Gounod
"The Taming of the Shrew" . . . . Goetz

[1]Upton, *Reminiscence and Appreciation*, p. 248.

"Lakmé" ....Delibes
"The Magic Flute" ....Mozart
"The Huguenots"................................Meyerbeer
"Aïda" ....Verdi
"Martha" ....Flotow
"Nero"...Rubinstein

To drill so large a company in so large a repertoire to the excellence attained here was a great labor.

With rare éclat the New York engagement ended. The company went on tour of the principal cities of the country. There it had from the press nothing but praise. I have not found among the reviews any other note but wondering applause for the singular completeness and worth of every performance. Boston in particular was captivated (in its newspapers) and declared that the highest artistic expectations had been more than realized. "No such performance of any opera had ever been heard here before," said the *Transcript*, and so in a sentence condensed the opinion of all the other writers. "It is not too much to say," observed the *Advertiser*, "that no person in the crowded and distinguished auditory had ever seen in this country any representation by any other organization nearly commensurate with this."

Philadelphia, Baltimore, Washington, and Chicago repeated these triumphs. According to every appearance, Theodore Thomas had attained to a summit of honor no other conductor had reached at any time in any country.

I hate to dwell farther upon the labors of this tireless person; they are too disturbing to us that, being normal, have mind upon our ease. Yet it is to be recorded as fact that while he was immersed in the vast sea of details pertaining to the American Opera he was going on with his regular orchestra and choral work as if he had nothing else to do. He even went a little beyond his regular work. Instead of nine series of concerts he gave this year eleven: the regular Philharmonic in New York; the regular Philharmonic in Brooklyn; the regular concerts in Philadelphia, Jersey City, Orange, Newark, and New Haven; twenty-four young people's concerts in New York, and twenty-four popular concerts; eight popular concerts in Brooklyn; two Liederkranz concerts of vocal music. These with rehearsals of orchestra and regular choruses besides the necessary rehearsals of the Opera Company. The wonder is twofold, that he found enough hours in the day for so many activities and then that any frame of flesh and nerves could have endured such a multiplicity of cares, bores, aggrieved geniuses, flaunted artists, fiends, lunatics, and exertions.

As to the Opera Company, remember that all the musical world had fixed its eyes upon this venture, mostly with scepticism. Nothing good in art could come out of America; this was the fixed belief of most foreigners, being obligingly reinforced therein by the general assent of Americans themselves. Yet here was proof to the contrary, or all the critics were liars. Something more than good had come out of America, something artistically great and memorable, something that set a new high standard of excellence. It had come about chiefly through the faith and persistence of one man. He would have been not of mortal compound if he had not felt a profound gratification. And yet, under the surface, all this was at work to provide his ruin.

The season ended in a flare of praise, and immediately after came on the Seventh Biennial Cincinnati Festival, which Thomas managed and conducted with the usual success, and next, without interim, the season of summer-night concerts in Chicago. The only rest he had that year consisted of a few days at his seaside home between the ending of his Chicago engagement and the beginning of rehearsals in New York for the next opera season.

The first year of the American Opera Company had been as full of financial trouble as of artistic delight. There had been great acclaim everywhere, but if the houses had been twice as great they could hardly have met the expenses of such an organization. Mr. Thomas's idea from the beginning, shared, I think, by Mrs. Thurber, had been a great enterprise in education for which the accumulated wealth of the country would be glad to pay. This he understood to be the meaning of the imposing list of millionaires on the incorporation papers. He knew there would be a deficit; deficits were inevitable. But he felt that, as these wealthy men had derived their fortunes from American opportunity, they would be glad of a chance to return thanks by upholding a great work for the public good. Particularly in view of the fact that the deficit, when divided among so many, would be for each a negligible sum. Mr. Carnegie alone, the president of the Company, could have met all the default and never have felt it, and in that list were twenty other men as rich as he.[1]

There is a kind of innocent paranoia of idealism as difficult to exorcise as its ranker prototype. From his youth Thomas had clung to this conception of American wealth, clung to it so fatuously that he would not even stop, in such a case as the American Opera Company, to question the foundations of his belief. He was now to learn, to his pained amazement, that the musical education of the American public had left out the American millionaire, even when pledged, one might think, to support a great project in musical education. When the year's work was wound up, it appeared that the American Opera Company was much in debt, and its incorporators and backers refused to meet these obligations or to contribute any farther to its existence.

For this apparently chill and cruel desertion there was more extenuation than Mrs. Thurber would admit. It is likely that the deficit part of the program was never explained to the gentlemen that played angel to the first launching. The notion

---

[1]This was before he had formed his great steel combination.

that any enterprise taking money from the public must be self-sustaining to justify its existence is bred in the Anglo-Saxon bone and has more manifestations than in music. Whatever others may have dreamed, the eminent gentlemen that Mrs. Thurber's eloquence and the popularity of her husband had induced to join in the American Opera Company believed they were starting a business enterprise like any other, and when they heard that it had not paid its way in one whole season of experiment, they called it a failure and scrambled ashore.

This was only natural. But there were other influences at work to the vast injury of the venture. Whenever in this world there is an abundance of praise or an eminence long continued there will also develop a revolt against it. Mr. Thomas had overdone his job. In a yachtsman's phrase, he had overstood his mark. An element in New York felt there had been too much Thomas; Thomas the king of the orchestra world, Thomas the great creator and leader of choruses, Thomas at the Philharmonic, Thomas with his own orchestra, Thomas here, Thomas there, and now Thomas surpassing everybody (in the public prints at least) with the brilliancy of his operatic productions. Professional and other jealousies, the New Yorker's love of novelty and change, the division of its musical world into hostile camps, were other factors. Dr. Damrosch had died suddenly and lamentably in 1885, but the faction that had been devoted to him was farther than ever from reconciliation to the immense vogue of his rival. The orchestral war now shifted into the opera war. Another opera company was then playing in New York. Thomas had incontestably eclipsed it. This naturally caused resentment. Another orchestra was forming[1] and another rival beginning to attract much attention. Here were sources of other troubles.

It is also to be admitted that the chief subject of these remarks had a considerable but unconscious proficiency in the

---

[1]Mrs. Thomas, pp. 276–277.

gentle art of making enemies. We have seen how largely gratuitous was his reputation as an autocrat, so far as he had one, but
any practitioner of his directness of speech would be sure to
offend many persons used to the obese circumlocutions with
which we have agreed to adorn our purposes. His lack of *savoir
faire* was a handicap that arose from the pressure upon him.
"Wi' these to oversee ye'll note I've little time to burn on social
repartee," was his idea of it. His conception of life was work;
when he was not at work he was thinking about work, an employment that seemed to him more important than drinking
tea and talking earnestly about nothing with persons that had
a superfluity of time but no sense of its value. It is difficult to
deal with these things without creating a wrong impression of
the man. He seemed to many taciturn and hardly amiable.
They did not know him. Under the defensive armor of impassive
reticence with which he got through the world, he was genial,
warm-hearted, kindly, unselfish, and almost singularly con-
siderate of others. "The easiest man in the world to get along
with," testified Frederick J. Wessels, so long his manager and
confidant, who knew him better than any other man ever had
a chance to know him.

As to thoughtfulness for others, please note. When released
from the strain of a concert, his physical man demanding food,
he liked to come home, have hot toast and a glass of wine, and so
to bed. Once it occurred to him that somebody must sit up to
make that toast, and maybe light a fire for it. He would never
afterward have toast at home.

With other dreams he had cherished one of a pension fund for
old musicians. There being nothing of the kind, he had from his
own lean purse, and even in adversity, helped the players that
because of age were retired from his orchestra.

When his daughter was married, he went out into the street,
fetched in all the waiting coachmen, gathered the other em-

ployed persons, served them himself with wedding cake and champagne, and entertained them as the other guests had been entertained.

These are but indices. I have one other, a great scene that eclipses them all and comes down to the primal springs of human emotions.

In 1870, nearly all the members of his orchestra are German. There is one exception, the principal player upon the horn, a Frenchman whom I will call Du Bois.

When the news comes of the battle of Sedan, September, 1870, the German members of the orchestra petition Thomas that at the rehearsal that day they may wind up with a performance of somebody's fantasia on he "Wacht am Rhein," or some other patriotic German jubilate, to celebrate the victory of the Vaterland. Thomas consents.

So when the rehearsal is over he turns to the Frenchman and says:

"That is all for to-day, Mr. Du Bois. You are excused."

Du Bois sits still and says nothing.

"We are going to do something that may cause you pain, Mr. Du Bois," says Thomas again, "and I think you had better withdraw, if you please."

Du Bois sits still and says nothing.

Thomas lifts his eyebrows and then his baton and the orchestra soars into the "Wacht" or whatever it is, playing fit to blow off the roof and Du Bois playing with the rest, but with the tears running down his cheeks. As the end is reached, Thomas drops his baton, strides over to Du Bois and throwing his arm around him says:

"My boy, I tried to save you from this and you would not let me."

"I know you did, Mr. Thomas," gulps Du Bois, "but my duty is with the orchestra. Whatever it plays, I must play too."

"Come!" cries Thomas, and lifts him to his feet. So with his arm still around him he leads him out in front of the stand and turns around facing the players.

By one of those strange psychological impulses that seize upon the souls of men, every player springs to his feet, stands at attention, and then salutes the Frenchman. Thomas with his arm still around him leads him away. As they pass out of the door a tender-hearted German cries:

"*Hoch der Du Bois!* and God bless him!" And all the men cry together:

"*Hoch!*" But now there is no triumph but a note of fellow feeling.[1]

Autocrat and all, he was father confessor to the men in his band. If any of them was in trouble, personal, domestic, or financial, he went straight to "the Old Man," and found sympathy and help. Upon pretentious mediocrity he had no mercy and he kept the discipline in his ranks as taut as a violin string. He had once as concert master one of the best violinists in America, a most talented as well as likable man, who fell unguardedly to speaking of himself as the "assistant conductor" or "associate conductor" of the orchestra. At that time Thomas had no such office in his organization. When the news came to his ears, with one winged sentence he dismissed the offender, rare and admirable artist as he was.

This Thomasian habit of terse utterance did his reputation much harm. Comes, for example, a hopeful composer with a perfectly grand composition he (or she) is sure Mr. Thomas will rejoice to play. Thomas, who will listen to anybody and try anything, accepts the composition for examination and at home that night studies it over with maybe a ton of others. In a day or two, Genius returns to pick up his laurel wreath. Thomas hands the piece back and says:

"Sorry; it will not do."

---

[1] I am indebted for this incident to one of Theodore Thomas's oldest living friends.

FRAGMENT OF A THOMAS SCORE

Part of the first page of his orchestration of the overture to "Alceste," prepared for the American Opera Company. (*Courtesy of the Newberry Library, Chicago*)

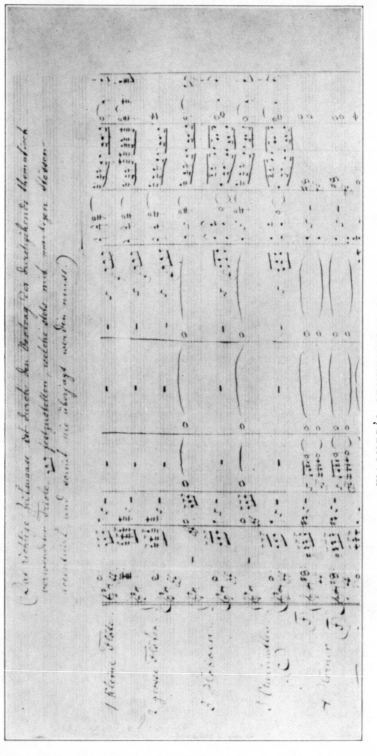

WAGNER'S CENTENNIAL MARCH

Part of the first page of score in Wagner's own writing. (*Courtesy of the Newberry Library, Chicago*)

"Why not?"

"Not good enough."

So then Genius goes away swearing mad and through all his circle of acquaintance spreads the word that Thomas is an autocrat, or maybe an old bear.

There were sixteen other persons waiting in line that day to have speech with the autocrat. He could not bandy linked sweetness long drawn out with all of them.

Generally speaking, he was not popular with newspaper men. The story of the Cincinnati episode was widely disseminated in the craft, but there were other reasons. He needed a good press agent and never knew it; for himself, he was the worst press agent that ever lived. He thought his work ought to do all the speaking for him. By another limitation of his mind, he was never able to put himself in the critic's or reporter's place. He seems never to have reflected that the bitter assaults on his programs, to take one example that made him writhe, arose from a total ignorance of what he was aiming at. The critic looked upon a Thomas program as he would have looked upon any other: as a thing designed to please people and show the excellence of orchestra and leader. He never suspected that the Thomas program was designed only to fill a certain place in a series of programs that stretched over many years and had for purpose to educate, not to entertain.

He never suspecting this, Thomas never told him; being true to form but poor in policy. It was always a defect in the Thomas system that he did not take the public into his confidence. He would not even defend himself against mendacious assault. All his life he pursued one style of tactics when attacked. He drew down his lips and said nothing.

The length to which he carried his rugged integrity sometimes made trouble for him. One day there came to him a newspaper man he knew fairly well, and said:

"Mr. Thomas, I have lost my place on the *Daily Balloon.*

You know Mr. Blank, our editor. I want you to do me a favor.
I know he will reinstate me if you ask him."

Thomas saw, what any other wise man in the same conditions
would have seen, that it was impossible for him to ask favors or
be under obligations to any editor. Another man would have
escaped by the near-by route of generalities or the popular
gate of an insincere promise.

"I can't interfere in such a case," said Thomas coldly,
making another enemy and one that pursued him for years.

But to come back to that battered concern, the American
Opera Company, with which these meanderings have little to
do. There was still one other reason why it was ill-starred, and
the strongest reason of all. It was plagued with the worst name
it could have been christened with.

Outside of the realm of the demonstrable, most ideas commonly held about nations are fallacious. There is a general belief
that Americans are narrowly nationalistic, blind and boastful
chauvins, always assertive of their own measureless superiority.
This is as true as the other common beliefs that the French are
volatile and erratic, the English frank and sturdy, and the Jap-
anese full of all guile and subtlety. In point of fact, as the
shrewdest English observer of these times has pointed out, the
Americans are the only people in the world that hate themselves.
"American Opera" connoted bad opera. To this day, "American artist" means to the average American soul inferior artist;
"American composer" means inferior composer. If doubt is entertained on this head, witness the fate of the "American
composer" programs in the experience of any grand orchestra.[1]
In 1886, the fundamental scepticism about American art was
even less convinced against itself; the fixed American habit of
demanding importations was not at all discouraged. A majority
of Thomas's solo singers were Americans. What in any other

---

[1]In Chicago, for instance.

country would have been a source of strength was in this a well-spring of evil.

But the books were balanced at the end of the first season, and there was that deficit staring Mrs. Thurber in the face with no resources available. In this emergency some agile mind suggested that the company reorganize under the elastic laws of New Jersey and so be able, like many other less worthy enterprises, to sidestep inconvenient litigation. This plan had also the advantage of a change of name that would drop the handicap of "American." "The National Opera Company of New Jersey" was formed to succeed to the assets of the "American," and as Mr. Carnegie's overshoes seem to have been misplaced about that time, Mr. Thomas, in an evil hour for himself, was induced to take the presidency.

For the season of 1886–1887 he felt that he could not longer carry the burden of so many enterprises.[1] He did not attempt to repeat the varied activities of the previous year, but retained the New York and Brooklyn Philharmonics and a few others. Most of his thought was now centered upon the opera. In a business way, this was a sacrifice, for the greater part of his income was derived from his concert work. But in his fifty-second year he began at last to feel the strain of so many cares, and having to choose between the two, chose the opera, to which he felt himself bound by honor.

The season began in New York with a renewal of all the artistic triumphs of the previous year. Toward the close, Thomas gave the first American production of Rubinstein's "Nero." Of this the New York *World* said that it was "placed upon the stage on a scale of splendor never before given to opera in this country, with scenes, pictures, and groupings of extraordinary magnificence, culminating with the burning of Rome; and sung with enthusiasm, intelligence, and artistic de-

---

[1] *Musical Courier*, February 2, 1887.

votion." It called the performance "an overwhelming success," and "marking an epoch in great opera in English."

Next came a long tour across the continent. At San Francisco the company made a marvelous hit, so that the people insisted upon one more night than had been contracted for. The next jump was to be to Kansas City. To comply with the San Francisco demand, it was necessary to hire three extra trains and race them at top speed. "Nero" was scheduled for the last night in San Francisco. The final scene is the destruction of Rome. Steam, conducted through pipes laid under the stage, was to be turned on to represent the smoke of the burning city. Something went wrong with the apparatus. When the signal was given to turn the valve there was a devastating explosion, fragments of the main pipe shot into the air, and out poured a great cloud of steam, not from many places, as ordered, but from one.

The chorus shrieked and started to run, the orchestra stopped, the players sprang from their seats. As before, the only perfectly cool man in the place was Theodore Thomas.

"Go on!" he hissed, and continued to beat as if nothing had happened. "Go on! Go on! Go on!" The orchestra pulled itself together, the chorus caught up a note, the voices quickly rose and the scene ended, half smothered in steam, illumined with fire effects the stage manager had not dreamed of, but radiant with glory. People said it was the best fire scene ever put upon any stage and the newspapers praised Thomas for arranging it.

The curtain once down, the company was hustled to the trains and a race against time began, halfway across the continent. Some of the players took with their watches the speed on level stretches and were startled to find they were moving at seventy miles an hour. On the locomotive of the train that bore the orchestra, the terrific pace produced a hot box. In a few minutes a tongue of flame stretched back of the engine tender and was plainly visible as they went around curves. Stops were made and the crew tried to subdue the monster. It always broke out again. When they reached Albuquerque and could change engines, so much time had been lost that it seemed impossible the engagement at Kansas City could be kept. The only Thomas boast was that he had never been late at concert or rehearsal. His record of so many years seemed now certain to be ruined. Kind friends commiserated him, and indeed it meant more to him than to anybody else. Whatever he may have felt, he maintained outwardly the aplomb that was so famous and so curiously inconsistent with the artistic temperament.

"We'll make it, all right," he said over and over to the puckered brows about him. "I know these railroads." It appears that in the last stretches of the race the cars went around curves on two wheels, and the timid among the company sat thinking of their latter end. They made Kansas City in time to whisk themselves into costumes and evening clothes and do "Lohengrin."

I suggested to the member of the orchestra furnishing this chapter that it must have been a poor performance.

"Not at all," said he warmly. "I have never known it to go better. We were too excited to be tired. Sometimes a performance on bare nerves is the best in the world."

I asked about Thomas. He said:

"I think he was never more self-possessed. The sight of him doing his work in that sure way after all he had been through was an incredible stimulant. I remember feeling as if I had drunk a highball."

But financially the National Opera Company fared no better than its predecessor. Under whatsoever name, the rich men of America would give little or nothing to keep alive an enterprise that had showed a deficit. Mrs. Thurber, unable to raise any money, was at her wit's end. At last the day came when there were no funds to pay salaries, and then a day when the members of the chorus and the subordinates, being without specie, were without food. At this juncture Thomas stepped in. He had himself received no salary from the beginning of the season but he now paid the living expenses of the penniless and at his own charges carried them back to New York. Repeated appeals to the directorate brought no response. He managed to fill the engagements as far as Buffalo, and there he gave up the fight. The next week the National Opera Company was no more.

As a going and musical concern. In the way of trouble-making it hung for years around his neck. He was only its hired man and one of its aggrieved creditors, but because of his prominence, and because he was the figure-head president, scores of persons that had claims against the thing hounded him with bills, collectors, lawyers, process-servers, and suits.[1] For what it may be worth here, I observe that among those that indefatigably pursued him were members of the company whose food he had bought and whose fare he had paid from his own slender means. The courts quickly decided that he was in no way responsible for any of the company's debts, but the necessity of defending himself entailed so heavy an expense that it effected his ruin. All his little savings were swept away. For the third time in his life he found himself financially drained and flaccid.

It was only the beginning of a chapter of disasters. With the old dogged courage he pulled himself together and set to work at the age of fifty-two to retrieve his fortunes. That summer he gave the usual concert series in Chicago and in the fall returned to New York expecting to resume his various musical enterprises.

He found things strangely changed.

The old constituency that, following him so many years, had seemed so faithful, now had largely drifted away. A popularity once deemed permanent had largely dissolved. The change per-

[1]Autobiography, p. 95; Upton, *Reminiscence and Appreciation*, pp. 190–192.

plexed as much as it hurt him, but is not now mysterious. He did not know the fact, but he had committed the unpardonable sin: he had wrought impiously toward the great American deity, which is Success. How had he? Why, if he had not failed himself he had been connected with something that had failed, and failed notoriously. He had better have committed forgery or burglary. The newspapers were full of the wreck of the opera company. In such cases we wise men do not discriminate. It was a colossal wreck, Thomas was on board; enough, he goes down with the rest. I do not exaggerate. The melancholy backwash of that submersion, for the time being, at least, shattered his prestige and flattened out his business.

Nothing ever happens for but one cause. With the perverseness that has made fate assume the imagery of an imp, upon the melancholy aftermath of the opera fiasco thronged coincident troubles. A new and formidable rival had appeared.

Anton Seidl came to New York in 1885 to succeed Dr. Damrosch as leader of the German Opera. He carried with him an immense prestige, for he had been Wagner's right-hand man at Baireuth. In the United States he soon attained to a great and deserved popularity. As a conductor of opera, and particularly of Wagnerian opera, he made many interesting revelations. After a year or two of brilliant success in opera leading, he formed an orchestra, chiefly from his opera band, and started a series of concerts.

These attracted much attention from the strong and novel readings he gave of Wagnerian cruces. The discerning felt that having been so close to the Master, he read with impeccable authority. It was a time when Wagner was enthroned and in spirit seemed to shake the spheres. While Thomas was ruining himself with the ill-starred American Opera Company, the new conductor was drawing to himself a great and devoted following.

He had many advantages and potent. He looked like a musician; Thomas would be taken at first glance for a fairly prosperous merchant or industrialist. Looks are a great matter when one comes to conducting. Personally, I have always been in favor of a school of pulchritude for all ambitious young conductors, with particular attention to be paid to hair. If I should say that more than one musician in the United States has made his way to renown on the basis of hair I should be guilty of an extravagance that all Right Minded Persons would condemn. Yet, on the other hand, how rash would be he that spoke contumeliously of the historic importance of hair! In Seidl's case attractive looks were united to superb musicianship, great gifts in conducting, and a manner that charmed because of its simple sincerity. He was musician and man.

Thomas continued to lead the Philharmonic and to keep his own orchestra together, but the tide was running against him. Instead of making money, he lost it.

The *Musical Courier*, after noting[1] that, in the season just closing, Thomas had directed his orchestra through sixty concerts, said editorially:

The marvelous attention to detail which Mr. Thomas exacts from his men never interferes with that breadth of interpretation that is now recognized as something peculiarly his own.

But, alas, there is an obverse side of the medal, and it is the painful truth that financially these concerts have not been a success. . . . There is at the end of the season a large deficit that Mr. Thomas, with his usual large-hearted generosity, has made up from his own private purse, a generous act that deserves to be recorded on something more enduring than paper.

He was playing then in Steinway Hall, and it appears from the records that he was not always filling it even when he produced some of his best programs and did some of his best work. The fashion of the times was all for Wagner and the younger conductor that was believed to know all the recondite secrets of the great magician. Nothing seemed stranger than to remem-

_____
[1]April 18, 1888.

ber that in a way Thomas had brought this upon himself. The Wagner craze that was so much his undoing he had started and assiduously fed. Even after he must hold himself disillusioned as to Wagner's character, he had continued flawlessly loyal to him as an artist, had preached his gospel and spread his following.

At Steinway Hall that spring, 1888, he was playing Friday afternoon and repeating the program Saturday night. One Friday afternoon, he produced a new composition with which the audience manifested great delight, but the playing of which wholly disgusted the leader. A rehearsal cost him about $350— at the end of a disastrous season. Nevertheless, he called a rehearsal for Saturday morning to polish and refine a bit of playing with which public and critics were abundantly satisfied.

Everything about a performance had to conform to his conception of excellence, even in matters no bigger than a pinhead. In this same unlucky season at the Steinway Hall he was to give a composition in which the piccolo suddenly appeared, played eight notes, and was not again heard from. In those days extra players were paid for each performance, and full price if they did no more than hit the drum one stroke. Thomas ordered the piccolo player from the outside to play those eight notes. He had been losing money all the season and was in a situation not far from desperate. The manager objected to the extra expense, and in view of the sharp exigencies of the exchequer, took his courage in his hands and intimated that the eight notes could perfectly well be played on the flute and not a human being would know the difference.

Mr. Thomas bent on the rash man a withering look and said: "Stuff! One would—the most important of all. I'd know it."

"Other orchestras don't do such things," sulked the manager.

"I don't conduct other orchestras—I conduct just this one."

"It isn't worth the cost."

"Anything is worth any cost that is right. Why debate? Please get the man."[1]

To make good his losses in the city he went on tour. But here again everything was changed. The Interstate Commerce Law had been passed and greatly increased the expenses of traveling companies. His own godchild, the Boston Symphony, had been diligently covering the provincial field and now largely occupied it. Thomas was so far from feeling jealousy of the newcomer that he first desired and proposed to have the Boston Symphony give concerts in New York itself.[2] But magnanimity does not pay hotel bills, and when he was done with the traveling that spring it was with dismay that he contemplated the results. For the first time he began to doubt his future. Up to this season, he had been sustained in defeat by a persisting faith in his calling and mission. It must have been a bitter hour when he was forced to question whether his mission were not at an end and his calling in doubt.

He led the Cincinnati Musical Festival again that May, 1888, and it seemed to many observers better than any of its forerunners. It was followed by a month's rest and then another summer-night series in Chicago, where (with Theresa Carreño at the piano) he gave the first performance of MacDowell's concerto, and produced many stimulative programs. Neither his skill nor his will failed him, but the upstream struggle was too hard.

One more disappointment fell upon him that might have been spared. He was again deluded by the mirage about an orchestral hall, the vision he had pursued so long and fatuously. His phantom rich men now reappeared with a promise and a project. Then, as before, they vanished. At the close of his Chicago season he called his orchestra together and made what amounted

---

[1]Communicated by an old member of the Theodore Thomas Orchestra who heard the conversation.

[2]*Musical Herald*, November, 1888, p. 60.

to an acknowledgment of defeat, new upon those lips. It was an address,[1] full of simple dignity, without complaint or fault-finding, in which the old lion faced the bitter truth. It was unfair, he said, to keep them in ignorance of a situation in which their interest was involved no less than his. He told them plainly that the chances were that he should have comparatively few engagements in New York the coming winter. He had been offered a series of winter concerts in Chicago but it seemed impracticable to travel back and forth so many times. The only way to keep the organization together in its existing shape was to give up New York and spend the entire winter touring through the West and he was sure that this the members would not wish to do. He felt compelled therefore to announce to them that they were free to make any engagements they could for the coming season, but he asked them to notify him when they were thus employed and to hold themselves, so far as possible, ready to fill engagements with him in New York if occasion should arise.

That is to say, after twenty-six years, the famous Theodore Thomas Orchestra, the pride of his life, was in effect disbanded.

The news struck the musical world aghast. "Theodore Thomas Retires—The Orchestra Disbanded and Scattered" are the headlines under which the New York *Tribune* made the startling announcement. In the article following it said:

Theodore Thomas is a man of lofty ideals. He has labored for twenty years to place his concerts on the loftiest plane of excellence, and is profoundly convinced that a permanent organization under his sole artistic direction can alone yield results satisfactory to himself. Not wishing to lower the standard that he himself set, being unwilling to subject his future work to injurious comparison with his past achievements, he prefers to abandon the concerts outside of New York rather than to go on with a band organized for these few occasions. This is the substance of his explanation concerning the concerts in other cities than New York.

[1]Autobiography, pp. 97–99.

Home support alone can make a permanent orchestra possible, and this support was denied him last season, as all readers of the *Tribune* have been told. If it were only a question of money, he says, he might raise it, but the problem is not solved simply by an offer of funds to defray a possible loss in case the local concerts are continued. He would have to draw for such funds or guarantees on his friends, and this he is unwilling to do so long as he does not see a prospect of success.

This prospect is obstructed among other things by the absence of a hall suitable for his entertainments and agreeable to the public. He therefore deems it the course of wise self-preservation to cease the struggle in which he had so long been engaged and devote himself to the Philharmonic Society and such other engagements as offer a livelihood for himself. "For I must make a living," he adds.

The *Musical Courier*, reprinting this article,[1] commented that it was not the absence of an adequate hall that explained the financial failure of the previous year, for Thomas had not been able to fill Steinway. It was due to his loss of prestige. Said the editor:

Theodore Thomas is the most prominent figure in musical art in America. He has done more for the development and popularization of classical and modern music of the highest order in the United States than all other musical conductors combined, and more than any other individual, as a matter of course. And yet, like other fallible human beings, Mr. Thomas made a serious and dangerous mistake when he permitted his name and his services to be used by the Thurber American Opera schemers. He has never recovered from the loss of prestige that resulted from the unhappy alliance with the managers of the American opera failure, and prestige is one of the most necessary adjuncts to the successful career of a public man, such as Mr. Thomas has been.

Mr. Thomas's charmed name had not sufficient magnetism to attract audiences to the American Opera performances, for the public had no confidence in Mrs. Thurber's company, and since those days Mr. Thomas has lost prestige with the public here.

---

[1] September 26, 1888.

But, the editor concludes, if Mr. Thomas had gone on another year with his Steinway Hall performances by his own orchestra he would have done better that season of 1888–1889 than in the previous season:

It requires time for the public to forget failure, and his connection with the Thurber schemers was fast fading from memory.

The scheme of "the Thurber schemers," so called, was to give opera in American by American singers and their crime in which Thomas was accessory was in not knowing from the beginning that this would never do in America.

All misfortunes seemed to come upon him at once. From Chicago he went back to Fairhaven to find Mrs. Thomas so ill that she must be removed to New York and placed under special medical care. All that winter she continued to be desperately sick and Mr. Thomas to worry about her. He went on with the Philharmonic as before, and a few times gathered together the former members of his orchestra and gave concerts; but these were not satisfactory to himself and not eminently successful with the public. He was never at ease conducting men that had played under other leadership and been insufficiently rehearsed. One fact will show to those that knew him what this season meant to him. It had been his fixed habit from the beginning of his career to preserve every program he played. This winter, for the first time in his life, he kept nothing. From the close of his summer nights in Chicago in August until almost a year later the program record is a blank.

All that winter Mrs. Thomas slowly sank before his eyes and despite every effort to save her. On April 4, 1889, she died. Although he had been so long warned of it, the blow stunned him. Upon her he had been dependent for the only comfort he knew in his troubles and upon his home for his one unfailing refuge. Mrs. Thomas was worthy of all the confidence he placed in her, most kindly, sympathetic, understanding, tactful, and so the true companion for such a man with such a work to do. It appears from the statements of his friends and family that for weeks after her passing he was like a man in a trance, incapable of work, incapable of fixing his thoughts. From this condition he was rescued by his children, and when the time came he was able to go to Chicago and resume his summer-night concerts for the season of 1889. But even so late as September he was writing to a sympathetic friend:

I am not exactly sad, but I realize that I am not normal; I seem to have no memory, and do the most curious things. . . . I tried to work this evening, but it is of no use. I cannot work. I am not myself any more. I do not know myself. The only explanation I can give is that this is the terrible reaction of the strain of the last twenty years of my life. But I ought to have some common sense and know that by and by everything will come into satisfactory shape again. But what is common sense? I have none.[1]

The self-revelation was new in him, the composed and quiet. That he should write in any such vein is more significant of his state of collapse than the words he used. It was only to his closest friends that he let his hurts be known. He turned to the world the old face of calm, or nearly so.

Some singular telepathic instinct it must have been that at this juncture of crisis brought him for consolation a most extraordinary tribute of goodwill and esteem. The idea originated in Minneapolis, where for years he had been regarded as the Gamaliel of music and where the Minneapolis Philharmonic Society had been founded as the result of his inspiration. I think it was David Blakely, that good man, that made the suggestion; the letter sounds like him. However this may be, there now appeared in the New York *Tribune* a communication from Minneapolis signed "Many Music Lovers," urging Thomas to undertake a tour of the country that would be in the nature of

---

[1]Mrs. Thomas, p. 333.

a national testimonial. Knowing Thomas fairly well, the writer was careful to explain that nothing was intended in the nature of a benefit, but quite differently, said the letter:

Let him simply take his orchestra and give in the various cities a *quid pro quo*, and more, as he always does, for all that he receives; but let the tour be understood to be a distinctive opportunity for the people to testify the high estimate they place upon Mr. Thomas's life-work in behalf of the music of this country. If Mr. Thomas doubts that there is a deep feeling of regard for him among the musicians and people of America, and that, whatever may be said of the sharp points of his character, they are ready to testify to it, let him give them an opportunity in the way now suggested. Minneapolis will be glad of the coveted opportunity to testify to other cities throughout the country the high esteem and sincere admiration that are felt by the people everywhere both for the man and his work.

We are to note now that the suggestion, without the least press agenting from any source and advanced in only this one letter to one newspaper, went of itself across the country. City after city took it up, Thomas began to be deluged with invitations, and before long found himself caught up by a movement of the kind he most disliked. He was not so much superman that he did not relish applause, but he had an instinctive horror of being, in his own phrase, "lionized." He was now in for more lionizing than any other musician had received in this country. In all these places, local committees had been appointed without delay, the preparations had begun for an unexampled demonstration, and there was no escape.

Even New York itself, which is not believed to be susceptible to any emotions so far known among men, took fire at the thought and came in with a request that it be included in what the Minneapolis suggestors had called the "triumphant march." The wording of the letter in which New York made its request[1]

---

[1]Mrs. Thomas has the letter and signatures and Mr. Thomas's response at pp. 335–337.

should have been enough to assuage almost any human grief.
It said:

Your public service of this kind [meaning the development of the
musical sense of the country] has been so signal that to call attention to it on the eve of a tour such as is contemplated is but to
refresh the grateful memory of lovers and students of music throughout the country, and to secure their cordial coöperation in earnestly
promoting the success of the projected series of popular concerts,
which will be peculiarly significant among our centennial commemora-
tions [it was the one hundredth anniversary of the adoption of the
Constitution] as illustrating in themselves the character and degree
of the advance of the public taste, knowledge and skill in music.

There was a marvelous list of signers, containing more well-
known names than any other like document I can remember.
Carl Schurz's name was almost the first; then came William M.
Evarts, J. Q. A. Ward, the sculptor, Edmund C. Stedman, the
poet, Chauncey M. Depew, Joseph H. Choate, Grover Cleve-
land, Theodore Roosevelt, Charles A. Dana, William R. Grace,
Parke Godwin, Frederic R. Coudert, Augustus St. Gaudens,
Brander Matthews, Moncure D. Conway, J. Pierpont Morgan,
Andrew Carnegie, William Steinway, and a multitude of others.

Thomas, of course, acceded to this proposal, and in his letter
to the committee offered to add to the popular interest in the
tour by playing "request" programs, if the local committees
would take steps to discover what compositions communities
most desired to hear. But it appears that while he responded
politely and cordially to these convincing manifestations of a
widespread sympathy, they only served to lower his spirits, and
this for a reason that the friendly outsiders would never guess.

He felt that he had lost his hold upon his players. Therefore
he could not give to the public the perfection of work that he
desired and (in his thinkings) the public was entitled to have.

Not his hold upon the affection and support of his players,
these he would always have; but his hold upon the quality of

their work. Since misfortune had come upon him and his orchestra had been disbanded, these artists had been playing for dances, in theaters, and wherever they could find employment, with the inevitable result that they had to his mind shattered the quality in which he used to delight. This for him always took the joy from any plaudits. In fact, it made applause only so much more gall and wormwood. Applause under such conditions showed that after all the people were not yet trained to discriminate between merely good work and the best.

The triumphal march began in Brooklyn, October 9, and ended in New York about a month later. Twenty-five cities were visited with results that went beyond even the happy expectations of the Minneapolis Philharmonics.[1] The testimony to "the high esteem and sincere admiration felt by the people everywhere for the man and his work" was unequivocal. If Thomas's depression had sprung from any wound of vanity it would have been ended now. Everybody applauded him, the country honored him, the newspapers headlined him, telling with emphasis and sometimes with accuracy the values of his work.

What more could he want? Well, the thing he wanted was something that only an artist could understand. He wanted a chance to do always his best work and in the gloomy prospect ahead of him nothing seemed less likely. He wanted his permanent orchestra, he wanted a home for it, he wanted the men that played with him not to play with anybody else. Without these attributes, the performances would be only torment to his

---

[1]Except, strangely enough, in Brooklyn. See Otis, pp. 22–23. Otis attended the concert there and was struck with the small size of the audience. But Chicago made up for the defect.

According to the *Musical Courier* of October 30, 1889, the tour was the most successful in a financial way Thomas had ever undertaken, the receipts averaging $2,000 a night. The *Courier*, on October 16, had said: "if there ever was a man who deserved the eternal gratitude of the music-loving people of America, that man is Theodore Thomas. He has labored long and earnestly in the cause, and his labors have borne glorious fruit." The New York *Herald* printed an editorial in which it said: "Theodore Thomas richly deserves the laurel wreath that was handed to him in the Metropolitan Opera House Wednesday night. To him more than to any other individual the people are indebted for the great progress high-class music has made in America."

sensitive ear. He had set his heart upon a goal. Say that it was not in reality so important as he thought; that, in spite of his disappointment, the development of public taste he had undertaken was still real and great; that all this should have consoled him. Men are not so consoled. In his mind, the failure of twenty-seven years of incessant toil to win a permanent place among the city's institutions obscured all else.

These reflections were aside from his deep-seated sense of the loss of his wife's companionship and the sting that still remained of the disbanding of his orchestra. There were other things to disturb him that would have driven from the field a smaller man. The worst was the outlook in New York. He could do nothing there that he longed to do; the things he could do only distressed him. Meanwhile, the star of Seidl rose as his seemed to decline. Being a flesh-and-blood man and not a fictional paragon, he was jealous about this; a measure of jealousy was inseparable from his sensitive make-up. In after days, for any such error, he made manly atonement.[1]

In these agonies of the spirit within, the near stoicism that was so singular a possession for a man of his temperament came to his relief, or perhaps he wrestled with Apollyon and at last conquered. By whatsoever route, he reached a point where he was willing to admit that his great hope had failed forever and to accept with resignation what he held to be defeat. In a letter to the lady who was afterward his second wife and was then Miss Rose Fay, he made the announcement.

"This life," he wrote, "is after all, mostly '*Entbehren sollst du —du sollst entbehren.*'"[2]

---

[1] "He was not without jealousy, and when Anton Seidl came to America, he looked upon him, unfortunately, as a rival rather than as a helper. But when he became familiar with Seidl's admirable work (with the Thomas Orchestra) at some of Mr. Grau's operatic performances in Chicago, he cordially offered his colleague his friendship and praise." (Review of Thomas's career in *The Nation*, New York, January, 1905. See also Finck, *My Adventures*, etc., pp. 176–177.)

[2] "Renounce thou shalt—thou shalt renounce." So it is usually translated, but it means more than that.

Upon that signal he gave over his dreams and settled himself to go through with what might be left. For the sake of his children and what he could still do for them, he would go on, but he seriously considered the leaving of orchestral work and the taking of a position somewhere as a professor of music in a dignified institution of learning.

After twenty-eight years of unremitting travail.

CHAPTER X

The Harbor of Refuge

HE WAS not yet done with the world nor the world with him. "Old age hath yet his honor and his toil," he might have sung if he had not been so resolutely hard set against any admission of age. "I will not grow old!" he wrote on his fifty-fourth birthday, and gave to the outcry the accent of an underscoring, which was unusual stress for him. As if he were still at the outset of a career, he had things good and bad left in his horoscope.

For the time being all seemed fairly bad. The season that followed the "triumphant march" he deemed to justify the worst he had ever thought of his situation. He continued to lead the New York and the Brooklyn Philharmonic concerts, but they were usually unsatisfactory to him. Every rehearsal was what he called a "fight." The term was not so belligerent as it sounds. What he meant was that at the rehearsals, which were too few and too hurried, he must strive with might and main to get the men back somewhere near the standard he desired. If by toil and trouble he succeeded for a time, he knew that the next week they would be playing again helter skelter and he would have all the work to do over again with still smaller chances of winning at it.

He had a conviction, in which he was probably right, that his mental mood was reflected in the work of the men he was conducting and that, being now in a state of persistent low pressure, the quality of the concerts suffered from this cause also. It fell to my own lot, as I am presently to relate, to observe some remarkable instances of this telepathy. One can easily see how the feeling that his depression flawed his work this season should operate as another depressant yielding more uneasiness about his work. He was thus going about a kind of spiritual spiral always tending to lower levels, and but for his devotion to his family and a certain event that on May 7, 1890, brought into his life the saving grace it needed, might have gone to final disaster.

On that day the profound and intolerable spiritual loneliness that had so long weighed upon him departed. He married Miss Rose Fay.

The wedding took place in the Church of the Ascension, Chicago. Clarence Eddy played the organ. He played part of a Beethoven Symphony. It was the Fifth.

The next day Thomas with his bride went to the conducting of the Cincinnati Festival of that year.

The man of many misfortunes could have had nothing befall him better to balance the hard blows of fate. Miss Fay belonged to a family whose services to the cause of Music in America have been genuine and historic. Her grandfather, Bishop John Hopkins, was known as "the Musical Bishop" for his efforts to spread musical taste and knowledge. Her sister Amy was a brilliant and famous pianist, and wrote a book still in wide demand called *Music Study in Germany*. Rose Fay was an artist, a musician, and a discriminating judge of musical excellence. Amy Fay's début, after her return from her studies abroad, had been made in Boston under Thomas's kindly leading, and so a friendship had grown up with all the family. Thomas turned to them in his troubles. Rose Fay was one of those women whose beauties of character are transparent in their faces. She was kind, gentle, sweet, wise, had long understood and shared Thomas's ideals, and was now the influence he most needed in his life.

There was also a brother in the Fay family whose potent, beneficent part in this story comes next.

When in a former chapter we had to deal with the railroad strike of 1877 and its effects upon Thomas's fortunes, I suggested that it would be well to remember the name of a young business man of Marquette, Michigan, whom the strike had brought into Chicago. Charles Norman Fay—that was the youth. Always after that summer he haunted every Thomas concert that came his way. From the beginning, all the Fays seem to have had an odd intuitive understanding of Thomas. If there is any such thing as spiritual kinship, it must have existed here. Charles Norman Fay was drawn to make Thomas's acquaintance even before his sister had appeared on a Thomas program. So far back as 1879 he had secured a letter of introduction and had used it, singularly enough, to address the object of his admiration upon the one topic always foremost in Thomas's own thought. Mr. Fay wanted to talk about a permanent orchestra. Only it was to be in Chicago, where Mr. Fay was then living, and Thomas had never thought of Chicago in that way.

Mr. Fay calmly proposed, he did, to go forth and raise the necessary guarantee fund among the Chicago business men. That was all—in 1879. The concept was not then available, but Mr. Fay never forgot it. For ten years he turned it over in his mind and of a sudden, in 1889, the road to it seemed to open. But he had better tell the story himself.

One day in 1889, I met him [meaning Thomas], on Fifth Avenue, and we turned into the old Delmonico's. He looked worn and worried, and I asked him why. There were reasons enough. There was mortal illness in his home; the American Opera Company, that short and melancholy chapter of good music and bad management, had swept away his savings; and almost worst of all, he had been obliged to give up his own permanent orchestra. To use his own words, "I have had to stop engaging my men by the year, and now I play with scratch orchestras. In order to keep my old orchestra together I have always had to travel constantly, winter and summer, the year around and year after year. Now I am fifty-three, too old to stand the traveling.

New York alone cannot support my orchestra, so it has had perforce to be disbanded."

For a moment, so bitter was his tone, I had nothing to reply, but finally I said: "Is there no one, no rich and generous man, to do here as Major Higginson has done in Boston—keep your orchestra going and pay the deficit?"

"No one," he answered. "I have told them often, those who say they are my friends, that for good work there must be a permanent orchestra; and for a permanent orchestra, which will not pay, there must be a subsidy. My work is known. I am old now and have no ax to grind. But they do not care. They think I have always kept the body and soul together somehow, and that I always will—that I have nowhere else to go. They treat me as a music merchant, a commercial proposition, subject to the laws of supply and demand."

My thoughts went back to those ten years of Summer Garden Concerts and to some powerful and devoted friends of Mr. Thomas and his music at home and I asked:

"Would you come to Chicago if we could give you a permanent orchestra?"

The answer, grim and sincere, and entirely destitute of humor, came back like a flash:

"I would go to hell if they gave me a permanent orchestra."[1]

In this Homeric style was born in a corner of Delmonico's one day in April, 1889, the Chicago Symphony Orchestra.

Mr. Fay went home and took up the task of securing in Chicago signers to a guarantee fund of $50,000 a year for three years. Because of his modesty, he leaves out part of the story. He really did it himself out of faith and fervor, that great job. With his extraordinary proposition and a paper in hand for signatures, he goes about among the business men of Chicago. Chicago is not New York. At the suggestion of Marshall Field he makes it fifty men at $1,000 each rather than ten men at $5,000 each. He goes on and he gets his fifty. Some subscribe that cannot afford to give $1,000. No matter; it is for Chicago. He wins through with his extraordinary proposition, he forms

---

[1] *Outlook Magazine*, February, 1910.

the Chicago Orchestra Association, "a corporation not for pecuniary profit," as the law directs. He gets his men together, he elects officers, December 17, 1890; for himself he takes the inconspicuous post of vice president, where he can do all the work and get no recognition. But the worst part of his job is done.

Meantime he had been communicating, step by step, with Thomas. Mr. Fay's idea was an orchestra of ninety men, engaged at whatsoever salaries might be necessary to bring them under Thomas's exclusive control, playing twice a week for full seasons of at least twenty weeks and all guaranteed against losses; the thing that Thomas had so long dreamed of. Yet he was at first sceptical of it. He had been disillusioned at last about the American rich men, and after his bitter experience in Cincinnati and with the American Opera Company, he felt that he had suffered enough. He thought with horror of again breaking up his home, and with another shudder of leaving New York, that dear old New York that many have left without a pang. Yet there was that point about the permanent orchestra. What could he not do if he had that, and his good old men around him? Beckel of the basses, Albert Ulrich the trumpeter, he knew they would go to Chicago or Jericho to play with him again. At last, he said he would accept the offer if the guarantee fund could be raised, being fairly well assured in his heart that it could not be. The next thing he knew came the word that the fund was all secured and pledged and here was the prospectus of the Chicago Orchestra Association and the contract for him to sign as on the dotted line.

Mr. Fay had drawn the contract. He knew what Thomas wanted and gave it to him. By most explicit declaration, the director was to have sole charge of the music, make the programs, select the soloists, arrange the choral and festival performances. "The intention of the Association being to lodge

in the hands of the Director," it said, "the power and responsibility for the attainment of the highest standard of artistic
excellence in all performances given by the Association."
"Responsibility!"—Mrs. Thomas tells us[1] that this word
at once caught Mr. Thomas's eye and gave him more satisfaction than anything else about the arrangement. Responsibility
for the artistic quality of the performances and a measure of
power to fit—all hand in glove with his ideals, although for the
first time recognized in a contract. After some consideration he
signed it, and with that pen stroke signaled the end of his long
career in New York.

Essentially, the sun setting had been murky. He that had
once been the popular idol now found himself, for no reason
anyone could put a name to, thrust aside and neglected. To
keep his head up, he had struck out in every direction where
there seemed to be a chance. In the spring of 1889, he had given
a series of extra concerts at Chickering Hall, paying especial
attention to the works of American composers.[2] They had
achieved some distinction but little returns. In the summer of
1890 he had tried a series of garden concerts at the Lenox
Lyceum. They were reported to be "artistically delightful but
pecuniarily unremunerative," so that they had been cut short
in June.[3] From 1882 to 1886, every hand had been raised in his
favor, and from 1888 to 1891 against him.

So he signed up for Chicago and shook off some of the bitter
reflections that belonged to these defeats. If Chicago was not
New York, it had offered him one thing that was better. He
was to have at last a guarantee to proceed upon, something
like permanence, and an uninterrupted chance to develop an
orchestra. His busy brain went instantly at work upon the

---

[1]P. 356.
[2]*Musical Herald*, March, 1889.
[3]*Ibid.*, September, 1890.

things he expected to do. He sent for his old men, signed on sixty of them to go with him; and the knowledge that he was again to have before him the familiar faces, that he could work with the hands he knew and trusted, buoyed him up with a content long strange to him.

The announcement was made in December, 1890, and to one still believing in human consistency the next manifestation must have seemed dumbfounding. Apparently, a community that one day was dead weary of Thomas and his works awoke the next to declare that he was indispensable. The old Thomas faction in the orchestra war, which had seemed scattered or indifferent, aroused itself to clamoring protest. Lose Theodore Thomas? It was like losing City Hall Park. A little of the feeling now displayed, if it had been shown earlier, would have made the protest unnecessary.

Perhaps Thomas himself was much to blame; perhaps taciturnity and his habitual mask before the public had more to do with his troubles than the supposed indifference of the New York public. At least, here is this seemingly significant fact that as soon as it was known that he was going away, three separate groups of men came to him and offered to raise guarantee funds of any amount if he would remain. He might have had his permanent orchestra in New York, he might even have had that orchestra building, that enduring home and center of music he had once been confident New York would erect. The discovery must have given him as much pain as astonishment. But for that Chicago contract he could have everything he wished at home and, as he well knew, Chicago was a desperate venture against heavy odds. Moreover, if any such things could have weighed with Theodore Thomas, his income in New York would have been more than twice the amount Chicago purposed to pay him. A suppler soul might have tried on plausible grounds to be released. Thomas had signed, he had given his word, and there was not a thought in his heart but to go straight ahead. His New York petitioners were dismissed with thanks, and he prepared to move in April to Chicago.

The last season with the Philharmonic must have touched him deeply, it was marked with so many expressions of good-will.[1] At the end of all was such a demonstration as even the Metropolitan Opera House had never seen. The place was packed to the last inch of its capacity. When the finale died away, the people rose and stood while the members of the Philharmonic presented to their old commander the great laurel wreath of farewell and tried to tell him their feelings about him, A series of farewell banquets followed, the Liederkranz, the Aschenbroedel, and other societies, and a great public demonstration, in particular, at which George William Curtis presided and delivered an address that deserves a place among the classics of American eloquence.[2]

The next day the Thomas household started for Chicago.

Disadvantages about the new field were many and real. It was a hazardous cast that Chicago could sustain a concert season of twenty weeks, and. to supply the deficit in receipts there was about it no such populous and easily reached region as surrounded New York; no Jersey City, Newark, Orange, New Haven, and the rest. Cities in the West were few, and with the exception of Milwaukee, far away. The population of Chicago itself was but about one fourth of its present numbers. Musical interest was strong, but no one need have thought it was extensive. Besides, the Auditorium, in which the concerts were to be given, was a vast, though beautiful, place in which an audience of the size Thomas could hope to draw, week in

---

[1]"The 12 years of [Thomas's] connection with the Philharmonic Society as its conductor were for the society a period of uninterrupted prosperity toward which he contributed greatly not only by his artistic zeal and skill, but also by voluntarily relinquishing, year after year, a portion of the sum which under his contract he was entitled to collect." (*Grove's Dictionary*, Vol. V, p. 88, edition 1910.)

[2]The New York *Times* of April 26th contained an article, prompted by this banquet, analyzing and highly praising the Thomas system of making programs.

and week out for a long season, would look like lost sheep. What bothered him most of all was that, while the acoustics of the place were perfect for some things, they were impossible for the best orchestral effects at which he aimed. All these considerations were discussed and well known. On one man's cool resolution they had no effect. Mr. Fay was sure of his Chicago.

As for Theodore Thomas, he had not proceeded long before the troubles began to gather thick upon him. Chicago being so evidently unable alone to support such an enterprise, it was early decided that an average of two concerts a week must be given in outside places. He had foreseen the geographical complexities of the new country and had written from New York that the out-of-town engagements should be arranged in tours. Thus he could visit a dozen places one after another without returning to Chicago, where for brief periods the concerts were to be suspended. The manager of that time knew naught of all this. He made arrangements for two of these outside concerts each week through the season. At the news, desolation fell upon the soul of Theodore Thomas. With any such mad gyrations about the country, away went all his rehearsals, and having thirty green men in the orchestra, more rehearsals, not fewer, were what he craved.

The first concert of the Chicago Symphony Orchestra took place in the Auditorium, October 17, 1891. Raphael Joseffy was the soloist and played the Tschaikowsky concerto. Other numbers were Wagner's "Faust" overture and Dvořák's "Husitzká." There also appeared on that first and fateful program in Chicago the composition that I believe of the whole range of orchestral literature meant most to him, his enduring favorite, the thing supreme to him artistically and musically, Beethoven's Fifth Symphony. On that first entrance upon the new field in Chicago he put up, as a kind of dedicatory prayer, the familiar

It will be seen that there was nothing of what was called "the popular" in this program. Nor, I may say, in any other of his regular series, that season or any other in Chicago; the Strauss waltz period was now far behind him; the "Linnet Polka" still farther. But in these Chicago programs he did not even compromise with the "Tell" overture or the perennial "Second Rhapsody." He had shot beyond them, also. One feature of his system of program making we have not noted. From the first concert he led he had pursued steadfastly the plan of playing a little ahead of the development of his audience. When he played the "Linnet Polka" he was playing to an audience whose musical taste was represented by him of the concertina. When he played the "Tell" overture he was playing to people that would have preferred the "Linnet Polka." When he came to Chicago he elevated his programs[1] relatively about the same distance above the average taste of his Chicago audiences and braced himself for the trouble that would follow.

His prophetic soul was not deceived about this. Trouble began early.

The second concert came October 24 and presented this uncompromising front:

Suite No. 3, in D major ....Bach
Aria, "O del mio dolce ardor," from " Paride ed Elena,"Gluck
                        (Sig. Galassi)
Symphony No. 2 in C major ....Schumann
Fantasia overture, "Hamlet" ....Tschaikowsky
"Wotan's Farewell" and "Magic Fire Scene," from
    "Die Walküre" ....Wagner

---

[1]Upton prints these in full, Vol. II, p. 292, *et seq.*

At the third concert he played Schubert's Unfinished and Saint-Saëns's No. 3. At the fourth, Schubert's C major and three selections from Wagner, by which time the murmurings began to be audible.[1]

No one in those audiences was as much dissatisfied with the lofty character of the music as Theodore Thomas was with the conditions under which he was playing. All that he had feared came to be true, with a superfluous margin of gadflies he had overlooked. The little company of the elect and others that gathered of a Friday afternoon and Saturday evening to listen to his offerings seemed forlorn and lonesome in the great Auditorium. To fill with sound so large a space, the orchestra must play in a way he despised and trample upon effects he most desired. Finally, he had not proceeded far before he saw signs that he was destined once more to have the press, or a part of it, on his back.

At the seventh concert he interjected a more varied program, having Mrs. Julie L. Wyman to help him with songs.

Overture, "Oberon" . . . . Weber
"Andante Cantabile," op. 27 . . . . Beethoven-Liszt
Aria from "Samson et Dalila" . . . . Saint-Saëns
"Tarentelle," for flute and clarinet . . . . Saint-Saëns
Fantasia for Violoncello, "Le Désir" . . . . Servais
Overture to "Tannhäuser" . . . . Wagner
"March Funèbre" . . . . Chopin-Thomas
"Fantasie di Bravura," for harp . . . . Schuecker
Songs:
       "At Twilight" . . . . Nevin
       "Ma Voisine" . . . . Goring Thomas
              (Mrs. Wyman)
"Intermezzo et Valse Lento"
"Pizzicato"
"Cortège de Bachus," from the ballet "Sylvia" . . . . Delibes

---

[1] Otis, p. 36.

This was neither the general conception of "popular" nor what wisdom had agreed he should do. A part of the press had expected a continuation of the summer-night concerts on the Lake Front. Mr. Thomas was pursuing a system of which his critics had never thought. He had consolidated the positions won on the Lake Front and now dug himself in upon a new line of entrenchments and waited, as he had so often waited before.

He played three other lighter programs and one "request" that season. The fact that one number thus requested was Brahms's Third might show to even the dullest fault-finders that he knew what he was about. It did not. With the ending of the season the Anvil Chorus rang out loud and clear.

A weekly journal sounded the first note of dismay. Could Mr. Thomas possibly succeed in Chicago if he persisted in giving it the kind of "musical diet" that had been indicated?[1] Toward the end of the season the complaints took more definite form.

"If it be desirable to educate 'the masses' to a liking for any certain style of music," said one critic, "sound policy dictates that some effective means be adopted for bringing 'the masses' aforesaid within the reach of educative influences and that the uniform and exclusive offering of what they will not tolerate is hardly to be reckoned among effective means. Mr. Thomas and his advisers seem to think otherwise, and if the Orchestral Association members are willing, for their own gratification, to pay the cost of what has been given them, nobody else has any right to object."[2]

He had landed nineteen symphonies and seven symphonic poems that season; twenty concerts, the last April 23, 1892. In the city, these were; meantime, there had been intermissions to allow of those terrific ordeals, the out-of-town and barn-hall engagements.

At the end, the books being balanced, an appalling fact was

---

[1]Chicago *Figaro*, October 7, 1891.
[2]Unidentified; but I think from the Chicago *Times*.

disclosed. The net deficit for the season was $53,613. Remembering well the American Opera Company, Thomas was prepared to see the whole thing blow up and himself once more adrift on the world. He did not know the Chicago business man. The guarantors made no complaint, found no fault, offered no suggestion. They quietly drew their checks, each for the amount required of him, and urged Mr. Thomas to proceed with his work.

The tours he must now make, poignantly irksome and troublesome to him, were to music in the West the gift of the gods. What had happened in Boston, New Haven, Rochester, Philadelphia, Baltimore, many years before, was now repeated in St. Paul, Minneapolis, Cleveland, Detroit, Omaha. That is, by returning regularly and often he developed in each community an always increasing demand for orchestral music, the kind of demand that grows the more it is gratified. For his second season in Chicago, 1892–1893, he was able to have the tours so arranged that they did not interfere with his rehearsals. This soothed his soul with concerts more nearly to his taste. I think the public never noticed the difference, but that was a point of little meaning to him; he had that unreasonable conscience to satisfy. Perhaps he thought at this time that his trench was too far advanced. In this second season he played only ten symphonies, and put in two Wagner programs and one Beethoven. On that Beethoven occasion he played the Ninth, which in his religion hardly ranged behind the Fifth. It was a novelty to Chicago. The first performance Friday afternoon did not go to the conductor's satisfaction. The stage interfered. Some of the chorus, which was furnished by the Apollo Musical Club, must stand where they could not see him. Because it was Friday afternoon, many of the men could not leave their businesses to sing, a fact suggesting much about his troubles. But on Saturday night everybody turned out, Mr. Thomas had altered the stage so that all could see him.

"When we rose to sing," says one of the chorus that night, "all doubts and fears seemed to vanish as we looked at him. His presence on the stand inspired confidence; it was an inspiration. 'Never mind the music! Look right at me! It will go all right,' were his words at the last rehearsal. Everything did go right."[1]

Perhaps he had no intention to yield anything to the growing complaints about the so-called heaviness of the menus he provided. Yielding could hardly be regarded as among the things he did oftenest or most gracefully. In any event, the net results of the second season showed little to spread an intoxication of joy. At the end the sum the guarantors must make good was $51,381.18.[2]

One fact had encouragement. The receipts from the Chicago concerts increased $10,000 over the first season. Apparently, then, he was slowly converting Chicago, in spite of itself and its newspapers.

Before long he had other things than the size of his audiences to distress him. His life seems to have been so ordered that without fault of his own he should never be quite free from grinding anxieties and bitter misfortune, and certainly no man ever less deserved the trouble that now befell him.

It was the time of the Chicago World's Fair, the great and really magnificent exposition with which we celebrated the four hundredth anniversary of the discovery of America. It should have been held in 1892, but the preparations were so vast that a year's postponement was necessary. When the time came to choose a director of the music for the Exposition, many voices acclaimed Theodore Thomas as the only man for such a place. It appears that Mr. Thomas did not want it.[3] His experiences with such things had not been uplifting, he had

---

[1]Otis, p. 41.
[2]Otis, p. 41.
[3]Chicago *Herald*, August 3, 1893.

full occupation with his regular work, and the soul of prophecy, which operated irregularly but sometimes accurately within him, foresaw a storm signal. By argument, appeal, and the efforts of Chicago friends to whom he was warmly attached, he was persuaded against his better judgment. But he made one condition.

This being agreed to, he projected himself into the task after his usual manner of high pressure. Naturally, he saw a spacious occasion. To be adequate, the general plan must be twofold. The exposition of music must show to the world America's accomplishment, and show to America the accomplishment of the world. He conceived on one side a grand design of bringing to this demonstration the greatest living musicians to perform here the greatest modern works; on the other, to perform American compositions with American players and singers.

The first trouble was close at hand and grew out of his childlike innocence of the simplest arts of propaganda. Reporters sought him to ask what were his plans for the exposition's music. He replied that he thought he ought not to make them public at that time.[1] It was a natural and proper reply, but it struck the match in the powder house. If you will believe me, the orchestral war was still raging in New York. The anti-Thomas faction leaped with joy upon this response and proclaimed that Theodore Thomas intended to utilize his new position only to exploit himself; he and his orchestra were to furnish all the music.

At this the shots flew back and forth all along the line. Thomas was furiously denounced for "selfishness" and "intolerable egotism." Nobody thought of waiting to learn if these charges were true. Denounce first and learn afterward is the good old rule in such cases. In the United States at that time were as many as twenty or twenty-five thousand men, each of whom had clearly perceived from the beginning that he was

[1]Reported in *Musical Courier*, April 1, 1892.

much better equipped than Theodore Thomas to direct the music at the World's Fair. Some of these now added to the debate their earnest condemnation of his abominable conduct, which had confirmed their worst fears. The *Musical Courier* included in its denunciations William L. Tomlins, employed to direct the choruses at the Fair. He, too, according to the *Courier*, had shown no less than Thomas the spirit "dictatorial" and "arbitrary." "There is no intention," said the *Courier*, "to grant, as a matter of right, any coöperation to any musicians that might be suggested as coadjutors in the work of getting up the music of the Fair."[1] In a few weeks the *Courier* returned to the attack and rebuked Thomas for his "selfish and unpatriotic" course. "It is a case of devil take the hindmost, the hindmost in this case happening to be Messrs. Seidl, Damrosch, Van der Stucken, Nikisch, *et al.*" It proceeded to a wounding suggestion about the departure of Thomas from the New York field. "One is almost forced to the belief," it said, "that Mr. Thomas accepted his Western engagement with a view to securing for himself and his orchestra the rich crumbs of this feast."[2]

The *Courier* did not know, and could not learn, that the plans included the fullest recognition of all the musicians it said had been ignored and of many more beyond its ken.

News of the dissatisfaction began to go about the world. The London press, scenting a chance of disaster to the Fair, received it with joyous jeers, one of which prompted the *Courier* to this envenomed utterance:

The man that is pursuing the dictatorial and foolish policy of self-aggrandisement at Chicago, and who appears to believe that the World's Fair was especially gotten up for his individual glory, is not a native American.

There is not a native composer or musician that has the gall for

---

[1]August 17, 1892.
[2]September 14, 1892.

such an exhibition of abject selfishness and megalomania as Theodore Thomas possesses.[1]

A few words of explanation would have straightened this unhappy tangle, but the stiff-necked Thomas had nothing to say. Even now he would not depart from his lifelong rule of replying to no attack and objecting (in public) to no criticism. No doubt the *Courier* meant to be fair, but it was exasperated by this silence. The issue of September 21 contains a long editorial on the selfishness of Thomas and the duty to tell him plainly that "the music of the World's Fair is not his private investment" and that he is a public servant. It says:

Mr. Thomas, one of the famous conductors of the present day, a man of unquestioned and unquestionable ability, and in some sense, greatness, whose services to music in America deserve the gratitude of every musician and musical artist, is personally one of the smallest specimens of the envious, everyday *musikant* whose mental vision does not extend beyond the narrow horizon of his ridiculous prejudices.[2]

Whether the remedy for these deplorable conditions was to discharge Thomas or assassinate him was not disclosed. When no result of the attacks was to be observed except Thomas in his place and continuing to function, the assailants turned to George H. Wilson, who had been made Secretary of the Bureau of Music. The nature of Mr. Wilson's crimes before God and man I have not been able to gather. It appears that he came from Boston and had been connected there with the *Musical Herald*, but these can hardly be judged in him malefactions that should exclude him from human society.[3]

In due time the plans for music at the Fair were made known, when it was discovered that Thomas had not been sel-

[1]September 21, 1892.
[2]*Ibid.*
[3]*Courier*, November 30, 1898.

fish and had not appropriated all the honor to himself and had not disregarded the claims of other artists but carefully had remembered them all. What he had done was to create a gigantic plan for an exposition of music beyond anything that had so far been known. Whereupon a musical journal that had not been engaged in the uproar said editorially:

The programs for the hall concerts [at the World's Fair] have been selected with that taste and intelligence for which Mr. Thomas is well known. . . . The scheme has involved an amount of labor, forethought and expert skill that few can realize, but fortunately for its success, it is in the hands of a man no amount of labor can appall and who is not in the habit of being daunted by obstacles. He intends to make the World's Fair music the crowning triumph of his long and eventful career and to show the world the great progress that music has made and the flattering conditions of the art in this country.[1]

"Some of it will stick," observed a seasoned expert in mudslinging when reproached with the futility of his industry. He seems to have been a person of considerable acumen. Millions of mankind learned of the accusations against Thomas; hundreds took note when the accusations were disproved. A vague impression had been created that he was after all an undesirable fellow, mean, or selfish, or something; and this impression was to have its own unpalatable fruit in due season.

When the music for the formal opening of the Fair came to be played, wisdom was seen to be justified of the slow-pulsed and deliberate among her children, for in breadth of conception as in majesty of execution, no such music had been heard in this country.

The dedication exercises took place October 22, 1892. To perform his program, Thomas had a chorus of 5,500 trained voices, an orchestra of 200, two military bands, and two drum corps of fifty players each. He had secured from John K. Paine a "Columbus March and Hymn" with which he

[1]*Brainard's Musical World*, February, 1893.

opened the ceremonies, all the means at his command being utilized in supreme and solemn harmonics. The body of singers and performers was so great that it was impossible for many of them to see an ordinary baton, and Mr. Thomas used a white handkerchief instead. His peculiar skill or gift or whatever it was that enabled him to cause great conceptions to move smoothly to a perfect execution was never better seen. The drum corps were in balconies on each side of the wide stage of the vast building. When the time came to begin the musical rites Thomas stood forward in his usual unruffled and masterly way and signaled slightly to the drum crops, which began a long double roll, starting softly and swelling gradually until it filled all the building, and then dying away again as the conductor without apparent effort controlled it. Then with all his instruments at once he passed into the first strains of the March. The effect was of an overpowering splendor of harmonious sound.

The other music on the program consisted of the musical setting by George W. Chadwick of Harriet Munroe's "Dedicatory Ode," Mendelssohn's "To the Sons of Art," Händel's Hallelujah chorus from "The Messiah," "The Star-Spangled Banner," and the chorus, "In Praise of God." The singing of the Hallelujah chorus made an impression hardly to be described as only profound.[1] The perfect modulation and control of the 5,500 voices seemed almost supernatural, and even upon persons without interest in music it was deemed the greatest event of the day.

As to the programs at the Exposition, Thomas had made preparation for music that would satisfy all legitimate tastes and still be worthy and educational and expository of music's progress. He planned a daily free concert of a popular character in the great Festival Hall to be given by the regular Exposition

[1]At p. 46, Otis gives passages from his journal describing vividly all these things as he saw and heard them.

Consult also Upton, *Reminiscence and Appreciation*, pp. 194–198. Mrs. Thomas, pp. 380–384, has an interesting letter from another deeply impressed witness.

Orchestra, daily open-air concerts by military bands, frequent symphony concerts in the smaller Music Hall by the Exposition Orchestra and by visiting organizations, choral concerts by visiting choral societies and by the children's choruses; concerts in which famous European musicians should play or conduct their own works, chamber concerts, artists' recitals, musical festivals, concerts by women in the Women's Building, concerts by women's amateur musical clubs from all parts of the country.

For these purposes he had this Exposition Orchestra, which consisted of his own organization enlarged to 140, two military bands, a chorus of 1,000 adult voices, and a chorus of 1,200 children's voices, as the regular equipment of the Fair. The other talent was to be summoned from afar. Among these visiting organizations, for whose coming Thomas must arrange, were the Boston Symphony, led by Mr. Nikisch; the New York Philharmonic, led by his one-time rival, Anton Seidl; the New York Symphony, led by the son of his other rival, Dr. Damrosch. At that time these comprised all the notable orchestras in America, aside from his own. Twelve bands were brought in, among them Sousa's, the Iowa State Band, a band from Italy, the world-famous band of the Garde Républicain, Paris. Thirty choral societies, including some from abroad, gave concerts at different times. In addition to all this, Thomas planned a kind of national tournament for American composers, offering prizes for the best compositions along different lines, and found among them seven that could be produced at the Fair.

All this was more than remarkable and worthy; it attracted applausive attention everywhere as the greatest effort in music that had ever been made, and Thomas was lauded at home and abroad for skill and daring.

Well, then, in a purely philosophical way, mark how so noble a design was ruined and what ruined it.

CHAPTER XI

Waterloo at the World's Fair

TO UNDERSTAND what happened next, it is necessary to reconstruct Business America of thirty-two years ago— a feat difficult now but serviceable if accomplished, for it will refresh us with a fair way-mark of our social advance.

It was a time when competition, now becoming extinct or perhaps perfunctory, was keen, nervous, relentless, and conducted frankly after the notions of primitive man. It was a time when oil mills were burned, blown up, or ruined, factories wrecked, competitors dogged with hired spies, entangled if possible in woman scrapes, bankrupted by incredible underselling, or maybe shot at if they still proved deaf to reason.[1] It was a time when the picturesque description of competition as "cut throat" had more than a humorous significance. It was a time, hardly to be imagined now, when a feeling of bitter personal resentment was expected to attend all commercial rivalry, and in small towns competing grocers belonged to different churches and walked on different sides of the street.

With the rest, the makers of musical instruments, above all of the tinkling piano, were engaged in a fierce strife for territory and sales.

When Theodore Thomas, taking, against his judgment, the musical directorship of the World's Fair, made a condition about it, he must have had this in mind. The music must be kept separate from the exhibit of musical goods; that was his condition. He wanted music taken from the Department of

---

[1] Ida Tarbell, *The Standard Oil Company;* Herbert Casson, *Romance of the Reaper;* H. D. Lloyd, *Wealth and Commonwealth;* Thomas W. Lawson, *Frenzied Finance.*

Liberal Arts, where it had been placed by the original organization plan, and made a separate institution, answerable to the Board of Directors.

This was promised; things are easily promised. But it was not done, and of course Thomas did not discover that it had not been done until he stubbed his toe on the omission.

The Chicago World's Fair was planned upon a scale of magnificence that had never been attained in any such exposition, and included a great display of all goods and instruments pertaining to music.

About the time it was to be opened, the curious news was made public that certain Eastern manufacturers of pianos, and these of great renown, conspicuously the Steinways, had decided not to exhibit at the Chicago World's Fair.

The reasons that led to this decision my finite and feeble mind has always refused to grasp, but I have no doubt they had some relation to the arcana of salesmanship, which we are assured on eminent authority is at once the supreme aim, plexus, and glory of human existence.

The manufacturers of and dealers in pianos that had taken space at the Fair, chiefly Western houses, now demanded that instruments made by firms that did not exhibit should not be played on the Fair grounds.

They made this demand of Theodore Thomas and at once placed him in a position of helpless embarrassment.

It was a recognized and necessary principle in his profession that an artist must be allowed to choose his own instrument; if somebody else were to choose it for him he could never be expected to do his best work. But besides this, Thomas was tied up by documents. He had made arrangements and contracts with his soloists, many of whom were coming from abroad to appear at the Fair without compensation. Some had exclusive contracts with certain manufacturers, others were well known to be addicted by preference to instruments that they deemed the best under their touch. Thomas could not ask players to break their contracts, could not insist that pianists should play on pianos they held to be unsuited to them, and above all, he could not insult artists by asking them not to come when at his request and to honor him and his country they had generously engaged their services.

In this dilemma he seems to have done about all that reason and goodwill demanded. He explained the situation and offered to make no more arrangements with artists that used the tabooed instruments.

He might as well have talked to the winds. The fury of competition was now aroused that makes men mad, or something to that effect. The exhibiting manufacturers appealed over his head.

"We have spent a million dollars to exhibit here," they said. "Do you suppose we spent that money for our health? If we spent the money, we are entitled to the advertising that goes with a soloist's appearance. Let the soloists play on our pianos. They're just as good as a Steinway."

In this mood they sought George R. Davis, Director General of the World's Fair.

Mr. Davis had long been the astute Republican boss of Chicago, a fact to which he owed his Director Generalship. Practical politics had taught him many things. One of them was to be deferential to business men. He listened with a sympathetic ear to the indignant protests of the Sangamon County Piano and Jew's-harp Company and other representatives of the best business interests and promised that the evil should be rectified at once. No piano made by a house not exhibiting at the Fair should be played on the grounds. He would issue that order. They might be sure it would end their grievance.

So he issued the order. He seems to have been imperfectly informed not only as to the man with whom he was dealing but as to the situation wherein he stood.

About this, we had better have an explanation.

The Fair project had been launched in Chicago with a local corporation having a Board of Directors to make all the plans and arrangements.

Action of Congress was necessary to designate Chicago officially as the place where the four hundredth anniversary of the discovery of America should be fittingly celebrated with the national and governmental approval. Congress did this, and then created a National Commission of the World's Columbian Exposition, a body of an imposing port but ill-defined powers. Every state in the Union was represented in its membership; usually by a Congressman, a former Congressman, a sentient politician, or one long moribund. As usual with such bodies, it was a handy covert for what are termed, in our easy political argot, lame ducks. The National Commission was supposed to command many things. In the meantime, the Board of Directors of the World's Fair Corporation continued to function and also to command.

Mr. Davis's order about the forbidden pianos was duly served on Theodore Thomas, Director of Music, and by him gently cast into the waste basket. He was obeying the Board of Directors, which endorsed the position he had taken about these outlaw pianos and instructed him to proceed with his own plans.

This was in April, latter part of the month. Ignace Paderewski was scheduled to play at the Music Hall under Thomas on May 2. It was well known that ordinarily he played only upon a piano of the Steinway make. Director of Music Thomas made no move to prevent him from using the instrument of his choice.

The exhibiting piano manufacturers went in a rage to the Director General, and he went, in a rage of his own, to the National Commission. One of their subordinates was defying orders. The piano makers went along and appear to have expended much fiery eloquence. The National Commission was naturally indignant. Members declared that they would see if the authority of Congress, vested in them, was to be defied by an upstart musician, for who was this man Thomas, anyway?

Let me do justice to the protesting piano makers. Something more than the madness of much competition was involved in the controversy. In a way that would not now be understood, the fury of sectionalism was aiding (superfluously) the other fury of business. New York had wished to have the Fair. Before Congress she had competed with Chicago for the prize and had been defeated. The disappointment rankled, or the newspapers so pretended. Some of the New York journals printed many jibes and jests at Chicago's expense. Some went farther than that. The late Archibald Gordon wrote for the New York *Sun* a page about Chicago that was a classic for deliberate, lancet-like, and nerve-searching sarcasm. This in turn rankled in Western hearts otherwise amiable. The notion went through all the West that New York was hostile to the Fair and wished to see it fail. When the Eastern piano manufacturers withdrew their entries, they were generally though erroneously believed to be moved by New York's envy and malice, and from this to a conception of Theodore Thomas as an agent of Eastern deviltry the step was easy.

Two newspapers in Chicago, the *Herald* and the *Evening Post*, having the same ownership, took up the cause of the exhibiting piano makers. Crusading was part of the newspaper business then. They made a crusade of this. Newspaper crusades, to be productive of returns, must make headway. This seemed to stand still. Against eloquent leaders and vigorous news articles the Thomas front appeared unscathed. Naturally, then, what had been a bombardment became a furious assault by shock troops.

The salient was Theodore Thomas.

May 2 drew near. The National Commission was informed

that Thomas still refused to heed the Director General's order. On April 28 the Commission met and passed a resolution declaring that "no piano shall be used on the Exposition grounds except those represented by firms that make exhibits at the Fair."

This was not deemed strong enough. The representatives of Sangamon objected that Paderewski was about to play on a Steinway when he might as easily play on a Sangamon. Therefore this was added:

"That if any Steinway pianos are announced for concerts in the Exposition grounds, the Director General is authorized to send teams and dump the pianos outside the gates."

Even this was viewed as but feeble prophylactic, and ginger was added thus:

"That the bills announcing Mr. Paderewski's appearance at a concert with the Exposition Orchestra be taken down and Mr. Paderewski's name erased."

The bills were not taken down: Mr. Paderewski's name was not erased. On May 2, he appeared in Music Hall and played with the Exposition Orchestra under the leadership of Theodore Thomas; played on a Steinway piano. The villain of the piece had outwitted the aggregate wisdom of much statesmanship. The night before, a Steinway piano had been smuggled into the grounds labeled "Hardware," or something, and on this Mr. Paderewski performed. No teams were sent; the piano was not dumped outside the grounds or elsewhere, and in the face of the anathemas of a National Commission created by Congress, the concert proceeded with great applause. A Columbian Guard made some attempt to interfere. He was led from the place.[1]

Beyond this in contumacy it seemed impossible to go. The

---

[1] The Columbian Guards seem to have been another triumph of the politics of the day and to have been recruited chiefly in the slums of the great cities. The newspapers teem with bitter and astonishing complaints of their brutalities. For this reason, the appearance of the guard at the Paderewski concert caused excitement and the expectation of a riot.

next day, when the wrath of the Commissioners was the hottest, they sent a letter to Thomas requiring his presence before a committee or board to explain the use of a Steinway piano on the Exposition grounds in defiance of orders. To this request he paid no attention, partly because the old Friesland spirit of stubborn resistance was aroused within him and partly because he recognized the Board of Directors as alone having authority over him. When the fact became known, many of the Commissioners regarded his silence as a gratuitous insult to a body Congress had created.

The *Herald* and the *Post* vigorously denounced the whole proceeding. The *Herald* attacked Paderewski and his playing, asserting that to show his contempt for the country and the Commission he had substituted the works of foreigners—Chopin, Schumann, and other low persons—when he should have been playing honest American music. Both journals clamorously insisted day after day upon the immediate removal of Theodore Thomas. Some other newspapers assented in the interest of peace.

The Board of Directors went placidly on its way of directing; Thomas, whether placidly or otherwise, went on with his programs. Tardily, the condition on which he had insisted at the beginning had now been carried out. The Bureau of Music was a separate institution entirely distinct from the Department of Liberal Arts; the Director General could have nothing to say to him.

A body called the Board of Reference and Control now approached the issue, but seems to have taken fright early and passed it along to the Council of Administration, which called a meeting for May 4, when the whole question of Thomas and his defiance of orders was to be laid bare, with proper punition following.

The next event was one of those strange coincidences that fall in to confirm faith in the bewitchments of a personal devil.

Among the members of this Council of Administration was Mr. P. H. Lannon, a politician from Utah, a National Commissioner, and one that from the first had seemed most incensed at Thomas's defiance of the Director General. At the meeting that day he caused a sensation by arising to unroll a package of letters, which he read, and when he was through Theodore Thomas seemed overwhelmed, convicted, and forever disgraced.

To make this clear, it is necessary to explain that one of the exhibiting houses that had taken a prominent part in the piano fight was the famous Chicago firm of Lyon & Healy. It seems that Lyon & Healy had a harp they were trying to push, and to this end had sent instruments as presents or loans to certain members of the orchestra. Apparently, the letters Mr. Lannon read had been furnished to him by the firm. This was one of them, written by a harp player of the Exposition Orchestra:

Chicago, May 1, 1893.

LYON & HEALY
    DEAR SIRS:
    I am very sorry to let you know that this morning Theodore Thomas gave us notice that he would not allow us to play the Lyon & Healy harp in his orchestra. With the harp I myself was delighted which you so kindly sent to my disposition, but as you know yourself, one must do what Theodore Thomas wants.
    Thanking you very much for your great kindness, you can believe me that we cannot do otherwise. I myself will see that the two harps, 518 and 553, will be packed carefully. Then you will please send for them. If possible, I will come to your store in a few days to thank you personally.

Very respectfully,
MISS A. BREITSCHUCK.

The other letter[1] was from the principal harpist and seemed to indicate that Mr. Thomas not only favored certain firms but countenanced something that looked like blackmail.

---

[1] All the documents in this chapter are copied from the files of the Chicago *Herald.*

Chicago, October 13, 1892.

LYON & HEALY
    DEAR SIRS:
    I take the liberty of inquiring if you are desirous of my taking any interest in the Lyon & Healy harp. If so, I must insist that you give me a written agreement guaranteeing me a fee of $1,000 a year and 10 per ce..t. on every harp sold through my influence, whether the party is a buyer or scholar. Furthermore, I must have two Lyon & Healy harps at my disposition, one for orchestra and one for solo use. For all of which I promise to play the Lyon & Healy harp in or out of Chicago and inspect and approve all harps leaving the factory. . . . If you are not inclined to accept my proposition, naturally I will lose interest in the Lyon & Healy harp, inasmuch as I have a proposal of representing a European firm during and after the World's Fair.
                                              EDMUND SCHUECKER.

These letters made the case plain to every politician in the Commission. Thomas had been paid by Steinway & Sons to keep all but the Steinway harps out of his orchestra. All the charges of bribery were clearly sustained. This is no man to be Director of Music at the great World's Fair. Out with him!

The champions of the piano makers exulted. "Other Queer Doings of Theodore Thomas" was the headline in the *Herald*. As to the woman harpist's letter, it said that "Theodore Thomas had compelled her to discard a satisfactory harp and play on one with which she was not familiar." As a result of what it called "Startling Charges Brought Against Theodore Thomas Yesterday," it gave the news that he was to be investigated by a special committee of six members of the National Commission. With every expression of an outraged sense of justice, the *Herald* and the *Evening Post* demanded his instant removal from the place he had dishonored. A few other journals echoed this demand. Many persons now began to see clearly that Theodore Thomas was not the kind of man they had taken him to be. He was in the pay of interests antagonistic to the Fair, the pride and joy of Chicago's being. Some were con-

THE THOMAS SMILE

A snapshot at a Cincinnati festival. Reprinted by permission
from Philo A. Otis's "The Chicago Symphony Orchestra"

CHORAL HALL—WORLD'S FAIR OF 1893
From the Chicago Historical Society Collection

vinced that as a conductor he must be equally unworthy. Perhaps he was not a musician at all.

The trial court constituted by the National Commission lost no time in its pursuit of the criminal.

The first meeting was held on the evening of May 5 at the Palmer House. Seven indignant makers of pianos from Sangamon and elsewhere were present. They brought with them lawyers to conduct their case against the Music Director. The *Herald*[1] reports them as saying to the committee concerning the letter of the harpist, that "while she did not tell which instrument she was required to use, it was generally understood that Theodore Thomas would compel her to use one made by his New York friends." And again, according to the *Herald*, "Theodore Thomas, an officer of the Fair, is boycotting our instruments. He is compelling players who are artists, satisfied with ours, to lay them aside and take other instruments." He never allowed an opportunity to go by when he could serve one New York firm, they said. One of the witnesses declared that this firm "had saved the Musical Director from bankruptcy when he was about to go under." This made clear to all business men why he had boycotted Sangamon.

On the morning of Monday, May 8, President Higinbotham of the Directorate of the Fair was giving in Music Hall an elaborate formal breakfast to the visiting naval officers of the world at which Mr. Thomas was a guest. In the middle of the repast, according to the gleeful account in the *Herald*, one of the biggest Columbian guards on the force pushed his way into the hall and laid this stern message on Mr. Thomas's plate:

Chicago, Ill., May 8, 1893.

THEODORE THOMAS, Music Hall.
    DEAR SIR:
    The committee appointed by the World's Columbian Commission to investigate alleged abuses in the musical department detrimental

[1]May 6, 1891.

to the welfare of the World's Columbian Exposition desires your presence this day at 2 o'clock P.M. at the committee room, Administration Building adjacent the office of Secretary John T. Dickinson.

Very truly yours,

P. H. LANNON,
Chairman.

"Mr. Thomas's lips curled ironically," says the *Herald,* "as he turned to the big guard and remarked 'Tell the honorable gentleman I'll be there.' Then he resumed breakfast."

Theodore Thomas to the bar! You are accused of treason to the sacred cause of profits. How say you, Guilty or Not Guilty?

Similar subpœnas were issued for Edmund Schuecker and Miss Breitschuck.[1]

Mr. Thomas went to trial first. Lawyers had been employed, shrewd and experienced, to cross-question him and make sure that he should not escape by evasion or trick. "Do you mean to tell me, Mr. Thmoas . . .?"; "Do you wish this intelligent Commission to understand that . . .?" and so on.

All the Chicago newspapers of that day have excellent accounts of the proceedings. I select that of the *Herald,* as being the paper least likely to be prejudiced in Thomas's behalf. It says that when he arrived before the appointed hour, "he looked jaded and worn out. His face was flushed and furrowed with deep wrinkles. He said he was tired."

"I am a very busy and a very much annoyed man," he said as he sank into a chair and leaned on the table. As a matter of fact, he had a concert to conduct at 3 o'clock and the hour was approaching.

"I have been chased by sheriffs, but through all these years I have worked for a cause and not for personal gain. Believe me, gentlemen," he added, in a tone that appealed to the Commissioners, "I did not do the things these men accuse me of doing."

As to the charge of serving the hated Steinways, "I care no

---

[1] Not a regular member of the orchestra but engaged for the Exposition period.

more for that firm than I care for Jones," he exclaimed. "I
neither suggest nor favor instruments of any manufacture. It
happens that the most eminent artists use the New York piano
and for that reason, and that alone, those instruments will be
heard in Music Hall."

"But it is said you selected those artists because they used a New
York instrument," said Commissioner Lannon, shaking a fat finger
at the excited witness.

"That is false, entirely false. I did not know what instrument they
used."

After explaining at some length that he had no interest in the exhibition of pianos and that it was only the artistic phase of music that
interested him, Mr. Thomas was questioned in regard to the order
forbidding members of his orchestra to play a Lyon & Healy harp.
The Music Director astonished the Commissioners when he talked
about that incident.

"I positively knew nothing about the order until it was read to me
from the newspapers," he said.

"Didn't you compel your players to discard the Lyon & Healy
harp?" Chairman Lannon asked in surprise.

"No, sir. I knew nothing of it. The order was issued by Edmund
Schuecker, leading harpist of our orchestra."

"Now, suppose several of your harpists should tell you they preferred the Lyon & Healy harp to the one sold by the New York firm.
What would you do about that?"

"I should immediately instruct them to play any instrument they
desired. That is the right of all artists and I should certainly insist
upon its being observed in my orchestra."

George H. Wilson, Secretary of the Department of Music,
was the next witness. He corroborated Thomas's statement
about the alleged harp order.

The real sensation of the day seems to have come when
Edmund Schuecker was called to the stand and told a story
that put the virtuous piano men in a different and rather an
awkward position.

At that stage of music in America, one must understand,

whenever an orchestra had a notable vacancy in its ranks or desired to increase its forces, it must send to Europe for the needed artists. We need not deny that some of these eminent ones came firmly resolved to acquire much wealth while sojourning in the land of the dollar and so return with a competence they could never expect to secure at home. In 1891, Mr. Thomas, reorganizing his orchestra for Chicago, needed a new harpist and sent to Germany for Schuecker, famous on the Continent both as performer and composer.

He told the committee that he arrived in Chicago in October, 1891, bringing two harps of the make called Erard, which he believed to be the best.

"James Healy met me at the train and asked me to call at his office. There he told me that Lyon & Healy would be glad to build a harp especially for me according to whatever model I should indicate and whatever color would best suit me, and that it would be ready for me at Christmas. Scarcely had the harp been in my house a day when Mr. Healy called again and wanted me to give him a testimonial for the Lyon & Healy harp. I desired to postpone this until I had become better acquainted with the instrument, but no time was granted me, the cause assigned being that the new catalogue was to be published immediately and that the firm wished to insert my testimonial. It was agreed that I was to receive 10 per cent. on each of their harps that was sold through me. I gave them the testimonial they desired and for a time everything went smoothly.

"Last fall, a pupil of mine bought a Lyon & Healy harp. I demanded my commission, which was promptly refused on the ground that the gentleman had contemplated the purchase of a harp a year ago. As I noticed they did not seem inclined to keep their promise, I wrote the letter that was published in yesterday's *Herald*, for I did not see why I should advocate their instruments and act as their agent without receiving some compensation. They would not agree to my proposition and demanded that the harp they had sent me be returned. I also demanded that the testimonial I had given them be returned, but with this request they refused to comply. At length I surrendered the harp to a sheriff whom they sent to the Auditorium for it."[1]

---

[1] Files of the *Herald*.

He said that when the orchestra was returning from Canada, where it had been playing, an intelligent United States Customs officer had seized his harp at the frontier and when he arrived at Chicago he had no instrument to play on. He had sent to Lyon & Healy to rent one. The answer he received was, "Not for $1,000 would we rent a harp for use in the Thomas orchestra." Thereupon he applied to another firm in Chicago and they sent him an Erard harp. He added that to mix the harp incident with the piano row was preposterous. The Steinways, about whom all the tempest swirled, did not make nor represent the Erard harp.

Thomas, he declared, had never attempted to interfere in any way with his free choice of any instrument. When Miss Breitschuck had testified, it was evident that the opponent of the Lyon & Healy harp was not Thomas but Mr. Schuecker himself, whose reasons were not less apparent.

After all this, members of the Commission assured *Herald* reporters that their impression was unchanged. Theodore Thomas "was partial to a New York concern and was using his position as Director of Music to bestow favors on his personal friends that could not be secured by exhibitors who were spending thousands of dollars in making displays at the Fair."

This damaging suggestion being further pursued, it appeared that what the Commissioners meant was that Paderewski had been allowed to play on a Steinway when he could not be induced to play on an instrument made by Sangamon, which had an exhibit on our grounds.

Meantime the committee that had been trying the case made up its report, finding Thomas guilty and recommending his removal. This is the verdict:

That no piano not exhibiting for award should be used in Music or Choral Hall during the Fair;

That the usefulness of Professor Thomas at the head of the Bureau of Music of the World's Columbian Exposition is so impaired that in our judgment his services be further dispensed with, and

That we recommend that the Director General be instructed to request his resignation.

But the *Herald* made note of a compromise suggested in quarters where the verdict was not viewed in the blithesome spirit manifested by the delegates from Arkansas, Utah, and Alaska. By this Mr. Thomas was to continue in office, but only on condition that he should undertake that thereafter no soloists should be employed except those that played on pianos exhibited at the Fair. "This condition will undoubtedly be bitterly opposed by Mr. Thomas," says the *Herald*, "but if he becomes convinced that his head is in danger it is believed that he will accept the terms."

As to this, the only response from the undaunted Thomas was the spectacle of him conducting his concerts as usual.

The report of the trial committee went now before the whole Commission, where it struck an unexpected snag. Mr. Lyman J. Gage had boasted some days before that the Commission was unanimous in its purpose to rid the Fair of this contemner of the rights of salesmanship. When the Commission met, Mr. Gage was proved to be but a scurvy prophet. Among those that had listened to Mr. Thomas's statement was General St. Clair, who was a Commissioner but not much of a politician. When the report came in he amazed the piano world by a speech in which he burned up the report and all engaged in making it. This was the more surprising because he had been counted as dependably in the anti-Thomas squadron. What had changed him, he said, was the obviously truthful statement of an obviously honest man. He challenged the committee and all others to show a word of testimony that had sustained any of the charges. "Where is it?" he cried. "Let us see it. Show it."

Some of the accusers had asserted that Thomas on the stand admitted foreknowledge that certain artists would play a Steinway or other instrument made by the loathsome opposition. Thomas had made no such admission; all such knowledge was exactly what he had explicitly denied. Any such action as was here contemplated would be utterly unjustifiable and contrary to the evidence.

The delegate from Arkansas responded to this. He wanted Theodore Thomas removed, "music or no music, bands or no bands," and this sentiment was approved by the majority of the Commission. The report was adopted, thirty-nine voting in favor of it, but the reporters noted that General St. Clair's plea was supported by twenty votes, where no opposition had been looked for.

By a special messenger, the Commission that afternoon sent to the Board of Directors the verdict demanding the resignation of "Professor Thomas."

"They will have a sweet time getting it," was the only comment of President Higinbotham.

Thomas continued to play as before.

Nothing else happening beyond bitter revilings in the *Herald* and *Evening Post*, Director General Davis despatched this letter:

Chicago, May 17, 1893.

Mr. THEODORE THOMAS, *Musical Director*,
Department of Liberal Arts,
World's Columbian Exposition.

DEAR SIR:

In compliance with a resolution adopted this day by the World's Columbian Commission, I have to request your resignation as Musical Director of the Department of Liberal Arts.

You will please turn over all property, records, and documents belonging to and appertaining to your office, to the Chief of the Department of Liberal Arts.

Respectfully yours,
GEORGE R. DAVIS,
Director General.

Thomas continued to play as before.

To be beaten in any campaign it has undertaken is for any newspaper bad business; bad in every sense. The *Herald* and its evening edition, the *Post*, having championed the cause of the piano makers to this impotent conclusion, were now compelled to turn their wrath upon the man they had undertaken to displace. Day after day their columns, news and editorial, bristled with attacks upon him. I will give a few examples that we may have a satisfying glimpse of both business and journalism a third of a century ago. In one issue of the *Herald*[1] I find this:

Mr. Thomas should have been leader of a barrack band in a mountainous camp in North Germany.

He is a small despot by nature; a dull and self-opinionated man, who has had unbounded opportunity in the land of his adoption and has disappointed, year after year, the sanguine friends who have been sympathetically petitioned to hold him up. A constitutional want of generosity, an unscrupulous resistance to reasonable appeals from every quarter and a thrift that has looked out for himself no matter who suffered in consequence, have been his dominant traits.

A musical director entering heartily upon his trust would have striven to make much use of the means of bringing the greatest possible number of people to Jackson Park.

Were he not the pragmatic curmudgeon he has always shown himself to be, he would have made national music one of the conspicuous features of the Fair.

The fallacy that Mr. Thomas is too classical is exploded. Were his faults on that side, he would not have failed to please Boston, where he is totally without prestige after repeated efforts to win success. He would not have failed where Seidl succeeded in New York and Brooklyn. It is not austere scholarship that makes Theodore Thomas unpopular—there are symphony orchestras that would not submit to his uncouth and rough-shod readings of the most exquisite works— it is that he is rough-shod; that with hoof of hussar he tries to ride down all that is opposed to his vanity, his selfishness, and his caprices.

---

[1] May 11.

If he had been a house breaker he would not have been so assailed. The outraged spirit of competitive business was avenged. Salesmanship was vindicated.

For some weeks the news and editorial columns of the *Herald* presented to the world a singular contradiction to the comments of the *Herald's* music critic. Day after day he wrote of the Thomas performances at the Fair in terms of unstinted eulogy. What the editor called "uncouth and rough-shod" the critic was praising for delicate shading and masterly interpretation. After a time to the Fair came the orchestral conductors that editorial wisdom had cited as examples of art better than Thomas's. The critic heard their work and decided that it was not better but worse. Somebody must have called the heed of editorial wisdom to this discrepancy, of which the public seems to have taken a humorous view. Of a sudden it stopped, and the hand of the music critic was seen no more in the *Herald's* columns. According to his statement,[1] he was summoned one afternoon into the presence of an editorial council where he was offered the immediate choice of denouncing the Thomas performances or of quitting the staff. He quit the staff.

The *Herald* now ridiculed as preposterous the notion that Theodore Thomas had ever been of any use to the cause of music in America.

Meantime, the Board of Directors of the Exposition Company, with whom alone Thomas had any contract and who alone had any control over him, unanimously supported him and insisted that he should continue upon the program he had designed for the Fair.

No answer being returned to Director General Davis's demand for his resignation, and the concerts proceeding daily as usual, the National Commission began to find itself in an exceedingly awkward position. With sound and fury it had demanded the head of Theodore Thomas on a charger, and the

---

[1]Made some years afterward to Frederick J. Wessels.

charger came back empty of the head but filled with the jeering comments of the press of the nation. The whole story of the Seven of Sangamon Against Art had been spread broadcast and aroused in some quarters an inextinguishable laughter and in others contempt and indignation. The Chicago *Tribune*, which from the first had denounced the course of the Commission, now asked derisively in what school of musical art a ward politician obtained his ability to analyse a symphony or the playing of it. As to the attacks on Thomas, it said they had gone far enough. All persons that knew anything of the man or his work would protest, said the *Tribune*,

... against this attempt to humiliate and persecute the man that has done more than any other for the cause of music in the United States, that has held his high and honorable position for forty years without swerving from what he believes to be the best interests of his art, and has labored patiently and courageously against a wilderness of obstacles and at great private sacrifice to maintain his high musical standard. In his long career no mercenary taint has attached to him. His bitterest enemies cannot point to any act of his that savors of self-seeking. He may have made mistakes, that is human; but he always has had a lofty ideal of his art and little patience with charlatans. It is too late in that long and honorable career for even members of the National Commission from the great art centers of Wyoming, Virginia, Utah, Kansas, and Arkansas to injure his fame.

Other journals were much less restrained. The New York *Times* called the attacks "an exhibition of the Yahoo press." The New York *World* said that the campaign "was conducted on the part of those that fought Thomas in a contemptible manner, and his firm and resolute defense was a satisfaction to all that admire the artist if not the man."

Freund's Weekly, musical review of New York said:

The glorious record of Theodore Thomas now spans many years. It is marked by the force, power, and command that come from undisputed and indisputable fitness and ability. A lifetime spent in the cause of music in its highest forms has culminated in the magnificent position he now occupies. In elevating him to it, Chicago elevated herself. His removal would be her eternal disgrace, and the world of art would demand to know who was responsible for the insanity that could drive her to trying to snatch the crown from her head and fling it foolishly away. Then would the petty rivalries of trade be proved to reign supreme in the councils of an exposition which was intended to be a beacon to the world, a phase of history of which every true American would be justly proud.

The storm continued to increase in all parts of the country. The Commission began to find itself naked and pelted with scornful comments. It seems now to have centered its powerful attention upon the necessary but difficult feat of saving its face. The *Herald*, in its issue of May 24, contains this news:

> Theodore Thomas will remain at the head of the World's Fair Bureau of Music, but shorn of his power of dictator and responsible to Director General Davis for the conduct of his department. . . . The meeting was called for the purpose of bringing the local directors and National Commissioners to a common ground in the insane Thomas controversy. The National Commission stood pledged to the removal of Mr. Thomas from the Bureau of Music for reasons of which the public is very well informed. It was no personal feeling against the great conductor that impelled Commissioner Lannon's committee to recommend his discharge. The Commissioners sensibly desire to protect the exhibitors that were loyal to the Fair and whose interests were in jeopardy through Mr. Thomas's partiality toward certain manufacturers of musical instruments.

Thomas continued to play as before.

Against this impregnable barrier the waves of competitive wrath breaking in vain, and likely so to continue, the Commission seems to have been struck with the thought that the best plan now was to bury from the public gaze and contempt a row so unseemly. It was agreed that Director General Davis should recall his demand for Thomas's resignation, an order was to be issued that the Director of Music should be thereafter responsible to the Director General of the Fair, and, the Director General was instructed "to protect the rights of exhibitors of musical instruments in Music and Festival Halls."

These resolutions being reported and passed, the Commission got itself, somewhat lamely, it must be admitted, out of the pillory, but the situation was not otherwise changed. The only authority Thomas could recognize was that of the Board of Directors, with which he had his contract and he was no more responsible to the Director General than he had been before.

The *Herald* and *Evening Post* resumed the daily cannonade. Now they attacked Thomas's programs and ridiculed his abilities. They said he was anti-American. As late as June 23 the *Herald* was saying:

Theodore Thomas is unable to discern any melody in a piece of music unless it emanates from a German composer. Mr. Thomas's musical taste is decidedly foreign. All airs except those of the Fatherland are vicious in his ears. He loves the German musicians and he abhors all others. It seems never to have occurred to Mr. Thomas that it would be proper for him as musical director of the Exposition to consult the wishes of the people in the arrangement of his programs.

The public really likes "Yankee Doodle" when well played better than a Wagnerian symphony in E.

Meantime, how was it really with the man about whom all this tempest was raging? As if he were treading the fires of Malebolge. Only those that understood his peculiar make-up could know what horrors or what torments his soul passed through. After forty years of public life he was still wholly un-hardened to publicity. The politician grows a crust about him like a turtle's shell; the charlatan enjoys notoriety even when it comes with slings. The artist is without defense; every shaft pierces and is barbed by his own bitter reflections. Of all the artists of his time, he was probably the most given to these self-torturings. Over a single cruel and unjust assault he would brood all night. Day after day he issued from his house and took up the task assigned to him in Music Hall, took it up and bore it so that the public generally believed he was untouched. But his face of unconcern was play-acting. Under it he had received a deadly hurt. A few friends knew what was going on in him and looked upon the whole drama with acute alarm. At least one of whom I have knowledge took up every day his morning newspaper with a sense of terror, expecting to read that Theodore Thomas had committed suicide. The glee with which the assailant newspapers recorded late in May that the attacks upon him had made him ill had basis of fact. It was only by the sternest exercise of his iron will that he forced himself to arise to his daily duty. He was sick of the whole controversy before it was twenty-four hours old and sick of his place. He would have been glad to get out at the first explosion and let the Seven of Sangamon have their own way, but he had in his complex make-up a peculiar sense of loyalty to his friends. He had been induced by them, though against his judgment, to undertake this work. It would be intolerable to desert them. For the first and only time, so far as I can discover, he committed to paper some of his feelings about the injustice that had been visited upon him. To his intimate friend, George Upton, he wrote:

I cannot tell you what pain these attacks have given me. My age and my record should have protected me from them. But let it pass. Art is long.[1]

That was all.

He continued at his post and guided week by week an extraordinary succession of great musical events. Paderewski stayed in this country only to produce for him his new piano concerto. E. A. MacDowell and Arthur Foote appeared in new compositions of their own; Amalia Materna, Lillian Nordica, Plunkett Greene, Christine Nielson Dreier, and other great

---

[1]Upton, *Reminiscence and Appreciation*, p. 177.

soloists sang for him; the choruses of the New York Liederkranz, Brooklyn Arion, Cleveland Vocal Society, American
Union of Swedish Societies, and many other organizations gave
concerts; there were Beethoven programs, Schubert, Schumann,
Brahms, Wagner, Raff, American composers' programs.
This continued until August. For the rest of the season he
had planned still greater things, the Ninth Symphony to be
performed under the leadership of Hans Richter, Saint-Saëns to
come to America and for three weeks to conduct his own and
other works, and so on. But all this came to nothing. It was the
year of the great financial panic; business was stricken almost
with paralysis; so great a fear swept over the country that many
in no position to be hurt believed themselves ruined. In these
conditions the attendance at the Fair fell off until it seemed
likely the enterprise would end in bankruptcy. A cry went up
that expenses must be cut. It gave to the unappeased instrument makers the opportunity they wanted. Since expenses
were to be cut the place to begin was with the Bureau of Music,
which was useless, anyway. They succeeded in bringing about
a condition in which no money could be had to pay the working
musicians. As he could not conscientiously encourage these to
continue under such conditions, Thomas gave up the fight and
resigned. Not to the National Commission; to the Board of
Directors, to which alone he felt responsible. This was on
August 12, and he went as quickly as possible to his summer
home at Fairhaven, for he was weary in body and wearier in
spirit. He was glad of a chance to go away and salve his hurts.
In a few weeks the country recovered from its hysteria about
business and money, the attendance at the Exposition suddenly
increased, from the imminent prospect of bankruptcy the
treasury showed an astonishing surplus, and the crowds that
now thronged the Exposition grounds began to ask why there
was no good music.
The Board of Directors had accepted Thomas's resignation

only because it seemed impossible to ask him to stay when there was no money with which to pay his players. It now pulled itself together and, with many other citizens, sent him an urgent message asking him to return and resume his labors and programs. The members of the disbanded Exposition Orchestra united in a similar request, offering to leave any engagements they might have since made if they could play again with him. The opportunity for such a brilliant return upon his enemies might have appealed to another man. It meant nothing to Thomas. He declined all importunities to resume his position and until the opening of his next Chicago season remained in seclusion at Fairhaven.

It is likely that others that knew him well may have a different opinion, but my own conviction is clear that Theodore Thomas never recovered from these blows. The loss of money and even of prestige was nothing to him. The destruction of the great plans he had made for music at the Exposition was a disappointment that he could have borne with fortitude, being but too familiar with such sour company. But what dug deep was the attack upon his business integrity. In his long career, in all his troubles, in the ruin that had three times fallen upon him, he had preserved unimpeached and unimpeachable the highest sense of personal honor. He had sacrificed himself and his interests many a time that the last constructive obligation on his part should be more than met. His word was so highly respected that often men and associations did business with him under no contract and sought for none, for widely it had been acknowledged that his mere statement was better than any covenant or any oath. If he had said he would do anything he would do it, or die. There had never rested upon him the shadow of a hint of departure from the one straight way of rectitude. In him appeared, about small things as about great, a certain insuperable scorn of deceit. If I may be allowed a personal testimony; I have known many men in many lands and under many conditions; I have known no man whose honesty was more crystalline. To be charged now with what to one of his creed would have been an intolerable betrayal of the most sacred obligations to the public, to his art and to his personal honor, was more than he could stand. That the greater part of the press, with the country at large, warmly repudiated the charge was no potent consolation to him. It could not dull the real hurt. In the face of such a record such a charge had been made.

I think he was never quite the same afterward. I think that even the knowledge of his own innocence did not sustain him as such knowledge is supposed to sustain. The *mens conscia sibi recti* has certain penalties also. The wrongdoer often holds his hardihood by the reflection that he took a chance and it turned against him; the sense of injustice sharpens and drives the dagger for the man that has done no wrong and is still condemned. Thomas had neither the strange egotism that sustains some public men in great crises nor the cynical philosophy that enables others to shed troubles as a mantle sheds rain. Always after this experience he showed the usual outward countenance of composure and self-command. To his friends and his family he was not less genial, kindly, self-effacing, and entertaining. He laughed and joked as before. But there was now perceptible an undercurrent of melancholy and sometimes a touch of bitterness that had not been known in him before. I shall go farther and express a thought that is likely to be controverted and is possibly wrong. But it seemed to me that for a time his mental state affected his work. He was still the great conductor after that fiery ordeal, still the conscientious artist, giving to the interpretation of great works all his best of insight and devotion. But the old masterly confidence and spiritual serenity were gone, and I think with them went much of the joy in his art. It seems to me that with a man of his temperament, nothing else could be expected.

AFTER THE WORLD'S FAIR
Thomas in his later years

FREDERICK STOCK
Thomas's successor. Conductor of the Chicago Symphony
Orchestra

CHAPTER XII

The Realities of Chicago

ONE other irony of this career was that opportunities for which he longed were continually opening when he could take no advantage of them. He was now convinced that his coming to Chicago had been an error. The deficit of the second season was one ugly fact; the prostration of the city after the Fair and the business panic was another. It had yet to be demonstrated that Chicago's musical interest, even if times had been normal, was strong enough to justify the hazard in which he had risked so much. On the other hand, Boston had firmly established its orchestra, Major Higginson was in a position to supply from his own purse all of its defaults, whatever these might be, and Boston was the center and capital of a great and populous musical world. He had often regretted that the chance Chicago gave him had not appeared in Boston.

Just at the moment when the outlook seemed most dubious, the thing he had longed for actually happened. Arthur Nikisch, who had successfully conducted the Boston Symphony for several seasons, desired to return to Europe, and Major Higginson offered the directorship to Thomas. There was every attraction in the offer. Aside from the matter of money, which Thomas, after his debts had been paid, regarded with unconcern, there was the indescribable charm to him of playing in a city well advanced in musical education, so that he should no longer be obliged to keep his programs at a lower level than agreed with his best ideals. It must have seemed to him a superfluous buffet of fate that this should come to him at such a time. He had no contract with the Chicago Orchestra Association, but he had what was to his mind a stronger obligation. He had set his hand to the work there and would not turn back. Besides, the men that had given money to make an orchestra in Chicago had given it because of him and their faith in him. He would not desert them. He refused Boston's call and turned himself doggedly to the dreary prospect before him.

This looked so bad at the beginning of the third season that he confidently expected it would be his last in Chicago, and another year would see him thrust back upon New York to face unemployment in his fifty-ninth year. The times were the hardest Chicago had ever known; they were hard everywhere in the United States that winter, but hardest in Chicago because of the collapse that followed the ballooning of the Fair. Hence decreased concert attendance, diminished receipts. By rigid economy the expenses were so reduced that the loss was $2,400 less than in the second season, despite the smaller attendance; receipts, $66,000, net loss, $49,000.[1] But the Association had now to make this good with an extra subscription, a contingency no one had expected. It is high tribute to the character of the men that were backing such a doubtful adventure that they met the demand without a murmur and for another year the orchestra was saved.

The Cincinnati Festival, the eleventh since he had founded these great musical events, came now like an anodyne. In all his troubles he had groped for efficacious remedies. One was to do something around his home that caused the children amusement, and another was his art. If he had not on hand a great plan for a festival or for a performance of the Ninth, he betook himself within the safe asylum of composition, to which he was not ordinarily addicted. One of the brightest of his works, a March, full of melody and sunshine, was composed when he was in the depths of despair about his orchestra and himself.

He buried himself in the Festival of 1894, and was pleasantly

----

[1]Otis, p. 57.

absorbed in the work of choruses and orchestra, when the destiny or chance or whatever it was that pursued him so malignantly hunted him out, even in this retreat. I have made mention of the singular affection he had always felt for New York, that chill foster mother of his, his home when he was young, the birthplace of his children, the city that had given him his first successes. Other communities might be good in one way or another: one was fairer to look at and another was farther advanced in music, but where was there to the New Yorker another New York? With all the poignancies of recollected gladness, he looked back upon the years he had spent in building the Philharmonic, those years of endeavors with visible results. Now, in the midst of his Cincinnati engagement, his friends in New York came to him with an offer of a guarantee fund ample to sustain him and his orchestra and assure his future. They did more than merely to hold this out to him in a long envelope. They sent a committee, a committee of his dearest and closest friends, to plead and argue with him. While an evening program was on, they waylaid him with this enticing proposal. It appears that before such temptation his usual calm was shaken.[1] So much it meant—peace and sufficiency, an end to harrowing anxiety, a triumphal return to New York, a home there the rest of his days. One may believe that he was sorely tried. But iron was still strong in his blood. He had given his word in Chicago; men had believed in it. To desert them, so long as they were willing to fight, he held to be akin to poltroonery, and so, refusing New York as he had refused Boston, he went on with his load.

A part of it, there is no denying, was the attitude of the press toward him and his attitude toward the press. This pivotal matter should be made clear. Theodore Thomas never lacked warm, eloquent, and effective championship among the newspapers of America. The majority, critics and writers, even a

---

[1]Otis, p. 58; Mrs. Thomas, p. 429.

fair majority, never wavered in their support of him and his art. But he was so constituted that this fact weighed little against unfair, untruthful, and malicious assault. On the other hand, and this was the strange thing, he was not avid of praise. In that expressed distaste for lionizing, he was quite honest: anything fulsome or extravagant in his behalf filled him with dismay and then with disgust. "Never was a musician more free from personal vanity,"[1] said George Upton, who understood him so thoroughly. But his very lack of ordinary vanity came, in an odd way, to be another source of weakness to him. Hundreds of other men, attacked and criticized, have been able to erase blame with praise and so move on serenely. His comparatively small delight in personal eulogy deprived Thomas of this useful adjunct.

In Chicago, now, a part of the press seemed to him animated by an implacable hatred. Salesmanship and Sangamon had been largely pacified by the ending of the World's Fair, but trouble came back to the programs, that old familiar fountain of bitter waters. Too much of the Wagnerian symphony in E and not enough of jig and "Home, Sweet Home," burdened the rasping complaints. The exact utility of these campaigns seemed to the impartial observer fairly doubtful. It was well known that Thomas would not change though all the oracles at once should cry against him. There was nothing to do with him except to endure him with a shrug and think how much better a program the critic could make. But this view, obvious as it was, could never have occurred to some of the Chicago journalists. For years they never ceased to expound his duty to this obdurate person. For instance:

During two seasons, with every possible influence united in his behalf, a deficiency of about $80,000 was created for the liberal guarantors of the Chicago Orchestral Association to pay out of their own pockets. The prospects for a Third Season under the gloomy auspices

[1] *Musical Memories*, p. 182.

now existing are such that unless Mr. Thomas is lost to all sense of gratitude he will relieve the friends who have stood by him from any further unreasonable and hopeless expense.[1]

The guarantors did not wish to be relieved. One of the curiosities of this story is the sharp contrast the business men of Chicago afforded with the conduct of the backers of the American Opera. The Chicago men never whimpered nor wavered, never complained about the quality of the music Thomas was furnishing, never intimated that the losses were contrary to business principles, never suggested that if he would play dance tunes he could fill the Auditorium and so ease them of the burden of their guarantees. That this was the truth was plain enough to all, but they never said it. The only word they had for Theodore Thomas was a word of warmest encouragement to keep upon his own chosen path, and I think this fact ought to have some of the admiring emphasis it deserves. Their faith would cost them dear, but they did not leave it, shrewd business men, and all that. And when we come to pay to Chicago, musical capital, some of the tribute due for its wonderful achievements, I hope to see a few wreaths for the Chicago business man. I do not know his equal for capacity of vision and for courage in following an ideal. If sometimes we have thought harsh thoughts about the encrusted selfishness of business elsewhere, they dissolve or ought to dissolve, before the astonishing record of men like these.

Men and women. The good women that had so often appeared in the Thomas story were not absent here. One of them, Mrs. John J. Glessner, stands out. With her to lead, they worked in a magnificent zeal to keep this hard-beset bark from sinking; they sold season tickets, they dragooned their society friends into knowledge of what the effort was all about, into subscribing for boxes, at last into a genuine interest. They

---

[1]Cited by Otis, p. 53. I have been unable to identify the clipping, but I think it is from the Chicago *Times*.

cheered Thomas in his despondent hours; like Mrs. Gillespie, in Philadelphia, with wit and courage they championed a good cause because they knew it was good.

To provide for part of the deficit, the season of 1894–1895 was extended by a long tour through the Western states. Traveling again. Twenty years had passed since Theodore Thomas had announced that he would do no more of it; here he was—still bound to the dreary treadmill. In his sixtieth year he found it worse than irksome. The broken rest, bad food, late hours, the noise and confusion, the jolting of the train, told too much upon his nervous system, weakened by worry and over-labor. On this tour he gave sometimes two concerts a day; when there was but one concert he would have a rehearsal, which was still more fatiguing. His letters to his wife show a growing depression.[1] For years he had been suffering from catarrh and rheumatism; traveling made these ailments worse, or he thought it did. The hotels were bad—once even bad enough to have bedbugs. He began to think seriously that his life work in music was done and he had better seek another way of livelihood. He wrote to his wife:

As to traveling again next year with the orchestra, I doubt if I can bring myself to make that sacrifice. I feel that I have done my share, and that the country and the people need time to develop now before we can expect an art appreciation. Consequently we must work only for the "many headed instrument," the orchestra, and I fear that would be suicidal for me. In one sense I am through with my life work. The personal satisfaction of showing what I could do under favorable circumstances I shall never get—or it must come quickly—but that may be nothing more than vanity. A man over sixty ought not to overwork as I do and I think I must find some suitable occupation and learn to live on a smaller income.[2]

[1]Mrs. Thomas prints several of these in Chap. XIX. They are to be read with recollection of the fact that if he had accepted the offer from Boston or from New York he would have spared himself the suffering he endured.

[2]Mrs. Thomas, p. 430.

Otis, at p. 67, has a good summary of this traveling business and what it meant to Thomas.

Close-paring economies were needful to enable the Association to survive. On this trip, the manager of that time, bent upon making a showing, began to lodge the men wherever he could get the cheapest rates and regardless of other considerations. At last he went over the bounds of patience by hiring rooms that for more reasons than physical untidiness were unbearable. The men went to Mr. Ulrich, who found their complaints just and sought Thomas with a plain recital of facts.

"Send Mr. Blank here," said Thomas, naming the manager. By the time the manager appeared the fires were hot.

"What do you mean by lodging these men in sties?" Thomas burst out before the manager could open his head.

Mr. Blank, discountenanced, as most persons were when they encountered The Thomas dight for battle, stammered that he had tried only to save money. "You know how poor we are, Mr. Thomas. We must reduce expenses."

"Well, reduce them some other way," crackled the irate Thomas.

The manager must have lost his wits, for he ventured to observe that after all the men that were complaining were the least important in the orchestra. He could have said nothing worse.

"Important!" shouted Thomas. "Who's important? Every man in this orchestra is as important as every other, and entitled to the best we can give him, and I don't care a damn whether he plays the first violin or the twenty-second triangle."

One night he got to bed at twelve, and congratulated himself that the hour was early. He fell asleep about one, awoke at three, lay awake until five, arose and walked until seven, when the train left. At one place there were no hotel accommodations ready and he must sit in an office while the manager scoured the city for rooms.

"I have done enough," said Theodore Thomas. "A younger man must take up the load."

While he was on this unlucky tour, which lasted two months and was for him a prolonged agony, he received another offer of leadership in Boston. He was half determined to abandon the attempt in Chicago, but would not leave it to take anything better, and for the third time refused an opportunity that had every attraction for him. A sense of honor like that would seem to atone for more "sharp points" in character than he is known to have exhibited. At the same time he wrote to Norman Fay that he could not consent to carry on the work in Chicago beyond another year, and the trustees should look for a younger man to take his place. He wished this to be laid before the trustees for action. Mr. Fay was too wise to act upon a letter written in evident despondency and physical distress, and held the matter over until Thomas should return. When the abominable tour was over and he was back again among the kind friends of Chicago, he felt he must go on so long as he could stand.[1]

The trustees, who had no idea of what had been in his mind, took this happy occasion to give a public dinner in his honor as a testimonial to his four years of work. The people responded to the idea in true Chicago fashion and made the occasion such an overwhelming expression of affection and gratitude that he was more than ever resolved to remain with a community so finely loyal.

The good women had their part in these saving graces. Thirty-six of them, headed by Mrs. Glessner, had an affair of their own. Before the public dinner they called at Mr. Thomas's house and presented to him a great silver punch bowl, pitcher, and ladle, properly engraved with their sentiments.[2] Instead of resigning, he went to Europe, enjoyed the first real holiday he had ever had, spent his days in art galleries, and came back

---

[1]Otis, p. 69.
[2]Otis, pp. 69–70.

calm in spirit and rested in body. This was the summer of 1895. Even the catarrh, which he had attributed to the Chicago climate, and the rheumatism, which, with the fiendish malignity of the disease, had settled in his right arm (of all places), departed under these sunnier conditions, and with alacrity and some confidence he began the season of 1895–1896.

He had good reason to feel encouraged, even he, for it was evident now his methods of tuition were slowly winning out in Chicago, as they would win anywhere. He was divesting the symphony of its terrors; he was showing Chicago, as he had showed New York, that this frightful beast could be tamed and domesticated. His native wit helped the demonstration. When the dissatisfaction with the "Wagnerian Symphony in E" was at its height in the second season, a kind of informal committee, composed of genuine friends of his that had allowed themselves to be swept off their feet by clamor, came to see him.

Mr. Thomas received them blandly, but seemed to observe them out of the tail of his eye.

"Mr. Thomas," said the spokesman, when no more time could be wasted in commonplace, "it has seemed to us that we should like to make a little suggestion, if we may."

"Go right on," said Thomas genially, "I am always glad to have suggestions from anybody," which was true; strangely enough.

"Well, it has occurred to us, Mr. Thomas, that the programs at the concerts would be more attractive to the general public if you did not play so many symphonies."

"Yes?" said Thomas, without the least truculence, "but there is one thing we must remember about that. You see, we are still much behind Boston in the symphony record. Just observe. Last season we played only ten symphonies and the Boston orchestra played fifteen. Now, we don't want it to be said that Chicago is inferior in musical taste to Boston. We must keep up Chicago's good name. Chicago can't play second fiddle to any city on earth. I am sure you will agree with me about that."

They did. There was no more complaint from this source about the symphonies.[1]

He must make two tours this winter, and as usual they oppressed his spirit. One thing he always complained about was the overheating of the hotels, which he believed was bad for his catarrhal weakness and gave colds to the men. He had other troubles. At Detroit there was some small difficulty about a soloist, and the newspapers embellished a trifling incident to make a sensation. At Pittsburgh, he fell into one of those civil wars in musical circles that now and then arose to add to his miseries. Two musical factions contended in the city. One having engaged the Thomas Orchestra, the other went forth on that account to make the engagement a failure.[2] It must have nearly succeeded, for Thomas wrote that he played there to the smallest audiences of his life and on the last night tickets were given away to secure a passable showing in the seats.

At this very time when he felt despondent about the apparently indifferent reception he had in some of these places, there was preparing for him in his old home a signal demonstration of applause. It had been arranged that at the close of the regular Chicago season he should take the orchestra on a tour of the Eastern cities, over part of the Highway he had traveled so often in other days. New York was included, and as soon as the engagement there was announced, musicians and public awoke to a lively interest. So far back as February, he had the cheering news· that the Metropolitan Opera House, where he was to play, was already virtually sold out. In Brooklyn and Philadelphia, even then, all the seats were taken.

He had, nevertheless, as much anxiety as pleasure from this

---

[1]Thomas has a reference to this incident in his Autobiography, p. 104.
[2]Letter to Mrs. Thomas.

prospect. Discontent with the quality of the performance was at all times a kind of monster that pursued him. He had in Chicago sixty men that he had brought from New York and thirty that he had added from local ranks. The two divisions were upon unequal footing, for the reason that when he went on a Western tour, because of the expense, he could take but sixty men with him, and of course chose the sixty of the regular force, the old Theodore Thomas Orchestra. This necessarily allowed the remaining thirty to accept other engagements and he was never sure of men that played otherwise than under him.[1] He yearned to have the Eastern tours something that he could look back upon with satisfaction, and as he must have with him the full force of ninety men, he doubted whether the work of the extra thirty would not take all the joy out of life.

Months in advance he made all his programs for the tour and rehearsed and drilled every man, regular and extra.

So far as New York was concerned, he had another reason for uneasiness, but one that only his intimate friends suspected. The old wounds of that terrific combat in Chicago, the hand-to-hand struggle with the Seven of Sangamon, still bothered him. He believed that with a large part of the press he had become personally unpopular, an obsession almost morbid. Of the psychology of press attacks he was the last man in the world to know anything. It never occurred to him that waves of liking and disliking sweep over the newspapers as over the public the newspapers serve, nor that such things have as much permanence and enduring importance as summer clouds. For a time all attention is fixed upon one man. Whatever he does is reported and lauded. Then public, or reporters, or all together, seem to weary of the repetition of his name. Now for a time he is anathema and nothing he does is well done. Thomas, not

---

[1] Mrs. Thomas, pp. 439–440.

On one of these tours he was obliged to play a Liszt concerto without rehearsal and when many of the men had never seen it before.

having the least gift for publicity, had been through both extremes of this phenomenon without beginning to understand it, any more than he understood propaganda's devious ways. When journalists met him he was coldly polite but did not conceal the fact that he had other things upon his mind and might be glad to have them elsewhere. Without a doubt he had created thus a feeling of antagonism even in the days of his greatest vogue in New York. When the time of conflict and doubt came on, these latent animosities crept out like snakes in spring and some of them hurt when they stung. They had helped to create or to foster that former belief of his that New York was weary of him and now they helped to make him feel that his reception in his old home might be hostile (in the printed word), and was certain to be acutely critical.

He made no error about the attitude of the press, or a part of it. For an old New Yorker and one that had labored thirty years or more for the benefit of the New York public, the reception he had in print was not of the kind that sets the joyful pulse athrob. One newspaper remarked after the first concert:

The Chicago Orchestra is a well-trained organization of mediocrities. If Mr. Thomas had a better orchestra he would naturally make better music.[1]

Another, speaking of the performance of Dvořák's "New World" symphony, said that "it would require half a column to enumerate the things Mr. Thomas does not know about this work."[2]

Henry T. Finck, long renowned as one of the scholarly and authoritative critics of the country, wrote in the *Evening Post* a totally different judgment. He declared that the Thomas train-

---

[1]See Otis, p. 79.

[2]Some of this must have been reflex of the orchestra war. The *Musical Courier* of April 1, 1896, in an apparently impartial review, praised the orchestra's work highly and said it was better than any New York band could do, giving as one reason the fact that the Chicago orchestra evidently rehearsed and the New York orchestras did not.

ing had won in this orchestra to a preëminent excellence, and held all the performances to be good. The public, having no prejudices in the matter and paying its usual tribute of indifference to the deep-breathing on Mount Olympus, hailed with enthusiasm the return of the man that had chiefly created the American understanding of orchestral music. At the close of the first concert Thomas was presented on the stage with a magnificent laurel wreath. The next night came the presentation of a wonderful silver loving cup, the fair thought of Paderewski. He was not in the country at the time, but arranged to have the gift made in his absence. It bore this inscription, which touched Thomas deeply:

> To Theodore Thomas, the great conductor,
> the true man, and the cherished friend,
> in admiration and love,
> from Ignace Paderewski.

All tributes, all applause, and all notes of affection were eclipsed by the unusual testimonial that marked the last concert. Musicians and music lovers of New York combined to do him a signal honor. As soon as the intermission in the program was reached, a committee headed by Gerritt Smith marched upon the stage and presented to Mr. Thomas a massive piece of plate, designed by a Tiffany artist, a great center-piece of silver, two hundred ounces in weight. The design was symbolic of Thomas's work and triumphs, particularly in the introducing of new works.[1]

At the Cincinnati Biennial Festival this year he gave two novelties, Saint-Saëns "Samson et Dalila" and Tinel's "Francis." For the Saint-Saëns work he was obliged to have certain specially made instruments to produce the required effects.[2]

---

[1]*Musical Courier*, March 25, 1896.

[2]Mrs. Thomas, p. 446. It seems that Saint-Saëns happened to see the instruments in Thomas's hotel room in Paris and played them for Thomas's delight.

That summer, 1896, he began the construction of a summer home in the White Mountains, near Bethlehem, New Hampshire, on a small tract of wild land he had bought two years before at the suggestion of Mrs. Glessner. Always afterward he spent his summers at this Felsengarten, and gained thereby. The dry air of the mountains usually subdued the Chicago catarrh in about three weeks. Besides, he developed a new interest, invaluable to one of his years and cares. He became a kind of landscape gardener. The place was on the side of a mountain and rough with boulders and outcropping rock. Thomas, crowbar or spade in hand, went about beautifying it. You can see from this that all the arts are akin and all practitioners of one art have sympathetic insight into others. He had never before considered landscape gardening, but now, of his own notion and on his own design, he transformed the rude place into a bower of beauty. Part of each day he spent in his study, working upon the scores for the next season; the rest, if the weather was possible, he passed out of doors.

But with all this he could not free himself from the overhanging shadow of a hostile press. If newspapers represented public opinion, then he was all on the wrong track with his programs, and leading the guarantors of the orchestra only the farther into financial bogs. After turning this over in his mind that summer, he came to a characteristic conclusion as to where lay his duty. The men that were so bravely meeting year after year the deficit he was causing them might feel in their hearts that the quest was futile and might regret that they ever embarked upon it. He wrote to the trustees of the Orchestra Association frankly stating the facts and offering to resign if the trustees so wished. Then the experiment might be tried fairly of playing more popular music. For himself, he said, he was not willing to lower in any way the standard he had set, but he deemed it most unfair to ask the guarantors to continue to support a policy that possibly they might not approve. At the same time he called attention to the fact that some things had been achieved by their unselfish contributions to art. In no other city of the world was there an annual series of forty-eight orchestral concerts of the highest class attended by so large an average audience. In no city of Europe was there an orchestra of the size and merit of the Chicago orchestra that was not maintained by a large subsidy in addition to the box-office receipts. And in no other city of the world except Boston was there such an orchestra maintained exclusively for concert purposes. It seemed then that despite all adverse comments the Chicago public had proved its readiness to support its orchestra. In relatively greater numbers than in European cities, Chicago people attended orchestral concerts.[1]

The trustees instantly refused to consider any suggestion that Thomas should retire or that another style in music was needed. Yet at the time the whole concern seemed to slide toward ruin. The losses had been reduced, but of the first guarantors some had died, some had met with reverses and so had dropped out. Instead of the original $50,000 a year, about $23,000 was all that could be counted upon. The survivors could contemplate this record of annual deficits:[2]

First season,	1891–1892	$53,907.09
Second season,	1892–1893	51,381.18
Third season,	1893–1894	48,972.21
Fourth season,	1894–1895	34,474.92
Fifth season,	1895–1896	27,159.73
Sixth season,	1896–1897	27,036.23

In strange ways, misadventure seemed to hang upon the skirts of the enterprise so that any body of supporters might reasonably have held it to be bewitched and given it up. The first Eastern tour having reaped a surplus, a second was held

[1]Printed in full by Mrs. Thomas at pp. 455–457.
[2]Compiled from the treasurer's reports, printed by Otis.

to be demanded by good business principles. It only depressed the Association with a total net loss of $15,000, adding that amount to the deck load of debt that before had seemed about to sink it. The same orchestra, the same leader, and now people cared for neither. Far be it from me to suggest solution of a mystery that has bogged experts; I can but recite the facts. Even in Brooklyn, old-time fief of the Thomas domain, where he was reputed to be forever lord paramount, barely enough currency was taken to pay the fee of Lillian Nordica, the soloist. In Providence, Rhode Island, Ysaye with the orchestra charmed the people so little that the receipts fell below his charges.[1]

Wise men suggested many expedients to lure the reluctant dollar from the public's purse. All failed. Thomas himself had a brilliant thought about it. He proposed and carried out a great pageant and ball at the Auditorium, designed for it scenes and costumes, and did for it what he had never done before and never did afterward. With his whole great orchestra he played for people to dance. It was all beautiful.[2] Four thousand persons were expected to attend. Fewer than five hundred appeared, and the harvest when gathered was another increase of debt.

The People's Institute was created on the West Side of Chicago, and many persons thought the occasion would be good for the orchestra to dedicate the Institute's hall and receive cash thereby. After an allowance of $100 for expenses, the next $500 was to go to the orchestra, and all receipts beyond this were to be divided with the Institute. Thomas made an unusually attractive program, and the total receipts were $96.30.

Alexandre Guilmant, the French organist, came in the season of 1897–1898 to play with the orchestra, and Chicago musicians gave a dinner in his honor, Thomas being present. It was like a chapter from Boswell at The Mitre.

---

[1] Otis, p. 99.
[2] Otis, p. 92.

"Don't you think, Mr. Thomas," says Frederick Grant Gleason, to start the musical Dr. Johnson, "don't you think that Mozart and Beethoven will become antiquated and Wagner will be the composer of the future?"

And now he is off and away! The words from the mouth of Thomas the taciturn, Thomas the autocrat, come tumbling in a flood. For half an hour the table sits in awe, listening to this eloquent discourse. He finds he cannot adequately express himself while seated; he must get to his feet and walk to and fro, while the lightnings flash and the thunders roll.[1]

"Bach, Händel, Mozart, Beethoven were sons of God! Wagner was an egotist! All sensuousness! Beethoven worked for humanity. There are three epochs in the history of art. First, the Greek; second, the period that produced Shakespeare; third, the period that gave to the world Beethoven!"

M. Guilmant understands this imperfectly, being ill versed in the language, but it is translated to him. He says:

"Surely, Mr. Thomas, you cannot ignore the author of 'Lohengrin' and 'Siegfried,' works the French people are now learning to appreciate. I am told you were the first to play Wagner's music in America."

"Mozart and Beethoven will live!" cries Dr. Johnson Thomas. "Wagner may and may not," and beyond this he will make no concession.

Against the financial disaster of the second Eastern tour, vanity might have set the memorable outburst of enthusiasm over his appearance in Boston. It is likely that, at this time, musical criticism was as highly developed in Boston as in any city in the world, as judiciously analytical, as free from personal bias. To be hailed by such judges as the faultless conductor and rarely inspired interpreter would have been balm enough for any hurts except such as his.[2] Of the New York concerts,

[1] Otis, pp. 96–97.
[2] Boston *Journal*, March 23, 1898.

Harper's Weekly published a long, carefully considered estimate and summary, crowning him as the first of all artists in his line.[1] I think he was gratified by this but not elated. Something else was at work within him.

For more than forty years he had been pouring out upon his work that great fund of vitality with which he had been endowed. He seems to have been of the physical order of Napoleon; the men that do not need the normal allotment of sleep and rest. Night after night, when he was on tour, he had no more than three hours' sleep. Even when at home it was his custom to arise while other men slept and get him to his desk. Perhaps to him it was not work; certainly it was not toilsome through the years when his health remained to him. It seemed more like the regular performance of an inevitable function, like the beating of his heart or the action of his lungs. He had no facility for idleness, and little for the relaxing of tension by which the human machine is saving from breaking. The mornings at his mountain home were always spent upon the scores he was to play the following season, often in marking the bowing. I think no other conductor of his time went forth to such labors. He would take a score, spread it before him, hold his left hand as if it grasped a violin, his right as if it held a bow, and thus in imagination play the violin parts, stopping to mark the bowing with a pencil. These marks were then by MacNichol, the incomparable librarian, or by his assistant, copied for all the violins. In this way he secured that perfection of unison that remains in the minds of all that heard him a grateful and delicious memory.

As an example of his prodigality of labor I come back to Beethoven's Fifth, that favorite triumph of Gothic art, playing so curious a part in his story. He knew it so well that he once offered a wager that he could write it backward from memory, every movement of it. Yet whenever it appeared on his pro-

[1] March 10, 1898.

grams he studied it afresh as if it were all new.[1] To such an undertaking as a Cincinnati Festival he gave months of intensive study. Alone, he prepared the programs, choosing from the range of musical literature compositions that would best fit what he had determined should be the dominant thought for the occasion. Alone, he chose from the grand army of singers the men and women that could best render these selections. Alone, he carried on the correspondence with them, prepared the scores and the choruses, arranged all particulars of each concert, conducted the rehearsals, studied new effects in decoration, conferred with musicians, scene painters, copyists, carpenters, florists, what not, having meantime his regular duties with the orchestra and others. This was an energy truly prodigious, but not more than his endurance. It is the multiplicity of cares rather than their intensity that breaks men down. He had more details to carry than one memory would hold; hence the little notebook's eloquent story of multiform activities.

Only a frame of extraordinary strength and a life most carefully ordered could support such a burden. At last even his abnormal equipment began to fail under the strain he had unsparingly laid upon it. Mrs. Thomas tells us[2] that after the Cincinnati Festival of 1898, a triumph of all his resources in program making and conducting, he was so tired that for a month he sat every day in his chair, moveless and inert, his head drooped forward in a kind of coma. For the first time even out-of-doors had no spell upon him; he lifted not a hand to adorn Felsengarten. Gradually his exhausted powers returned, and by the end of summer he was something like himself again. But he doubted whether he could get through another festival, and but for his personal affection for the men that so many years had helped him carry out this great work he would have given it up.

[1] Upton, *Reminiscence and Appreciation*, p. 231. "He had conducted the Fifth Symphony hundreds of times, and yet every time that he took it up the performance showed the influence of fresh care in phrasing or tone-quality."
[2] P. 480.

By the end of the season of 1897–1898 the Association's debt had become $30,000 and there was no chance that the next season's increase of attendance would reduce it. No company of men in such conditions could be expected to go on. Thomas knew this as well as anybody; he thought the game was nearly up. Even he underestimated the spiritual and the idealistic in the Chicagoan. Mr. Fay, whose resolute spirit was unshaken in all these emergencies, suggested a dinner to which should be invited the most prominent men in various lines of industry. When they arrived he explained in the frankest fashion the situation. The Orchestra Association owed $30,000 and faced extinction. Should Chicago admit defeat in this the most notable experiment in pure art the country had ever known? That was enough. On the spot the men at that dinner contributed the $30,000 needed to liquidate the existing debt and then $30,000 more to make sure that the Association should not again be in jeopardy—$60,000, equal to $120,000 now, set down in about thirty minutes. What was it Gungl and others said about musical taste and public spirit in America? Let me not even seem to suggest Chauvin and his vaunts, but I am not acquainted with another country where one can do such things.

In the next season there came to Theodore Thomas, by a rare relenting of fate, a gift of fortune for which he never ceased thereafter to be grateful. One of the burdens of his career had been the business end of his enterprises, the blood supply of their existence. He never pretended to be much in the business way; yet he had been compelled year after year to look with minutest care after details of affairs that if sordid were needful. He had tried many a manager, often good men and capable, but business manager with him meant a combination of rare gifts. One so furnished came to him now in the person of Frederick J. Wessels, himself a musician but having also a genius for management. From this time on, he so directed all the business of the orchestra, the festivals, the traveling, that Mr.

Thomas had never to give it a thought. Mr. Wessels had this priceless advantage, that he was, and had long been, personally interested in Thomas's plans and ideas, understood them and desired to see them carried out. By an odd coincidence, his own ancestry was North German; his is a great name in Ost Friesland, and when I was in Esens I encountered many traces of his tribe. The substance of the benefaction of Wessels was to be revealed later. For that present Thomas had his usual sufficiency of troubles, with an overplus. The press, or a part of it, was crustier than ever about his programs. When these changed not, the next natural course was to belabor the obstinate heretic that sloughed off all this priceless counsel. Soon after the beginning of the season of 1899 he deemed that even apostleship did not oblige him longer to emulate St. Lawrence on the gridiron. Mr. Otis's diary contains this entry:

November 16 (1899). Thursday evening. At the opera to hear Calvé, Campanari, Susanne Adams and De Lucia in "Carmen." Met Wessels after first act, who handed me a letter from Mr. Thomas, tendering his resignation, to take effect May 1, 1901. Bizet's lovely music had little interest for me after reading this letter.

The next week it was laid before the Board of Trustees, thus:

MR. PRESIDENT AND GENTLEMEN:

I consider it my duty to acquaint you with a decision I have arrived at, and to give you all the time possible in which to make your arrangements.

I wish to return to the East after the season of 1900–1901. I regret more than I can tell you that I cannot end my life of usefulness here in Chicago, where I have met more friendships and public spirit than anywhere else, but the climate does not allow me to end my life here happily.

I wish to return to the East before my professional usefulness weakens, although I do not feel sure that any work will offer itself there that I shall be willing to accept.

I thank you for the kind feeling I have always met with from you, and above all I desire to express my appreciation of the generous support that you have given to music in this country in your effort to establish an art institution of the highest standard in Chicago.

In all sincerity and with respect,

THEODORE THOMAS.

Chicago, November 14, 1899.

Two weeks passed without a response, the trustees being set too much adrift to make answer. Thomas, becoming impatient, demanded an interview with Mr. Otis, who was Secretary of the Orchestra Association.

The next morning he came to my office in a very despondent mood, and sinking wearily into a chair asked:

"Have the trustees acted on my letter of resignation?"

Going to the safe, I took the letter from a drawer and handed it back to Mr. Thomas, but he declined to take it.

"No, Mr. Otis, I am in earnest. I am through. I cannot stand these continual attacks by the newspapers on my programs; the Chicago climate affects my hearing and makes my life a burden: the Auditorium is too large for symphony concerts; if we are to remain here we must have a smaller hall."

I could see that the real cause for his action was the attitude of the press.

"Why do you read the newspapers, Mr. Thomas? They do not pay the salaries of the orchestra. The trustees have never once commented on your programs. We have paid the losses cheerfully and without a word of complaint. Go on with your work; make the programs as you have always done, without regard to the newspapers.[1]

A few days later there was a meeting of the trustees and Thomas attended. He wished his resignation acted upon then and there; no longer, he said, could he manage to endure the bitter attacks of the press; he must retire. Thereupon one of the trustees said quietly:

"We do not wish to think of your resignation, Mr. Thomas. You are engaged to play only the great works of ancient and

---

[1]Otis, p. 114.

modern times, and nothing else. If there are any deficits in giving the concerts, we will take care of them."

He was a business man that said this, head of a great manufacturing concern. He must have been able to pack much conviction into few words for it appears that the incident closed with this speech.

"Mr. Thomas," says Mr. Otis, "never again suggested his resignation, but went on with his work, going 'from strength to strength' with progress ever increasing in the favor of the people."[1]

He had never been so much discouraged that he thought to turn from the next great Cincinnati Festival, 1900; even the memory of his narrow escape from physical disaster at the last Festival could not hold him back from this. After two years of planning he burst upon responsive Cincinnati with another great program, and if we may judge by the comments, another historic success. This time the years had their way with him. He had mind upon his health, for he got him early to bed, rested when he could, restrained his appalling energies, and came through without wreck.

And now observe a curious thing. It was the season of 1900–1901 in Chicago. Where were the critics that had so long denounced his programs, driven him toward resignation and foreshown his total failure? Gone to their final rout and silencing, it appears. His programs changed not, yet a strange, unearthly stillness fell upon prophets that before had known well that this kind of thing would never do. Apparently, he was proving this season that from the first concert played by the Chicago Orchestra he had been right. He had insisted upon his own thought-out plan of inspired education; he saw now the results. This year, for the first time, he ventured upon a Beethoven cycle, a series of four concerts composed of only symphonies and other works that had been denounced as impossible, and

[1]Otis, p. 115.

behold, the people came out in greater numbers than ever before and understood and liked what he played. Blessed be obstinacy in a cause of righteousness! Lo, the benevolent autocrat, bearing home the crown! If he had played what the critics wished him to play and pilloried him for not playing, would he have won to any such triumph? Say rather he would have carved ruin for all concerned. The Chicago Orchestra would have passed long before to the junk heap of forgotten things.

Who, then, is practical? Who is the real business man?

In one way there was no limit to the reality of his victory. Forty years before he had set the symphony as the emblem of his success, if he was to succeed. For nearly a quarter of a century he had maneuvered, feinted, marched, and countermarched to win that prize and overcome the popular antipathy. In New York he had led the public inch by inch with symphonies in fragments; the second movement of the Second, introduced in a casual way between the "Blue Danube Waltz" and the "Invitation to the Dance"; the second movement of the Seventh, cunningly disguised, as the old-style family physician concealed castor oil in syrup. Chicago in 1891 was hardly better; I have recorded his trouble there on this same point. Observe, then, that on the occasion of this cycle the first program contained one symphony, and the great piano concerto No. 4, which is equal to another, and each of the remaining programs contained two symphonies. The people used to object to one in a season. Now they accepted two every evening. Accepted them and applauded them and, what was worth more, mastered them at last. He shall have it, we said long ago. He has it now and here.

Not so much elsewhere, as he was most painfully reminded. There were the tours. He had always hated this work, and now, with infirmities increasing upon him, found it almost unendurable. He thought he was too old to be shunted and slung about the land over the American railroad system, giving concerts that always wrung his artistic soul because he could not make them what he desired. Sometimes the railroad tracks were so rough that the instruments were broken in transit. Once the company spent eleven consecutive nights in sleeping cars.[1] Cold halls were common. Sometimes in the North the fingers of pianists and violinists would grow so stiff with the cold it seemed impossible they could play. In the South the hotels of that period seemed even worse than those of the North. Often they had to play in churches, with temporary scaffolding put down on each side of the pulpit, sometimes on carpenters' saw horses only too visible. There is always a feeling of restraint in a church; nobody likes to let go there; the invisible threads of feeling and sympathy that must connect players and audience are largely inoperative in such a place. The sternly basic necessity of the tour being revenue, one might think that Thomas could have summoned philosophy and overlooked artistry for cash. He would have been shocked at such a suggestion. To give a performance that fell short of his ideals was always a bitterness, be the audience one of thousands in New York or one of scores in Painted Post. He never became inured to these troubles, even after forty years of concert giving. I should think nothing else about him more difficult to account for than this. As a rule, men past sixty are willing (or glad) to make compromises, accept their lot, and give up resistance. This man never lowered his standard nor ceased to vex himself about shortcomings. An inadequate performance was as painful to him at sixty-five as it had been at thirty.

Once in a Southern city there came a variation of the usual miseries. Orchestra and leader were to take part in a festival. The local chorus was large, apparently well trained, assumably efficient. In the middle of a number this chorus must have been possessed by some devil of mischance, for here it came blundering in, four bars ahead of the right place.

Mr. Wessels and others that knew turned faint and sick; the

---

[1]Mr. Wessels's reminiscences, *Chicago Daily News*, January 7, 1927.

whole performance tottered on the edge of irreparable wreck. For an instant a horrible discord arose; the next all difficulty had vanished, orchestra and chorus were sailing on in sweetest amity, and so to the end.

As they were walking to the hotel that evening Mr. Wessels said:

"I wish you would tell me how you did that."

"Why, certainly," said Thomas, with his quizzical look. "You see, I just jumped the orchestra ahead four bars."

This is all he would ever say about it, but if we knew the means by which he made this leap we might have a glimpse of the psychology of the baton that to the layman seems so mysterious.

His letters home on this, which proved to be his last concert tour, reveal his dissatisfaction with conditions as much as his intense longing to be through and at home. With Mrs. Thomas he had now transformed what was at first only a bungalow at Felsengarten into a permanent residence, where he had more delight and peace than he had known before in all his life. He had the north countryman's innate feeling for the homestead. It centered upon Felsengarten and the rest of the year he was spiritually looking forward to the few weeks he could spend with his own spade upon his own grounds. All his life he had longed for something of this kind, and he was sixty-five years old before he got it.

CHAPTER XIII

At a Morning Rehearsal

MOST of my time from 1900 to 1905 being cast upon Chicago, I was enabled to renew my acquaintance with Mr. Thomas there and to follow his work. He was then giving regular concerts on the Friday afternoon and Saturday evening of each week through a season of twenty-four weeks. Monday, Tuesday, Wednesday, and Thursday mornings were spent in rehearsal, ten o'clock to noon. The concerts were in the great Chicago Auditorium; the rehearsals upon its stage.

As a rule, outsiders were not admitted to these practising bouts, but by hard petitioning I won an exception in my favor and formed a habit of attending at least one rehearsal every week. In that vast space I sat the one auditor of a deeply interesting procedure. In many ways, it had profit; for one, it made me better acquainted with the peculiar mind and methods of Theodore Thomas than I could have become from a hundred mere conversations.

I was not long in discovering one of the secrets of that extraordinary command over his players so many observers had talked about. Aside from the recondite psychology of a dominant nature, which never will be revealed to us, the thing was simple enough. He never once assumed the attitude that he wanted anything done only because he wanted it done.

"Do this because I tell you to do it," was never once suggested or hinted. His attitude was always, "We shall do this a certain way because we all know it is the best way and we are equally interested in having this work perfect." He did not say these words, you will understand, but conveyed always the sense of them: an odd illustration of spiritual democracy, if I may use that phrase, for nothing else can express it. From reading Stephen Fiske and others I had been led to expect Termagant; a kind of shouting, brow-beating, fault-finding, foot-stamping mogul of the baton. I was astonished to find that ordinarily he was the gentlest and most lovable old autocrat that ever went in shoe leather. At the same time, he was absolutely businesslike, absolutely certain of himself, firm, rigorous, insatiable of effort, but even when he called an individual player to task for error, I think he never aroused resentment in the wandering one. There was no humiliation in his corrective ardor, and that made the difference. After this I hardly have need to say that he never raved up and down the stage tearing his hair and cursing, as conductors of the old time were pictured, perhaps libelously. The Thomasian idea of venting wrath upon one that had forfeited his esteem was the sentence of excommunication. "Let him never speak to me again."

He displayed one attribute in his rehearsals that I have not heard of in other conductors, though it may not be so uncommon as I think. He seemed to know by an infallible instinct when the players were becoming weary and needed relaxation. It was remarkable to see how completely and quickly he changed his bearing at such a time. The moment before he had been urging them forward, repeating passages, softening shadows, bringing intensities into proper relations, polishing a phrase until it glittered. Now he dropped the baton, leaned over his stand and told a funny story or cracked a joke. When everybody had laughed and stretched out and known a moment's ease, he resumed the work as before. It struck me as strange that he could divine so surely when these periods of rest were needed, and much more wonderful that he could at will throw off the austere dignity supposed to pertain to his position, throw it off, put it on, throw it off, and never for a moment impair discipline or lose in any degree the respect and confidence of the men he commanded. I recall in the military service the many and lumbering devices that aim to keep intact an awesome distance between officers and men, and I think this was a remarkable person.

I once knew a famous conductor in another city whose stand was so marked and battered with the blows of his baton at rehearsals that it had to be painted. Mr. Thomas seldom rapped in rehearsal either to start or to stop, and never in public. He had the players' stands so arranged that he was visible over the top of each, and he required each player to look at him at least once in every bar. So, when he wished to stop he merely dropped his arms, which was signal enough.

"No, not tum-to-tum-tum-tum-tum, but this way," and then he would hum the phrase as he wished it and sometimes Leopold Kramer, the wonderful concert master, who generally understood Mr. Thomas's ideas, would play it on his violin to show the exact emphasis or whatever else the leader was seeking. "Now, then!" Thomas would call in his cheery and rather high voice, and away they would go. Four bars, and down fall the arms again. Still they have not hit upon the exact shade or turn he wants.

"Tum-tee-tum-t-e-e-tum-tum-tum," he corrects. "Now, then, once more," and so they go on. The violins have it all right this time, but the wood winds slip a little; they don't show the curl he wants on that "tee-tum-t-e-e-tum." So the wood winds try it alone. "Tum-t-e-e-tum," don't you see? It is the stress on that second "e" that he wants. On the next attempt they have it. Now all have it and that's out of the way.

"Four bars before No. 29," he cries. This is a device of his own. To facilitate rehearsal he has had the scores sub-divided and the sections numbered. Therefore when he indicates any place where he thinks drilling is necessary all know where to turn.

In my time, much had been said and written about his unusual powers of hearing, but nothing I had read about this seemed to equal the wonder of the actual feats I saw him unconsciously perform. One morning he was rehearsing D'Indy's "Symphony for Piano and Orchestra founded on a French Mountaineer's Song," and Rudolph Ganz, later the admired conductor of the St. Louis Symphony Orchestra, was playing the piano part. The first harpist was Enrico Tramonti, that marvelous master of a beautiful instrument, and the second harp was played by Walfried Singer, an excellent musician, who at times appeared in the second violins. D'Indy's symphony has a long cadenza in which strings, harps, wood winds, and everything else let go. They were swinging down this with great and glorious sound, it seemed to me, when of a sudden, Crash! went the baton on the stand, and everybody stopped short.

A dead and awful silence ensued in which Mr. Thomas was observed to be standing, baton in hand, glaring down upon the unfortunate Singer, who gazed back with eyes of mild alarm.

"Well?" said Thomas at last.

"It was only a wrong note, sir," piped the penitent one.

"O-h-h," said Thomas, transfixing the culprit with his eyes as one might spear a butterfly, "that was [pause] A-

                              L-   it?"

                              L- [pause] was

At another time he left the stand, walked to a certain player in the rear rank, pointed to the score and said quietly, oh, so quietly! but so distinctly, "That note is A sharp; you have twice played it A natural."

But this, I should explain, was an extra player, brought in from the outside for a special occasion, and not a regular member of the organization. In the early days at Chicago the limited finances necessitated this practice, afterward discontinued.

Walter Unger, who for many years sat at the first violoncello stand, and was a 'cellist of great distinction, used to be fond of telling this instance of Thomas's acuteness of hearing:

Unger had broken his violoncello and must have it repaired. The workman changed the position of the sound post. Next rehearsal, Unger had a short obbligato to play. When the rehearsal was over, Thomas said to him:

"Is that a new instrument you have there, Mr. Unger?"

He had detected the slight change in its tone.[1]

Everything to the Thomas mind must be exactly thus and so, and above all, the audience was not to be distracted with any interruption, even the slightest, of the regular and smoothly working machine.

The principal 'cellist in those years was Bruno Steindel, who had no great claims to personal pulchritude (some persons said he looked like a German bartender) but played the violoncello like an angel from heaven. I am not to be understood from what follows as implying that Mr. Steindel was more careless about his personal appearance than another man; so far as I can learn no one has ever been able to devise a posture of perfectly Apollonian grace while operating upon the violoncello. One week he was to be the soloist, playing Boellman's "Variations Symphoniques." He was rehearsing with the orchestra when I came in. After a time Mr. Thomas called someone to take the baton, left the stage, and came and sat down in the parquet near me.

"Well," he whispered, "what do you think?"

Of course I said that the performance was great.

"H-m-m," said he. "Do you see anything wrong?"

I said I did not.

"Hah," said he, "poor eye—very poor."

He strode down to the front, reached over the footlights, grasped Mr. Steindel's two feet, one in each hand, lifted them and planted them in positions far from those they had before occupied. Then he stepped back and observed the effect of the

---

[1]Upton, at p. 225 of *Reminiscence and Appreciation*, has a somewhat different version of this anecdote. I tell it as it was told to me.

changes, Mr. Steindel (with pathetic gravity) and the whole orchestra continuing the while to saw away. Next Mr. Thomas took a pencil from his pocket and marked on the stage the place for each Steindel foot. The difference was that before, the posture of Mr. Steindel had seemed a little awkward, not quite right, not sufficiently graceful, and now it seemed at ease and admirable. I doubt if anybody else, save possibly some specialist in such things, could have told what was wrong with the first pose, but certainly it gave one a vague discomfort of inharmony and therefore opposed one of Thomas's pet theories. Most conductors would have deemed it a thing too small to bother about. Thomas held that nothing was too small to bother about if related to the transfer of the feeling of the music.

He had a galvanic sense of humor but it was sometimes slightly saturnine. By the time he had reached sixty he had encountered the all-but-universal misfortune of civilized man and was becoming bald. The great stage of the Auditorium was a drafty place and his preternatural physical sensitiveness embraced the belief that he was an easy victim of colds; more than ever now because of the thin thatch left on his head. He determined to wear headgear at the rehearsals, and after the manner of a grim humor, appeared one day in a kind of jockey cap, light blue and velvet, I think, with a long peak. So helmeted he led the rehearsals. The next week a more orderly headgear, a black silk cap made by Mrs. Thomas, was to be observed. But as this did not provide for the concerts, where the stage drafts were all unabated, he came finally to admit that he must resort to a toupee. He got it, unusually well made and of a handsome gray. The first time he was to appear at a rehearsal thus accoutered he waited in his room until the players were in their places. Then he marched out before their astonished gaze and turned his back.

"Now laugh," said he, and added with peculiar emphasis, "once!"

He had boundless contempt for the musicians that went about seeking to advertise their calling in their dress or neckties. Except for the jockey cap, which was by way of jest, he was always attired with the utmost simplicity and compelled his players to go likewise. Changes among the personnel were few, but at the beginning of each season there were usually one or two new hands. Once there came a nice young man that could never have heard about the Thomas rule of unobtrusive demeanor, for he had luxuriant locks abundantly cultivated and wore a long flowing tie with other insignia of the tribe artistic. I saw him come in thus upholstered and wondered how long he or his outfit would last. Less than a day, apparently, for at the next rehearsal the youth appeared with a chastened demeanor and his hair well cropped. One of the players gave me the cue to the transformation. He said that throughout the first rehearsal Thomas had eyed the hirsute youth with manifest disfavor and at the end motioned him aside. Some of the amused players lingered to hear and see what should follow. Mr. Thomas, with his arms akimbo, stood and gazed sardonically at the waving field of hair. Then he laid a finger on the young man's arm and said with no unkind accent:

"Practice—practice—not pomade—makes the artist."

The young man went out and asked the way to a barber shop.

Another occasional attendant at rehearsals was Frau Lilli Lehmann, and she has with feeling told her gratitude for what they brought to her. She says that once she noticed in the tone quality of the orchestra something she had never found before. She gave herself up to the enchantment of it and presently discovered that it was of a double origin. First, the bowing together (which Thomas first of all the conductors of the world introduced), and second a subtle skill with which the different classes of instruments were introduced. When the wood winds came in they "suited their tone and sound color exactly to the instruments that had preceded them. Therefore they were not shrill or inharmonious as we are accustomed to hear them, but mingled with soft unobtrusiveness and melodiously in the volume of tone without one perceiving where they or the other instruments came in and dropped out."

She says she was at a rehearsal one morning when Thomas, after a pause, resumed work and then suddenly stopped, crying out:

"But, children, tune your instruments. It is quite unbearable!"

She says that she had a keen ear but was unable to detect anything wrong. She thought that later she might have been able to hear what Thomas had heard.[1]

The man that could fight his way through against determined opposition and could hold to his purpose in wreck and disaster, was yet so sensitive that a single harsh word or rude encounter might echo in him for hours, unsuspected by his fellows. One day Manager Wessels was in his office, bowed over some accounts, when the door was opened part way and Thomas thrust his head through the aperture.

"Busy?" says he.

"I have some things here that must be attended to," says Wessels, "but they can wait. What can I do for you?"

"Want to buy a hat," says Thomas from the doorway, in a tragic whisper, hand to his mouth.

"By all means, let's get the hat," says Wessels, and closes his desk.

In the hat store he takes the salesman aside, knowing fairly well what is the matter, explains who the visitor is and what he wants. The salesman smilingly brings out Mr. Thomas's idea of a hat, a simple, old-fashioned, unobtrusive felt. Mr. Wessels assures him that it is a good hat, perfect in fit and right in shape and Mr. Thomas goes back content, the new hat on his head.

---

[1] *My Pathway Through Life,* pp. 344–346. She adds: "Thomas was a man, take him all in all, to whom I should like to erect a monument, for he was a sound kernel in a rough shell."

The trouble had been that the last time he tried to buy a hat alone the salesman was impudent and offensive and the effect of that disagreeable experience still lingered in his mind.

He was then spending his summers at Felsengarten, returning to Chicago early in September. He told me once that the next four weeks after his return were to him the hardest of the year. They comprised what he called his "fighting rehearsals." Through the long summer vacation the members of the orchestra were playing helter-skelter, in summer gardens, theaters, for dances, under any chance leadership or none at all. In that time they drifted so far away from the symphony form that four weeks of drill were required to get them back to standard. This will seem wonderful only to those that have not glimpsed the peculiarly and unreasonably sensitive elements in the orchestral equation. Why, it is a fact that even from Saturday night to Monday morning, while the season was in full swing, the men would fall off, so that the Monday morning rehearsal was always the hardest. Monday was a hard day at best with Thomas, so full of cares and troubles that he did not go home until night and always had luncheon in his room with Mr. Wessels and some friend or friends. Once I stumbled in there when he was presiding at this repast. His desk was the table, and two or three towels made a tablecloth. In the center was a great bottle of beer, I should think a half-gallon bottle. The bill of fare was brief: a few thin sandwiches. When the scanty portions had disappeared, Mr. Thomas curled himself up in Mr. Wessels's chair, tucked his short legs under him, and observed with portentous gravity and a twinkling eye:

"It's funny you wouldn't offer a man a cigar."

In that chair his legs were not long enough to reach the floor, Mr. Wessels being the taller. The cigar being supplied and lighted, he looked about the circle, emitted a curl of smoke and said, swinging his legs emphatically:

"Listen. I have an observation to make. The curse of civilization is so many long-legged men. This world will never be truly right until they are massacred."

He felt strongly about the composers he admired and was always a little hurt when others failed to see in them the spiritual qualities he discerned. For a long time he thought Richard Strauss came near to Beethoven in the worth of his message, but after the appearance of the "Sinfonia Domestica" he concluded that Strauss was drifting out to sea. For "Death and Transfiguration" he had a profound reverence. While his admiration for Strauss was at its height, he was sitting one day at his desk, pencil in hand, sketching his programs for weeks in advance, as was his habit. Just then the figure of Manager Wessels passed the door.

"Come here a minute," said Thomas. "I am going to ask your advice. I will not promise to take it, but I'm going to ask for it. If you were making up a program and had the choice between Strauss's 'Thus Spake Zarathustra' and his 'Heldenleben,' which would you prefer?"

The moment was a trifle delicate for Wessels, who knew how strongly Thomas was drawn to Strauss and how he felt about all good artists. He warded off the question by bringing up a matter concerning the orchestra's business while with the other side of his mind he hunted for a good way to convey his opinion. At last he said:

"I was in a barber shop the other day to have my hair cut. When the barber was through he leaned over me and said:

"'Sea foam or dry shampo,' sah? Have you any preference, sah?' I said:

"'Yes, I have a strong preference. I prefer to have neither.'"

Thomas laughed a little, pulled his mustache a little, and with his pencil crossed both items from his list.

When he was aroused on a topic that interested him and there was no rehearsal or concert at hand, he talked easily, fluently, and with speech illuminated with research. There never was a better host at a dinner table, or one more charming. But about ordinary matters, he thought if a thing was settled it was settled, and why expend breath upon it?

Somebody asked him what kind of a performer on the horn he was in the days of his engagement in the naval band at Portsmouth.

"Damn bad," says Thomas, without hesitation or a quiver of mirth.

I once asked him to tell me the story of the American Opera Company. He told it. He said:

"Good intentions, bad management, no money."

His terminology was not only terse but satisfying. The question has often been rasied in late years what he would have thought of modern music if it had appeared in his time. I think I can contribute an indication of his probable attitude. In the years that I have now in mind I had often to go to New York and so utilized the chance to observe how and what the Eastern orchestras were doing. On one such visit a famous organization brought out with press trumpetings a new symphony by a budding German composer, who, I think, must have continued in the bud, for I have not since encountered his name on any program. At the time he was being hailed by some of the serious thinkers in music as the one sign of dawning in an otherwise desolate world. The composition with which he had favored us just then was a forerunner and most admirable specimen of what later developed into the cubist or ultra-modern school. So nearly as I could make out, it depicted life in a madhouse, a large, teeming madhouse, situated somewhere on the East Side of New York, near the elevated railroad, and in a street where there was much trucking on bad pavements. The first two movements seemed devoted to hysteria, the third to an interesting study of the pathology of acute mania, while the last, in which the elevated railroad fell down while all the inmates of the asylum screamed at once in different keys over a background of fish horns was one of the most remarkable things I had ever heard.

A considerable part of the audience received this contraption with ecstasy, a sure enough sign of the antiquity of a well-known affectation. I understood in New York that a copy of the work had been sent to Mr. Thomas with the expectation that he would give it a Chicago premier, and his judgment on it was awaited with interest. When I returned I mentioned to him casually that I had heard the composition in New York and it had seemed to be viewed with favor. He said:

"Musical mud."

For a man that lived by public favor, he had more capacity for self-effacement than any other I have known. I have mentioned elsewhere his singular lack of vanity, but he went far beyond the negative state of the virtue. At the close of each number of his program, while the audience was applauding the effort, he invariably managed to convey the impression that he was acknowledging the praise on behalf of the players but disclaiming it for himself. The exact means of this communication were mysterious to strangers but the effect was always the same. The conductor was merged in the company.[1]

One of my experiences with him illustrates the same rare trait. At a time when publicity might be of inestimable assistance to him and his projects, it fell to my lot to write for the magazine that then had the largest circulation and influence an article about him and his work. Some points being uncertain or disputed I must besiege him with questions. It was a case of taciturn witness and persistent examiner. He answered succinctly and kindly, but never volunteered a line of his own and displayed as lively an interest in the matter as he might in an article about the Parliament of Dijon. But one day, before I was done with the writing, Mrs. Thomas called me on the telephone

---

[1]Conf. Upton, *Reminiscence and Appreciation*, p. 223.

at my office and said that Mr. Thomas had thought of one request he should like to make about my article.

"Only too glad," said I. "What can I do for Mr. Thomas?"

"Mr. Thomas would like to have you say something nice
about the New York Philharmonic Society."

I thought of the many ladies and gentlemen in the musical
and theatrical way that had, in my observation, made obei-
sance before the merest chance of a splash of printer's ink and
concluded I had here something truly unusual.

He had much to do with the furthering of orchestral music in
America but nothing with the singular superstition that the
conductor produces all the music, causing it to flow at his will
out of the small end of his baton. I think he would have been
much amazed if he could have looked ahead and seen the extent
to which the public he was tutoring was to be ensnared with
this childlike belief. Since it is the fact that the conductor's real
work is done at rehearsals and not before the public, and since
he was so hard set against all affectations, he never pretended
anything to the contrary. With patient labor he drilled his
players to play each composition as he desired to have it played.
When the public performance came on he gave them the time
and with his left hand conveyed intelligences to them, but he
never did a sand dance about the platform and his every movement was not only graceful, as I have said, but usually restrained. I doubt he would be found for the fashion of these
times; Rutgers Square would not believe that he was conducting at all. Nevertheless, his methods must be admitted to have
had one advantage: they never diverted the thought of the
auditor from the music by impinging with a fear that the conductor was about to fall off the platform or leap through the
sky-border.

In yet another respect he was out of the present fashion. The
method of certain modern conductors, by which they signal os-
tentatiously to each variety of instrument when it shall come

in, never occurred to this simple soul. His naïve conviction was that if the gentlemen that played the oboe did not know enough to come in without being hooked in by a conductor's long prehensile forefinger they did not know enough to play at all and promptly rid himself of their presence. This was a benefaction to the men that remained, since it saved them any chance of an annoyance sometimes to be observed with pain in a later day, when the conductor signals in the wrong place. The discerning in Thomas's audiences shared in this good fortune. Nothing can be more disturbing to the thoughtful mind than to see a robustious leader signaling to the trombones to come in when the score requires the trombones to stay out.

Yet he had his own affluent means of communicating his purposes to the men that played before him. So far as the audience could see, he was doing little more than to beat the time with his right hand and baton, a thing that always caused grumbling among the superficial, if they had been used to directorial gymnastics. What the audience could not see was his face and eyes, eloquent with feeling and command, and the all-controlling movements of his left hand. This he held so that only the players could see it and to them it was never inarticulate. When he desired increasing emphasis he beckoned with it, palm toward himself; when he wished restraint he turned the palm the other way and made a repressing gesture. In the crescendo passages it rose; in diminuendo it was lowered. In all this as in so many other devices of his, the thought was to offer to the listener no distracting suggestions, but allow him to concentrate his mind on the music and nothing else.

I think the colors of music were as real to him as the color of glad grass is to us. I think he had no mental question about their reality. We may believe that since Tyndal and Merkel no one has been more profoundly engaged in inquiries as to the physics of musical sounds. The theory that the musical scale is a kind of spectrum with dark tints for the low and light for the high is held now by many persons. So far as I have been able to discover, he worked it out for himself before he had read any suggestion of it from others.

In his later years new musical compositions were shot at him from the ends of the earth and all the way between. He used to read them from the scores. He would say to Mr. Wessels:

"I have a new symphony by Humdinger. I'm trying it out. The colors seem to be about right. If they are, we shall do it at the concert of January 22," or some other date about six weeks ahead. In another day or two he would put his head in at Mr. Wessels's door and say: "The colors are all right in that, Humdinger. I have put it down for January 22."

About this time, Mr. Henry E. Voegeli, who was afterward so prominent in the business affairs of the orchestra, joined it as assistant manager and went ahead of one of its tours. He was then young and inexperienced in the managerial mysteries, but he did his work so excellently that Mr. Thomas sent for him to thank him personally, which was a way he had about such things. Mr. Voegeli, who was almost as much embarrassed as gratified by a recognition he had never expected, protested that what he had done was a little thing and not worth noticing.

"Young man, let me tell you something that I have learned in a long and fairly active life," said Thomas. "Every big thing is only a conglomerate of little things. Anybody that will look well after the little things will find the big thing taking care of itself."

His sense of punctuality amounted to an obsession; it is not fanciful to say that one could set one's watch by his appearance on the concert stage. In many years he had never varied from his rule of reaching the rehearsal at least fifteen minutes before its appointed time. For concerts he was usually in his room a full hour in advance. This habit had become so fixed upon him that if he was to take a train at ten o'clock he would appear at the station at nine. He would not tolerate tardiness;

it seemed to him the unpardonable crime in anybody—star or trombone player, it made no difference to him. Mr. Upton tells a story that shows the trait to have been early manifested and therefore, one may guess, inherent. It was away back in the days when Thomas was conducting opera in New York for Impresario Ullmann. Madame Frezzolini was the prima donna. A rehearsal had been called. Frezzolini exercised her prima donna prerogative and was late. Thomas sent the orchestra home and there was no rehearsal. When Ullmann, fuming, demanded that somebody be discharged, Thomas replied:

"Certainly. Discharge me. I am the only one responsible. If you don't and Signora Frezzolini continues to come late to rehearsals I will discharge myself."[1]

No excuse was accepted for tardiness; if a man was "bridged" in the old days in Chicago he could always use the tunnel. Or let him start early enough so that there need be no chance of accidents. Better an hour of waiting at the hall than ten minutes' delay on the stage.

Once, when the Chicago orchestra was on tour, Thomas, after an evening concert, called one of the 'cello players and the two had a midnight luncheon. Finding a billiard hall open, they went in and played billiards for an hour, after which they sat in the hotel office and told stories until three o'clock. A rehearsal had been called the next morning for ten. Thomas, as was his wont, appeared fifteen minutes ahead of time, looking as fresh and cool as Herrick's primrose filled with morning dew, which was also his wont. He could live easily on three hours of sleep. The 'cellist was absent and did not appear for twenty minutes. When he came Mr. Thomas laid down the baton and regarded him with a brow of thunder.

"Mr. Blank," he said sharply, "why do you come late to rehearsal?"

[1] *Reminiscence and Appreciation*, pp. 121-122.

"Why, Mr. Thomas," gasped the offender in much surprise, "you know how late it was when I went to bed."

"Late?" snapped Mr. Thomas. "How do you mean—late?" Then looking at him icily and without a glint of humor: "Why, where on earth did you go after you left me?"

Punctuality, accuracy—they were deities in his religion. I have not known another man so rectangular. When he decided to bring out the "Love Scene" from Richard Strauss's "Feuersnot" he believed it would be the first performance of the piece in America and so announced on the programs, which were printed some weeks in advance. Afterward he learned that on the same afternoon Walter Damrosch was to perform "Feuersnot" in New York. He obtained a copy of Mr. Damrosch's full program and saw that, whereas his own performance would come at 2.45 Chicago time, that of Mr. Damrosch would be at 3 o'clock, New York time. By the clock, therefore, he would be playing the piece before Mr. Damrosch. But in actuality, when he should start upon it, Mr. Damrosch would have come to the end of it. He had all the programs and announcements changed and the words "First time in America" stricken out.

He had funny little ways. At a concert, if the orchestra acquitted itself well, he would leave the score on the stand and make to the players a slight bow before he turned to acknowledge the plaudits of the audience. If the playing did not suit him he would drop the score on the floor and omit the bow. In that event it was fairly certain that the composition would reappear before long on his program, and meanwhile there would be diligent rehearsing and some rebukes.

Cool reasoning lay back of some of his noted peculiarities. Thus he always had two of everything—carried two watches, two pencils, two keys to each lock. The stopping of a watch or breaking of a mainspring was not to be allowed to interfere with the Thomasian punctuality. Two batons were always laid upon his stand with his scores. Twice I saw demonstrated the wisdom of this precaution. In an energetic movement the tip of the baton he was wielding caught in the music stand and was wrenched from his right hand. With his left he picked up the extra baton lying before him and proceeded without difficulty or interruption.

Someone asked him, not without scorn, about his habit of going to the concert hall or railroad station an hour ahead of the scheduled time. He said:

"Suppose the cab should break down? Suppose there should be a traffic jam? I have never missed an engagement. I will take no chances on missing one now."

He seemed to dislike to have himself referred to as in any way unusual or phenomenal. I once caused him annoyance by printing a story I had been told (not by him) that illustrated his remarkable powers of hearing. It was at a rehearsal for his great New York Musical Festival of 1882. He had an augmented company, including thirty-six violoncellos. The full orchestra was rehearsing a Wagnerian selection when he detected an error by a 'cellist at the last stand, went to him, and set him straight. He seemed to think an important item had been omitted in this account that divested the incident of any unusual quality. It lay in this, that noticing the wrong playing at the last 'cello stand, he looked in that direction and saw a player's hand in the wrong position. It was therefore perfectly easy to detect him and the instance was merely an ordinary one of fair eyesight. I do not know that his explication made the thing the less wonderful. In the midst of such billows of sound he caught the wrong notes.

He had one of those hard-gripping and indefeasible memories that are so intolerably annoying to the rest of us, having them not. He seemed never to forget anything. About this time he was making a tour with the orchestra throughout the Southern states. Late one night they came to a town where they must stay until morning for a train connection. As they were waiting in the hotel office for their baggage they heard a distant whistling.

"What's that?" asked one.

"Sounds like a locomotive," said another.

"Locomotive? Oh, no," said Mr. Thomas. "That's a steamboat on the Okmulgee River," or some such name.

It was. He had not heard such a steamer since the time more than forty years before, when as a boy he had traversed that region, but the note of it was tucked away somewhere in his infallible memory.

One year, just as the season was to open, Walfried Singer, the musician of whom I have before spoken, received an offer to appear at a concert in a neighboring town on Christmas Eve. To accept it he would have to be absent at the last of that week's morning rehearsals, a thing he knew Thomas was always against. Singer sought the assistance of Albert Ulrich, who for years filled the place of orchestral manager, quite different from that of manager of the orchestra. Mr. Ulrich consulted Mr. Thomas.

"Why, certainly," said Thomas, "if he has a good opening, let him go. We can get along without him at one rehearsal."

This was about eleven weeks before the time. Meanwhile the proposed concert fell through and Singer's engagement was canceled. He did not think it worth while to mention the fact to anybody, and on Thursday morning of Christmas week appeared at the rehearsal as usual.

"Hello!" said Thomas, as he filed past. "I thought you were to be absent to-day."[1]

I think he scorned everything in the nature of theatrics or posing; self-exploitation he loathed. In looking over his old programs (and he invariably drew up his programs with his own hand and sent the copy himself to the printer) I notice that he never once allowed himself to appear there with the

---

[1] Mason, at p. 202, has another illustration.

prefix "Mr." before his name, but merely as "Theo. Thomas."
Even when he was to be a soloist among other listed soloists,
this was the rule; even when he shared the conductorship with
another. "Conductors Mr. J. Mosenthal, Theo. Thomas";
"Soloists, Mr. August Kriesmann, Mr. George Matzka, Theo.
Thomas." He despised titles, great and small. All men he
called by their last names, if he knew them well; even famous
soloists. The only exception I have heard of was the case of
Mason, for whom he had a peculiar affection; Mason was always
"William." "We know each other well enough to drop these
stupid formalities," he said once to George Upton,[1] suggesting
that they cut out the "Mr." in addressing each other.

He was an iron-willed autocrat while he was rehearsing and
an easy-going democrat about everything else. He believed in
giving everybody a chance, and otherwise than as artists all
men looked about alike to him. Once in Cincinnati there had
been, after the last evening Festival performance, one of the
celebrations that the orchestra was accustomed to hold on gala
occasions. This lasted late. As usual, Thomas led all the fun.
It was daybreak when they emerged upon the street. At that
hour there were neither cabs nor street cars to be found, and
Thomas was a long distance from home. Someone commiserated
him upon the dismal walk ahead of him.

"Walk!" says Thomas. "I'm not going to walk. See that
milk cart? That goes up my way. I'm going home on that."

He summoned the astonished driver, hopped into the narrow
seat, put a cigar into his own mouth and another into the
driver's, and went off, gently humming "The Evening Star."

I have not known of another conductor that pursued so
resolutely the practice of affording his men a chance to appear
as soloists. Since soloists were necessary, why not pick them
from our own ranks? seemed to be his idea. At one time he had,
if I remember rightly, four in his first violin choir that had been

[1]*Reminiscence and Appreciation*, p. 248.

thus distinguished. Solo performances by 'cellists, harpists, viola players, clarinetists, flutists, oboists, the organist, and even by bass violinists are scattered through his programs. Some of the men had been with him for years and looked upon him as a father. Dear old Mr. Beckel, for instance, so many years his principal in the bass violin group. I suppose that if he had become convinced that Theodore Thomas's plans and the welfare of music in America required his death, he would have asked for two glasses of beer and then sent for the hemlock.

But I think that, speaking broadly, Thomas did not care for soloists and rather regarded the placing of them on programs as a concession to Philistia, a thing necessary but not really consistent with the best ideals and unpalatable to persons of a mature mind. Besides, his business was to teach orchestral music, the illimitable range of which should be enough for any rational being. He was a little disposed to sniff at the undeniable but hardly inspiring fact that many persons came to hear a famous soloist merely as they would go to see an okapi and with as little desire to be elated. Whether the performance was good or bad could make little difference to these. Yet he had delight in any competent artist appearing in concerto or otherwise, and among the soloists had some of his dearest friends; as Paderewski, for one example. He never forgot that he himself had been a concerto player, and regarded the violin concerto as perfectly legitimate and admirable, but always in his mind gulped a little at the piano's intrusion in these fields. "God never intended the piano to be played with an orchestra," he said.

He had also this peculiarity, that he was in great things or small always mindful of the rights and welfare of the audience. Their minds must not be distracted by sight or sound from the mood in which they could best receive the message of the music. It was partly for this reason that he introduced the uniform

bowing and why he held himself in restraint while he was conducting. Everything must be seemly, in good order, unobtrusive, harmonious. Suppose a player to show a striking peculiarity of dress. "Oh, see the man with the big necktie" some mind
in the a· ʹience would remark, and so remarking might lose
one of those strains in a symphony that he regarded as vital.
He allowed no sprawling about in their chairs by the players,
no conversation among them, and no act that might draw the
least comment. And, oh, boon beyond price, he allowed no
tuning on the stage before a performance!

Once we had for soloist a young woman from Boston, a brilliant violinist, but at that time young, very young, and as sub-
sequently appeared, nervous. At the rehearsal all had gone
well, but when she came out to play at the Friday afternoon
concert, she discovered that the position of the dais on which
Thomas stood was not to her liking and demanded to have it
moved. This grossly violated in more ways than one the Thomasian idea of the proprieties; also his rule about smooth performances. He would not delay the concert by calling for a
stage hand, so he himself shifted the stand to the lady's liking,
but, by this time, knowing him fairly well, I could see that he
was boiling with indignation. She should have mentioned at
rehearsal her preference about position and not have waited
until the audience was there. His theory about the relation of
mental moods to quality of orchestral performance was justified
that afternoon. The concerto did not go well and this young
woman did not play again with the Chicago orchestra.

I seldom knew him at rehearsal to play any composition,
except a novelty, all the way through. His practice was to pick
out the weak and difficult spots and drill at these until they
were perfect.

One reason for his potent influence upon his men was the
deep respect they had for his musicianship, first, and then for
his transparent integrity. The world at large is easily fooled by

FELSENGARTEN
Thomas's home in the White Mountains

FREDERICK J. WESSELS
For many years Thomas's friend, confidant, and business manager

pretentious incompetence, but two bodies here below are not fooled at all. A ship captain may fool his passengers, his owners, his underwriters, the press, and the public; he cannot fool his crew. With them, either he knows his business or he does not. It is so with the members of a grand orchestra and their leader. Conductors have been known in orchestral annals that lived and had honor and grew fat and died renowned whose men would crouch behind their stands that they might not see the baton's eccentric gyrations. Some there have been that were the subject of their players' everlasting mirth, and some whose players ran habitually half a beat behind. No such filigrees adorn the story of Theodore Thomas. Baton and men proceeded in faultless harmony and at the end all sound of all instruments seemed cut off as if with one huge knife, sharp and clean.

At one of the last rehearsals I attended everything went well, the difficult points were smoothed out easily, the tonality seemed perfect. About half-past eleven Thomas laid down his baton, made his little bow, and said, "Well done, children, well done! We can all go home now. Thank you, children!" He turned on them his big, kindly, genial smile. I had heard him say that before, and never thought that day I should not hear him say it again.

CHAPTER XIV
The Home-Coming

BUT what we are most concerned with is the development of the orchestra in America and the growth of musical taste.

How far the educational urge had reached in the next season in Chicago, 1901–1902, may be gauged from the fact that Thomas was able to go beyond his Beethoven boundaries of the previous year and to produce a "historical cycle" of six programs illustrating the evolution of orchestral music from the Sonata "Piane Forte," of Giovanni Gabrieli, Sixteenth Century, down to the Symphonie Pathétique of Tschaikowsky. Each of the six contained a symphony; the first, the second, and the last had two each. One of the features of the first evening was C. P. E. Bach's Symphony No. 1 in D major from the early part of the Eighteenth Century, which, as we have seen, was first played in the United States by Thomas on September 18, 1862. The other symphony of that evening was Haydn's E Flat. For the last program he played Brahms's Fourth (which may be regarded as doing fairly well in an educational way), Tschaikowsky's Sixth and the second piano concerto of Saint-Saëns. Other symphonies played in this cycle were Mozart's C major (K.551), Schubert's Eighth (B minor —the Unfinished), Beethoven's Third, Schumann's Third (Rhenish), and Berlioz's "Symphonie Fantastique." Surely here was a testing of the musical spirit in any community!

If his art was manifestly triumphant, his own life within himself continued to be sorely tried. I have spoken of the strength in him of the family tie. He had always been bound up in his children. In December, 1901, he was hit hard by the sudden death of his eldest son, Franz C. Thomas. The circumstances were strangely pathetic. It seemed as if this head were doomed beyond others to bear blows. The orchestra, which was more like a great family than a casual band of hired performers, cherished the custom of giving from time to time social and merry entertainments for themselves and their friends. These took place after an evening concert and were enlivened with burlesque, comic plays, and jests. Thomas was the life of such jocundity. He could enter into it with zest and loose upon it his singularly happy resources in fun making. The news of the death of Franz Thomas came on an evening when such an entertainment had been scheduled. The stricken father not only led the orchestra through the concert that evening, but he compelled himself to go through with the hilarity. Except to his friend Wessels, he would not so much as mention the misfortune that had fallen upon him.[1]

"If the members of the orchestra know of it," he said, "they will of course call off to-night's merrymaking. It will only spoil the evening for them."

The funeral took place in New York on a Friday afternoon. Mr. Wessels urged Mr. Thomas to cancel the Friday afternoon concert and go to New York for the funeral.

"I have no right to make the public mourn with me," said Mr. Thomas. "I have never missed a concert in my life. My duty is to stay here."

He led the concert that afternoon at the very hour when he knew his son's body was being laid in the earth.

His own ill health continued to increase, complicated with these griefs. He began to be aware that the end was approaching. A profound seriousness fell upon him, and as if to express what he felt of resignation and religious exaltation, he chose for the feature of the next Cincinnati Festival, which he thought

---

[1]Otis, p. 130.

would be the last he should conduct, Bach's Mass in B minor, that massive and splendid work. He seemed to have purposed to make this occasion, if it should indeed prove to be the last of his labors in Cincinnati, a kind of monument, for he devoted two years to its study. I have never heard of another instance where a conductor went to such lengths to secure accuracy and adequacy. He read everything about Bach that had been printed in English, French, German. He scrutinized every note and tested it. Says Mrs. Thomas justly of this colossal endeavor:

The score in which the results of his labors were annotated is unique in the world, for it represents the consensus of the opinions of all the great Bach experts of both Europe and America. There was not a trill nor a turn in the entire work that he did not study separately and write out in full, nor an instrument indicated that was not faithfully employed, although some of them had to be made especially and learned by the orchestra.[1]

One thing he was prevented by modern conditions from reproducing. He could not use in the great music hall of Cincinnati the small orchestra that was customary in Bach's time, but he made one of the same balance.

As a contrast to this classical orthodoxy, he gave Berlioz's Requiem Mass, and loosened the thunders. Besides an augmented orchestra, he had a brass band in each of the four corners of the stage, sixteen kettle drums, ten pairs of cymbals, a great chorus and the organ, and when all joined the effect was stupendous. He used at that festival four orchestras of different dimensions. Two hundred musicians played in the Berlioz Mass, 129 in the Bach Mass, 93 in the Beethoven Third Symphony, 100 in Wagner's "Meistersinger" Vorspiel. Of all the great festivals he conducted in Cincinnati, each a triumph of skill and scholarship, it seems to me this was the greatest.

---

[1] P. 496.

The season of 1903–1904 was marked by the visit to Chicago, at Mr. Thomas's invitation, of Richard Strauss. He appeared at the concerts of April 2 and 3, 1904, conducting his own tone poem, "Thus Spake Zarathustra," "Till Eulenspiegel," and the "Death and Transfiguration." Mme Strauss came with him and sang his songs. One of the largest audiences the Auditorium ever held listened to these concerts and gave the composer an extraordinary welcome. No other maker of music of his time was so well known to Chicago; Thomas had made him so. He held one rehearsal. When it was over, he took the orchestra by surprise with a little speech. He said:

Gentlemen, I came here in the pleasant expectation of finding a superior orchestra, but you have far surpassed my expectations, and I can say to you that I am delighted to know you as an orchestra of artists in whom beauty of tone, technical perfection and discipline are found in the highest degree. Gentlemen, such a rehearsal as that which we have held this morning is no labor but a great pleasure, and I thank you all for the hearty goodwill you have shown toward me.[1]

At the Cincinnati Festival of 1904, the last Thomas conducted, he gave Beethoven's "Missa Solemnis" and Ninth Symphony, which he regarded as almost the climax of Beethoven's greatness.

The programs for the regular orchestral season of 1903–1904 were the best he ever made and reveal a kind of farewell to his work as well as a consciousness of the advance that his constituency had achieved. Mrs. Thomas thinks that he desired to play all the greatest works in orchestral literature that he might hear them once more before he should leave them forever; the last salute of a musician to the masters he had loved and the cause he had served.

If he was easily deceived in business, he had a marvelous intuition about artists. Some persons have said that by merely

---

[1]March 31, 1904. Mrs. Thomas has this at p. 503.

looking at a candidate and hearing him talk he could tell, and err not, how much was real, how much paste. No doubt this belongs to the realm of fiction usually surrounding men that achieve, yet a singular thing happened this year to sustain the theory of his almost wizard intuition. There sat in the second row of the viola choir a young man of quiet bearing and unobtrusive ways, whose contributions to the orchestra had consisted of being always and promptly in his place, discharging his duties faithfully and playing the viola ably. Of a sudden the announcement was made that Thomas had chosen this young man, whose name was Frederick Stock, to be assistant conductor of the orchestra, a place unknown before in the Thomas story. Amazement sat upon many brows.

"What on earth does the Old Man think he has discovered now?" was the general comment. It appeared that Mr. Stock was without experience as a conductor and did not himself know what he could do with his new post. I may say that no one was more astonished than I, for I had long before picked the man that I thought was destined to succeed Mr. Thomas, and it was not Mr. Stock. The first violins in those days had a magnificent unison, tonality, and finish, and to my mind the next great conductor was to come from among their number, and I thought I could name him. Some of Mr. Thomas's friends even went to the length of inquiring of him in an injured way about this man Stock. I record with pride the fact that I was not among these, being capable of many foolish things but not quite of this one. Inquirers had for their pains little besides grim smile or cryptic sarcasm. One related to me that he fared still worse. "I think I am old enough and have been in this business long enough to know what I am about," said Thomas. It seems that the conversation ended abruptly at this point.

He certainly knew in this instance, at least. The man that he chose in such clairvoyant fashion turned out to be an orchestral genius, a conductor of extraordinary gifts, a marvelous student, interpreter, and educator, able to take up Mr. Thomas's work, carry it on, extend it; a man destined in his own way to be another great influence upon the life of Chicago and its musical development. Chicago owes to Theodore Thomas more than it can ever express by monuments or otherwise, and eminent in the list is his unerring prescience in the discovery of Frederick Stock.

He went to Felsengarten that summer of 1904, wearied from the exertions of the Cincinnati Festival and oppressed with the feeling that it was the last time he would conduct that noble enterprise, but cheered in his depression by the promise that before he should pass, one dream of his life, and that the most persistently baffling, might be realized.

This is a peculiar story and deserves a chapter to itself as a revelation of the American community in one of its strangest aspects. We are to remember that all these years Mr. Thomas had been combating in himself a growing dissatisfaction with the limitations that hampered him. His heart, set upon achieving certain effects in his work, fretted and wore itself out against the things that continually frustrated him. To say to him that his public did not then share his chagrin nor know of it nor have the ability to understand it, was all idle. The point with him was that if he had the chance to do what he wished to do, the public would come in time to understand all, rise to it, be blessed by it. It was here as it had been with every other stage of his story. He thought ahead of his public. There had been a time when people were ready to revolt against the playing of a symphony; now they understood and loved it. There had been a time when people resented Wagner; now they worshipped in the Wagnerian fane. Just as they had not perceived once why he kept on with his symphonies and insisted upon Wagner, he knew he could not at that time expect them to see why he was wholly dissatisfied with the present situation.

At last he made up his mind to go no farther with it.

From the beginning he had known that the Auditorium was not the place for orchestral concerts. It was so big that to fill it with sound he was obliged to employ a stress all out of keeping with his ideas and purposes, a stress that obliterated the finer points he wished the public to seize and assimilate. The stage was so ill adapted to an orchestra's use that he regarded it as hopeless. In the season of 1903–1904 he told me that he had tried thirteen different arrangements, now with sounding boards, now with raised seats, with shut-in spaces, with this kind of background, then with that, all that his years of studies in acoustics could suggest, and none of them had proved tolerable. At one time he had the basses divided and arranged on each side, as the Monaco orchestra has them to this day. Then he had them strung in a line across the back. Then he tried having them doubled up all at his left hand. Nothing would prevent what was to his ears a deadly misch-masch of sound where his passion was for clarity and sweet reasonableness.

But the public was fond of the Auditorium, which was and is a beautiful place, admirably adapted to spectacles, operas, and public meetings. In some respects its acoustics are marvelous; a speaker, for instance, finds them virtually perfect. Then again, room was ample at the Auditorium; it was so huge! If a Chicagoan had visiting friends, he knew that any time before the performance he could get seats. It was a comfortable place; one felt at ease there. At the suggestion that it was not adapted to the orchestra, citizens would have been amazed and exasperated. It was the place where they had learned to love Theodore Thomas and his work, and in such instances the sense of locality is like the sense of home. There were hundreds of good people in Chicago that would have been sure they could not enjoy that orchestra in any other hall.

Yet throughout the season of 1902–1903 Thomas felt more

and more that the place had become impossible. If any results were to survive his labors, the orchestra must have a permanent home. If the Chicago public was ever to reach that stage of musical perception and development he had hoped for it, he must have a hall where he could show veritable effects. Finally, he had that strong feeling that for him the end was not far off. If he was to realize his ambition he must move swiftly.

Slowly, a little amazedly, Chicago awoke to the fact that it faced a crisis about the orchestra of which it had been so proud. Mr. Thomas had made to the trustees of the Association a declaration in the shape of an ultimatum and one that seemed to many persons finicky, arbitrary, and unreasonable. He had announced that other quarters must be had for the orchestra or he would leave it.[1]

"It is useless to attempt to make an orchestra permanent without its own building," he said. "I found this to be the case in New York, and was obliged to give up my orchestra there for lack of such a building. Conditions in Chicago are similar. We now have here a large and cultivated public that demands the highest forms of music, and, I believe, would not be willing to give up the orchestra. But what is everybody's business is nobody's business, and the people will do nothing unless the situation is brought before them very strongly. I therefore ask you to announce to the general public that, unless in the next six months a sufficient endowment can be raised to provide a suitable building in which to carry on the work of our institution, I shall resign my position here and go elsewhere. I take this course because I believe it is the only way to arouse the public to quick and decisive action, and also because if it fails to do so, I think it is better to disband the orchestra now, before it piles up another large debt for the Association to pay."

The first reaction to this cool demand was almost of resent-

---

[1]The interesting documents pertaining to this story are printed in full by Otis, pp. 134–145.

ment. What was the matter with the Auditorium? It was well known to be one of the best public halls in the world. What was the matter with Mr. Thomas? The audiences were steadily increasing, the deficit was diminishing,[1] why disturb a prospect so pleasing? There would always be found in Chicago enough public-spirited men to make up any loss. Was Theodore Thomas becoming senile?

But there he stood, as so often before, immovable in his purposes. As so often before, if he had been more communicative to the public, he would have found his path easier. The press agent is the chief engineer of modern success; Theodore Thomas never grasped the fact. True to his own tradition, he said nothing more, and it was left to the rest of us to make the public understand the necessity of the change; the rest of us, with voices unauthoritative and, as it were, piping at second hand. I remember well the arguments we had to print, many times over, concerning the unsuitableness of the Auditorium and the advantages of a permanent home. I may say now, frankly, that at first we printed them without hope and as a matter of duty. I think there was not a newspaper man in Chicago that did not feel, as I felt, that the task was impossible.

The difficulties were too great. One that alone seemed insuperable was this feeling about the Auditorium. Men resented the criticisms upon it as an attack upon a local institution in one of the proudest communities on earth. Another that came near to wreck the whole project was a plan evolved from this feeling and aimed to placate it. Up to the end of the season of 1902–1903, or after eleven years of the experiment, the total expenses of the orchestra had been $1,383,000 and the box-office receipts $1,012,000; total deficit $371,000—in eleven seasons. But the orchestra was plainly winning its way. Let it stay two years more, or three, and it would become self-sustaining. If

---

[1]This was the common belief, but not quite justified. The receipts for the season of 1901–1902 were nearly $3,000 less than in the preceding season. (Otis, p. 136.)

anything was really wrong about the Auditorium, which all persons were reluctant to believe, remodel it so as to meet the objections of Mr. Thomas. These objections were mostly Greek to the man in the street, but anyway, they could surely be met. Then let us appeal for a guarantee fund to be placed at interest and provide with its income for any deficit.

To this the trustees would not consent, for a good and sufficient reason. Mr. Thomas would accept no compromise. With him it was all or nothing.

So, then, the trustees went forth to the testing that would determine whether the orchestra was to live or perish then and there. I should like to emphasize the remarkable fact that even in that moment of general doubt there were business men in Chicago that were not afraid of the issue but purposed to go ahead and do their duty by it no matter what might come. They now subscribed $100,000 and secured the option on a lot in Michigan Avenue as a site for the orchestra building, before any human being could feel reasonable confidence that there was to be any orchestra to house there. Stern moralists that are so fond of citing our derelictions in the way of materialism (and usually with grounds enough) should have their attention called to this pertinent fact; it shows the real Chicago better than many chapters about the smoke and the stockyards. Come, tell us: where else in the world was such a thing likely to happen? Where else, if we come to that, would anybody, at that time, have entertained the notion that a sufficient endowment fund for an orchestra could be raised by general subscription?

But we went at the task, some of us with wry faces and few with spontaneous enthusiasm. We told the public that unless this money should be raised, Mr. Thomas would end his long and honorable career by retiring under a defeat. We begged that the stigma of failure should not be placed upon Chicago, which had never before failed in anything. We retold the story of the growth of the musical interest in Chicago and its reaction upon the general life. The newspapers did this. They did it freely and ungrudgingly, as in Chicago the newspapers will always do anything that is plainly for the city's great welfare. They argued and pleaded and asked for subscriptions, and then we stood back to see what the results would be.

The money began to come in, not only from millionaires and such men of means as had hitherto paid the orchestra's deficit; it came from the public at large, including that great part of the public that is never supposed to know or care a stricken thing about classical music. The rich were asked to give, but it was the common run of humanity to whom we turned and that now spoke out. Working men, merchants, clerks, bookkeepers, school teachers, shop girls, scrub women—it is the most amazing thing I know of, but these were the people that responded. Between eight and nine thousand persons in the city of Chicago voluntarily sent in money to provide a symphony orchestra with a permanent home, sent in all told $750,000[1], and saved the day.

The announcement was made that enough had been secured to erect the building.

It was the summit and climax of Theodore Thomas's career. If he had been capable of self-exaltation he might have been puffed with just pride at a tribute without a parallel in history. He had gone through the depths of doubt and despondency when it seemed to him that all had been wasted and that essentially he had failed. He might now have seen that, instead of failing, he had won a strange and memorable success, for he had created the devotion to art that these people had so touchingly expressed, and there was probably not another man in the world that could have done it.

---

[1]The $100,000 paid for the option on the lot is not included in this sum. The $100,000 did not pay for the lot. It was necessary to give in addition a mortgage on it of $350,000. The men that subscribed the $100,000 turned it over at cost to the Orchestral Association. (Otis, p. 135.)

As soon as it was settled that the orchestra was to be saved and was to have, what no other orchestra had ever had, a permanent home built by the voluntary subscription of the public, Mr. Thomas brought out the plan that years before he had sketched for such a building.

"Notes on the Construction of Music Halls," it was called. It had reposed in his library until it had grown yellow. Now it came forth for to use. Daniel H. Burnham was the architect of the new building. He was Mr. Thomas's old-time friend and follower. So far as the limitations of the lot would allow, he put into practice every suggestion that Mr. Thomas had made. The exceptions were small and unimportant; in all essentials the building rose as he had imagined it. The dream was come true, the baffling road had an ending. The man that had been hammered so long by an uninformed press and pursued so long by disappointment and trouble had at last one unalloyed joy.

One other of less moment befell him in April of this year of 1904. I have mentioned the peculiar affection he cherished for the Philharmonic Society of New York, the organization he had joined as a boy and led to triumph as a man. One day there came a letter from the Philharmonics asking him to be their guest conductor and lead them in a concert in New York. They said:

It would be very delightful if you could open the season for us, but we should be only too glad if you could appear at the head of the orchestra at any concert of the season, at your choice. You are first in all our hearts, and we trust that you will give us the supreme pleasure of seeing you once more in the place where for so many years we loved to see you—at the conductor's desk of the Philharmonic Society of New York.

In the broken state of his health he felt that he could not undertake such a task, and declined it. The Philharmonics were not to be so answered. They sent to Chicago, Richard Arnold, so long their concert master, to argue and plead. Mr. Thomas was unable to resist this unusual mark of affection and esteem, and, against his judgment, finally consented to go.

The building had been assured before he left for Felsengarten. When he returned in the fall, it was well under way and architects and contractors promised it for early in December. But the satisfaction he felt in the fruition of his hopes in this one particular did not change his thought that he walked in the great shadow. About all he really hoped for now was that he might live to inaugurate the new building and adjust the orchestra to it. The doctors gave him no comfort. They reported that his heart was affected and his nervous system undone. He had more tangible signs of collapse in the failure at last of part of his remarkable auditory equipment. Because of the catarrh that had afflicted him, one ear had become almost totally deaf as the sight began to fail in one eye.

With an impulse that seems now pathetically expressive of what he must have had in his thoughts, he did not go at once from Felsengarten to Chicago at the close of the summer, as was his wont, but instead visited in Boston, Fairhaven, and New York, making a point of calling upon old friends and in effect bidding them good-bye, although he said no such word to anyone, and he still bore the old unruffled exterior.

The hope had been strong in him that the new hall might be ready for the beginning of the season. Delays had arisen, the inevitable delays. He was hit hard when he found that the first concerts of the new season must be given in the Auditorium. More than ever he was beset with the goading thought that he might not live to enter the new home. For the first time in his life he showed an extreme irritability.[1] At last the building was definitely promised for the middle of December and Mr. Thomas made up his dedication program, which was this:

---

[1] Mrs. Thomas, p. 534.

"Hail! Bright Abode" from "Tannhäuser".......Wagner
(Combined chorus from the Apollo
Club and the Mendelssohn Club, Chicago)
Dedicatory Address.........................George E. Adams
(Of the trustees)
"Death and Transfiguration"..................Richard Strauss
Symphony No. 5 C Minor ....Beethoven
"Hallelujah" from "The Messiah" ....Händel
(Chorus and Orchestra)

The Fifth Symphony was there—to mark this great occasion
of his career.

Fresh delays occurred in the building, and at one time it
seemed doubtful if the contractors could have it ready by
December 14, the date announced for the dedication. Mr.
Thomas was in a fever of unrest. At last the main hall was
ready for testing and with a front of calm but inward anxiety he
assembled the orchestra to try the acoustics. The composition
he selected was the "Tannhäuser" overture. In the midst of it
he signaled to Mr. Stock to come and take the baton while he
went about the hall listening in different corners. In the upper
gallery he stopped and danced six steps of a jig. The president
of the Association, with Mr. Fay and some others, sat in one
of the boxes, listening and waiting.

"Gentlemen, your hall is a success, a great success!" shouted
Mr. Thomas. On the spot he wrote a cable message to Mr. Burnham, who was then in Manila, a message of warmest congratula-
tions.

Nevertheless, the rehearsals for the dedicatory program must
be held in the Auditorium. Returning after some weeks in New
York I went the first morning to my old seat. The orchestra was
just starting upon the Fifth Symphony. I was shocked to observe that Mr. Thomas no longer stood before the band but was
seated on a kind of wooden horse with a back to it, plainly
manufactured for his use. I thought this an ill portent, for

him who had been so resolute and sturdy. The Fifth Symphony, it will be remembered, starts with its ominous and beautiful summons that had figured so often in his story, the

"Fate knocks at the door," men have called this. When the orchestra came that day to the modified repetition of this phrase that begins at the twenty-second bar, he stopped them and made them replay it until he had brought out in it what seemed to me a singularly foreboding and tragic staccato, much more than I had ever heard before in this passage, and an effect that he produced by leaning a little upon some instruments and lightening others. I sat through the whole rehearsal. It seemed to me that he was sadly depressed, a fact that made me wonder when I thought of the triumph that awaited him in a few days. When they reached the last movement, he did not stop them anywhere but let them play on as if at a concert, clear to the end, a thing most unusual for him. When it was over he lingered an instant, and I thought he was going to say something, but he only laid down his baton, made his little bow of thanks and dismissed them heavily. It was the last time he was to rehearse that symphony, in his mind the greatest of all.

The dedicatory concert went gloriously, with great singing, faultless playing, a surge of feeling from the audience that was rare, spontaneous, and electrifying. The goal won, the house built, the permanent orchestra, mirage of forty-three years, come real at last. Here it is; behold it, touch it, enter it; it has come real at last! In this life, moments of happiness so great and unalloyed were rare.

They were also evanescent. The press was once more attacking Theodore Thomas.

ORCHESTRA HALL, CHICAGO
The gift of the citizens to the institution Thomas had founded

THE THOMAS MONUMENT
Erected on Chicago's lake front

What for now, in the name of Heaven?

About the building. It was so different from the Auditorium; everything sounded so strange in it. How persistent was this mischance! A few words would have explained all. They never occurred to him. The trouble was simple and, like most ¬oubles, imaginary. As thus: The orchestra in the Auditorium and the orchestra in the new orchestral hall were different machines. The new hall had hardly a third of the depth of the old and its acoustics were so perfect that the slightest whisper on the stage was audible at the back of the upper gallery. For thirteen years the orchestra had been accustomed to play so it could make itself heard in the great hollow of the Auditorium. It was humanly impossible that in one concert or two or four it could perfectly adjust itself to conditions so different. This was what Thomas had foreseen and had labored hard to meet. The public, of course, had no suspicion of the truth that in a short time all the apparent harshness of the orchestra in its new quarters would be smoothed away. Thomas knew it well. I think he felt that Chicago by this time had won to some faith in him; it might have known that he would not stumble at the summit and crisis of his art. We would not entertain so reasonable and obvious a thought. The cry arose that after all the labor and sacrifice the new hall was a failure. Such a notion, though preposterous and without foundation, was something to startle the public with; a part of the press used it industriously and struck Theodore Thomas with one more poisoned shaft. It went to his heart. In the deliberate judgment of Mr. Upton[1] it contributed to the disaster that followed.

The new hall was still damp from undried plaster. Its stage doors were imperfectly fitted and admitted terrible drafts. To put forth every effort to adjust the orchestra to the new hall, Thomas held daily rehearsals in these unwholesome surroundings. He took a cold but stubbornly refused to exert the least

---

[1] *Reminiscence and Appreciation*, p. 110; Mrs. Thomas, p. 537.

care about himself; even when signs of influenza developed, he refused. The first regular concert in the new hall took place two days after the dedication and was the annual Beethoven memorial. The next was December 23, at which he played the second movement from the Second Symphony and some other lighter numbers, evidently designing a kind of popular program. His condition all this time steadily becoming worse, yet he resisted every entreaty to spare himself. On the Monday following Christmas he was to have a rehearsal as usual. It was evident now to all that he was carrying on by sheer will power. He arose that morning at the accustomed hour and started for the hall. At his own front door he collapsed and must be helped to his bed. It was the first rehearsal he had missed; in forty-three years of orchestra conducting, the first he had missed.

The next concerts, December 30 and 31, Mr. Stock must conduct while the word went over the city that Theodore Thomas was fighting for his life. There followed a strange thing; after all these years it seems to me as strange now as it seemed then. Theodore Thomas was of that world of classical music that is supposed to be inhabited by a comparatively small and select population. He had never trod the way of a general popularity. By all the usual standards, he should have been to the great mass of mankind either unknown or a figure without significance. It was his own sad conviction that to a great extent he had failed and to the generality of mankind he meant nothing. Yet it was the generality of mankind that now seemed to stand bareheaded at his bedside, understanding him perfectly, understanding what he had done and what he meant to his age. The whole city knew he was sick; the whole city asked from hour to hour about his condition.

On Friday, the 30, the day of a concert, pneumonia developed. Still the resistance of that iron constitution and powerful will was not overcome, and on the morning of Monday, January 2, the news was better. That afternoon, defeat began, and he lapsed into unconsciousness. At daybreak on the morning of January 4, 1905, he died.

About midnight he had roused himself, and then for a moment consciousness returned.

"I have had a beautiful vision," he said to Mrs. Thomas, "a beautiful vision," and lapsed again into coma.

I think he had. Beautiful visions he had known all his life and been led by them. Perhaps this was better than even the realized dream that came at the end of so much struggle only to be taken away as he gained it.

CHAPTER XV
Results

U PON the community where he had lived and served, the effect of his passing was something to be pondered then and remembered afterward. Great numbers of men and women that probably had never heard him play, whose interest in music one would suppose to be of the slightest, showed that they knew well his work and him and paid to both their simple tributes of respect. Perhaps they felt more by intuition than by gained wisdom that this man had followed lofty ideals and given himself unreservedly to a good aim. Therefore they honored him and mourned at his bier.

It is no figure of speech to say so. He died on Friday morning. Sunday afternoon there was held in the Auditorium, where he had been so long a familiar figure, a memorial service consisting of only music, the music that he had loved best to play. The great hall was filled to its utmost capacity. But what was extraordinary and to the last degree affecting, the streets about the building were packed all that afternoon with crowds of silent people. There was no funeral cortège, there was no hearse, no coffin, there was nothing to be seen; but by a common instinct these people gathered there and stood in the cold winds of a January afternoon that they might in some way manifest their respect for the dead. I have never known a thing more impressive. It showed how much this man had come to mean to the people he had tried to benefit. With bowed heads they stood while the memorial was in progress that scarcely any of them could hear.

In St. James's Episcopal Church were held the funeral services over this man of such profound religious feelings. On the list of pallbearers were the most distinguished citizens of Chicago, but the bearers of the casket were members of the orchestra; they would allow no other hands to carry it. The music was singularly solemn and touching—chorales played by the orchestra trombones and at the end, strains from his beloved Ninth Symphony.

The requiem program was given twice: on Saturday afternoon for ticket holders in the new Orchestra Hall, the place that was and is the monument to this life of patient endeavor; at the Auditorium, Sunday, for the public. Mr. Stock conducted. The profound feeling of the men and their leader seemed reflected in every note. This was their program:

Chorale......................................Bach
Symphony No. 3, the "Eroica"................Beethoven
                  (First two movements)
"Siegfried's Death March" from "Die Götter-
  dämmerung)..............................Wagner
Tone poem, "Death and Transfiguration" ....Richard Strauss

Among the great musicians of the world that laid their tributes upon this bier was one that had often played under his baton and knew well and sympathetically what he had tried to do and at what cost. Flowers she sent, this artiste, Fannie Bloomfield Zeisler, to be placed on the stage of Orchestra Hall. When they were revealed they had been formed into the shape of the opening bars of the Fifth Symphony:

Under the sign with which he had begun, so he ended.

A stone cross marks the spot where he lies in Mount Auburn cemetery, near Boston.

With the reaction from the world outside, we came next to understand that this was not a citizen of Chicago that had gone but a great national and international figure of a distinctive significance. Even his most devoted friends had not known to what a place he had won in the affections as well as the esteem of his countrymen. He had thought that he was hardly a name; it appeared now that he had been a potent verity. The press with one accord, great and small, without exception, from one side of the continent to the other, raised a voice of eloquent tribute. After all, what is detraction? Throughout his life this man had been assailed with all varieties of malignity from covert to savage. He had taken the storm in the face, he had held to his task, and now at the end all evil sayings and evil thoughts of him were as if they had not been. They seemed to fade from all men's minds, be annihilated and forgotten. Nothing was remembered but a life of unselfish service. All the evil might as well never have been written, all the fault-finding and the false reports.

> Life and the clouds are vanished: hate and fear
>   Have had their span
> Of time to hurt, and are not: he is here,
>   The sunlike man.

The newspapers that had been most cruel to him, the critics that had pursued him with unappeasable ill-will, joined the great unseen procession that followed his viewless corpse and buried it in wreaths no less real because imponderable. If the thought arose in some aware of the whole of this story that a little of the kindness now shown above his clay would have cheered the rough road he traveled while he lived, the thought was submerged in the fact that at last the world knew him for what he was.

Few other men that had not held official positions, no other man whose life had been led strictly for and in art, ever received such signal honor in America. Great memorial services were held in New York, Cincinnati, and other cities. Letters, telegrams, messages of condolence and sorrow came in a flood from all parts of the world. In places where one would not think the mention of his name ever to have been heard, there were expressions of regret. For once the artist of honest purpose seemed to win more glory than the soldier of much noise. Strange are the ways of the fate that hounded him! He died without knowing or suspecting the place he had won or the magnitude of the work he had accomplished.

But of that accomplishment no man in 1905 could have spoken oversurely. A force had been let loose in the country; its workings were not yet to be seen. On May 13, 1862, there was in the United States, besides the band before him, one orchestra entitled to be called of the due symphonic quality, and that feeble and dubious, with five concerts a year. When he left New York for Chicago, 1891, there were, in addition to his own, three others of assured and definite basis and one that led a fitful existence. Twenty-one years after his death I count in the United States fifty-one grand orchestras giving regular and competent seasons and hundreds of excellent smaller bands in the picture houses and hotels playing a grade of music that but for his sowing and the produce thereof would have been impossible. When he began, a knowledge of the joy of great music was the possession of a cultural sect so small as to seem now a thing for ridicule. Twenty-one years after his death a perception of such joys was becoming a national possession. When he began, a single movement of but one symphony was a sign for revolt to the handful of persons that had been tricked into hearing it. In December, 1926, by means of the joining of a grand orchestra and the radio, an audience estimated at two millions heard the whole of Beethoven's Fifth.

Among the cities of America that now maintain great orchestras playing always a higher grade of music than anyone dared to play in 1876, is Minneapolis. We need an example of the means by which the national redemption may be wrought. Let us take this at random.

It is a typical Western city; a city of rapid growth, of great material prosperity, of a mixed population. In 1862, it hardly existed except as a name; in 1876, it had about 35,000 inhabitants; in 1891, about 175,000; in 1926, close to half a million. An industrial city, manufacturing many things; an American city showing to the world that hard, materialistic American surface always deceptive to the foreigner.

Minneapolis, from its village days on the frontier, had an element of music lovers. When music did not come to them sufficiently to meet their yearnings, they went in search of it. In 1882, Theodore Thomas came to Chicago with his great musical festival of that year, almost a week of instrumental and vocal music performed by famous singers, choruses of many voices, an augmented orchestra. A band of the music lovers of Minneapolis went down to Chicago to hear these marvels. Among them was David Blakely, local apostle of good music, and happening to be good journalist as well as good musician. His journalistic experiences had taught him something about the public and what could be done with it. On the way home from Chicago he discussed with his fellow townsmen the possibilities of holding in Minneapolis such a festival as they had just attended in Chicago. Mr. Blakely said it could be done and they started then to do it.

The next year they brought Mr. Thomas to Minneapolis with all his famous singers and all his orchestra. They themselves had provided and trained the choruses. It was Chicago over again. People came from all the region around as they came to the State Fair. They went home to a hundred communities, their heads ringing with great music, their minds filled with new ideas of what man can really get out of this life of his.

The next year, Mr. Thomas came again and gave another great festival and drew other great crowds.

At that time the concert master in his organization was Frank Danz, whose father was also a musician, the leader of a theater orchestra in Minneapolis. Sometime afterward, the younger Danz gave up traveling and came to live in the same city with his father. At once the suggestion occurred to many persons. Here was a man that had been closely associated with Theodore Thomas, he must know all the secrets of orchestral success, the very man to start a local orchestra. Meantime, Thomas continued to visit Minneapolis and to multiply and foster the musical interest there. At last, Mr. Danz got together a group of musicians and began to give Sunday afternoon concerts in an upstairs hall in not quite the best region of the city; but concerts with competent musicians. From that beginning came the great Minneapolis Symphony Orchestra that for so many years has played regular seasons at home and been heard from coast to coast, heard with delight by the most critical audiences, heard and applauded in critical New York, once contemptuous of everything that came from any given spot more than two miles west of Hoboken.

There is still one more stage to this story. The creator and first conductor of the Minneapolis Orchestra was Emil Oberhoffer, a greatly gifted musician, thinker, and interpreter. One of Mr. Thomas's ideas had been to teach good music to children. Much could be done with the American if caught young, was his notion of it; show a youth good musical ways, and when he is old he will not depart therefrom. Out of this notion grew the children's concerts that have made so profound an impression in Chicago and elsewhere. Mr. Oberhoffer was particularly happy in the children's concerts he established and conducted in Minneapolis. Thence after some years he went to Los Angeles. Now this again was a place Mr. Thomas used to visit and do gardening in. So Los Angeles must have its symphony orchestra.

Mr. Oberhoffer went there to lead it and took along with him his plan for children's concerts. Go there now and observe the effect of them.

Meantime, as a result of all this, Minneapolis added to its public school system a department of instrumental music, with a supervisor and assistants that give all their time to promoting among the school children knowledge and skill in this branch of music. Recorded fruitage of this attention seemed remarkable. On January 1, 1927, each of the eight public high schools had two orchestras and a band composed wholly of students. The first orchestra in each school was nearly of symphony proportions. In the first orchestra of Central High School there were fiifty-three student players; in that of West High School, fifty-two. In each school, the first orchestra was recruited from the second as skill was developed. The bands were well balanced and most of them uniformed.

Orchestras and bands were meeting in school time and the members were receiving credits and markings as in any other study. They were being trained by specialists that had taken post-graduate work in orchestra conducting. The high schools were giving each year operas, or operettas and one or two oratorios, and for these the school orchestras were playing all the music.

The school orchestras and bands were playing for assemblies, for football games, for neighborhood concerts, and elsewhere. Credits were allowed for music study outside the schools.

There were also eight junior high schools in Minneapolis, and four of these were large enough to have each its two orchestras and a band. The other schools had each one orchestra.

There were ninety-six grade schools, and of these fifty-three had student orchestras. In the total of one hundred and fourteen school buildings in the city were seventy-one separate orchestra groups. The Board of Education had acquired a large library of orchestral parts and was adding to it. The Minneapolis

Symphony Orchestra, from which all of this came in a space
of ten years, was giving Young People's concerts on certain
afternoons. Every year there was a playing competition among
the student instrumentalists. The winner had the honor of appearing as a soloist with the Minneapolis Symphony Orchestra.
At the contest of December 17, 1926, the prize was won by a
high-school girl that played Liszt's piano concerto in E flat
major. Concerto-playing contests between the high schools had
developed an interest that indicated an approach to that pertaining to the athletic meets. At that time a final concert had
been planned at which six high schools were to play each a
movement from a concerto, to be accompanied by the orchestra
of that school, a consummation of effort the more astonishing
when it is remembered that ten years before in Minneapolis a
public school was considered fortunate if it possessed a piano.

On January 1, 1927, more than five thousand pupils in the
city's public schools were playing in school orchestras.[1]

The supervisor of instrumental music, whose care commanded
these great achievements, had been trained under Theodore
Thomas.

Direct cause, direct result.

I have cited here this one example. There are many more.
Many other cities are keeping pace step for step with all this
truly wonderful transformation. I might have said of Detroit,
for instance, all I have said of Minneapolis. Youthful America
is coming up with music in his soul. For many years Walter
Damrosch gave in New York at his morning symphony concerts for children excellent addresses and well-considered music.
Thousands of children whom he first inducted into the begin-
nings of this art became later its staunch supporters. In Chicago
Mr. Stock, who ever since the death of Theodore Thomas had

---

[1]For the facts here given about this memorable evolution I am indebted to a special
report drawn up by Miss Ruth Andersen, First Assistant Music Supervisor of the
Minneapolis Schools.

carried the Chicago orchestra to new and brilliant successes, was working wonders; a full season of children's concerts, one every other week, tickets carefully distributed through the public schools, two hundred free seats on the stage for the best scholars in every school, most intelligent, skilful discourses revealing the substance of musical principles, stereopticon slides to multiply interest and visualize the lessons, a whole great new constituency provided every year, classical music shot from that stage into a thousand homes in all parts of the city, most of which were otherwise inaccessible to its entrance.

The sowing and the reaping. When Theodore Thomas was going about the country, a virtual outcast from New York, living on lean hours of sleep, fighting managers, obdurate musicians, greedy hotel keepers, plunging into bankruptcy and struggling out, devoutly wishing he were at home and continuing to travel away from it, tortured with bad halls and performances that seemed to him inadequate, bombarded by journals that would not understand what he was trying to do, he started all this; it is his dreaming and planning. Truly, it seems to be the fact that the men of whom the world at the time takes little note are the conquerors, "the dreamers, the derided, the mad blind men that see." Little it means now that even he himself never knew how much he had won, the influence he had exerted upon his countrymen or the reverence in which his name was to be held. Only one dream of his life came true in his own time. He fell just inside the portal of the vision when it was realized. But the rest was secure.

Grateful Chicago has erected upon its beautiful lake front a monument to his memory. New Hampshire has named one of its mountains in his honor. Neither monument nor mountain seems more permanent than the effect of his life, for that will go on when there shall be no more trace of his name and little of the age in which he lived. If I say that no other man of his period exerted upon mankind an influence so great and lasting,

I shall be looked upon as lunatic, although that is what I honestly believe. Is it so mad a thought? Statesmen come and fill the world's horizon and din the world's ears and so pass with their rub-a-dubs. The conspicuous men of one generation are the scoffing of the next and forgotten by the next. Is there a reputation of Theodore Thomas's time that careful men would insure for two hundred years? His own is already perishing; but the thinkings of a people go on forever. There are thousands of homes in America where music is a pervasive influence because of this man's endeavors. The ramifications of such an influence will never stop.

A work so stupendous required a most unusual combination of endowments and qualities. Their mingling in this man seems outside of chance. So far as we can see now, with less of any of his attributes, less of iron will, less of the sense of a high summons, less of what was called his autocratic spirit, less of his human sympathies, even less of his sensitiveness, he could never have done it. An artist, he lived in the world of men; all human, he lived in the world of art. Forty-three years of ceaseless and often desperate struggle passed between the time he first raised a baton over a concert orchestra and the time when he laid it down forever. If any man ever sounded out this life and what life means and what life can give of labor, sorrow, pain, trouble, and the supernal joys of achievement, it was Theodore Thomas.

APPENDICES

A. THE GRAND ORCHESTRA IN THE UNITED STATES

(To January 1, 1927. Asterisk denotes organizations that travel or give concerts in neighboring cities.)
Compiled from Pierre V. R. Keys's Music Year Book, 1926–1927.

Place	Founded	Number of Players	Number of Concerts Annually	Conductor
New York				Willem Mengelberg
*Philharmonic	1842	103	84	Wilhelm Furtwaengler
				Henry Hadley
*Symphony Society	1878	101	61	Walter Damrosch
American Orchestral Society	1920	100		Chalmers Clifton
Sunday Symphony Society	1923	85	15	Josiah Zuro
Philadelphia, Pa.				
*Philadelphia Orchestra	1900	107	72	Leopold Stokowski
New Haven, Conn.				
Symphony Orchestra	1894	75	5	David Stanley Smith
Stamford, Conn.				
Symphony Orchestra	1924	62	3	Clayton Hotchkiss
Boston, Mass.				
*Symphony Orchestra	1881	107	101	Serge Koussevitzky
People's Symphony	1921	75		Stuart Mason
Bangor, Me.				
*Symphony Orchestra	1895	65	7	Adelbert Wells Sprague
Springfield, Mass.				
Symphony Orchestra	1921	79	3	Arthur H. Turner
Utica, N. Y.				
Symphony Orchestra	1923	70	8	Edgar J. Alderwick
Syracuse, N. Y.				
Symphony Orchestra	1921	85	20	Vladimir Shavitch
Rochester, N. Y.				
Philharmonic Orchestra	1923	104	10	Eugene Goossens
Cleveland, O.				
*Cleveland Orchestra	1917	87	120	Nicolai Sokoloff
Detroit, Mich.				
*Symphony Orchestra	1913	84	100	Ossip Gabrilowitsch
Grand Rapids, Mich.				
Symphony Orchestra	1919	65	12	Karl Wecker
Flint, Mich.				
Symphony Orchestra	1922	65	5	William W. Norton

Place	Founded	Number of Players	Number of Concerts Annually	Conductor
Cincinnati, O.				
*Symphony Orchestra	1894	97	87	Fritz Reiner
Chicago, Ill.				
*Symphony Orchestra	1891	95	145	Frederick Stock
Civic Orchestra	1919	75	7	Eric DeLamarter
Woman's Symphony	1925			Richard Czerwonky
Minneapolis, Minn.				
*Symphony Orchestra	1902	56	48	Henri Verbrugghen
Duluth, Minn.				
Symphony Orchestra		50	6	Fred G. Bradbury
Springfield, O.				
Civic Orchestra	1921	63	4	Charles L. Bauer
Springfield, Ill.				
Civic Orchestra	1921	45	6	Wallace Grieves
Davenport, Ia.				
*Tri-City Symphony Orchestra	1915	55	18	Ludwig Becker
St. Louis, Mo.				
*Symphony Orchestra	1879	78	65	Rudolph Ganz
Omaha, Neb.				
Omaha Symphony Orchestra	1924	70	6	Sandor Harmati
Kansas City, Mo.				
*Little Symphony Ochestra	1920	25	31	N. De Rubertis
Topeka, Kan.				
Händel Philharmonic Society		50	5	George W. Barnes
Nashville, Tenn.				
Symphony Orchestra	1920	60	10	F. Arthur Henkel
Mobile, Ala.				
Symphony Orchestra	1924	40	4	Claude Dahmer
Atlanta, Ga.				
Symphony Orchestra	1923	65	8	Enrico Leide
Charleston, S. C.				
Philharmonic Symphony Orchestra	1924	85	4	G. Theodore Wichmann
New Orleans, La.				
Symphony Orchestra	1925	60	5	Dr. Ernest E. Schuyten
Dallas, Tex.				
Symphony Society		60	5	Paul Van Katwijk
Pittsburgh, Pa.				
Symphony Orchestra	1926		10	Guest Conductor
Lancaster, Pa.				
Municipal Orchestra		70	3	John G. Brubaker
Baltimore, Md.				
Symphony Orchestra	1916			Gustave Strube

Place	Founded	Number of Players	Number of Concerts Annually	Conductor
Erie, Pa.				
Symphony Orchestra			12	Henry B. Vincent
Easton, Pa.				
Symphony Orchestra		75	7	Earle Laros
Allentown, Pa.				
Symphony Orchestra				Lloyd A. Moll
Reading, Pa.				
Symphony Orchestra		70		Walter A. Pfeiffer
Denver, Colo.				
Civic Symphony Ochestra	1922	102	12	Horace Tureman
Sacramento, Calif.				
Symphony Orchestra	1923	65	6	Franz Dicks
San Francisco, Calif.				
*Symphony Orchestra	1920		70	Alfred Hertz
Los Angeles, Calif.				
*Philharmonic Orchestra	1916	100	45	Walter Henry Rothwell
Redlands, Calif.				
Community Symphony Orchestra			48	Carl Kuehne
Portland, Ore.				
*Symphony Orchestra	1910	70	16	Willem Van Hoogstraten
Seattle, Wash.				
Symphony Orcnestra	1926	65		Karl Kruge
Seattle Civic Symphony	1920	70		Mme Davenport Engberg
Seattle Orchestra Society	1921	75		Francis J. Armstrong
Tacoma, Wash.				
Civic Orchestra	1924	70		David P. Nason

Interesting and significant comments belong to the foregoing list.

The excellent orchestra at Baltimore is maintained by the city and has been since its foundation in 1916. The city treasury meets the deficit; private subscriptions are not countenanced. The public reaps the benefit in good music at cheap prices: twenty-five, fifty, and seventy-five cents a seat are the prevailing charges. This is the first instance in America of an entirely municipal symphony orchestra.

In Denver, Colorado, the municipality contributes with an annual appropriation toward the orchestra's support. The rest is supplied, as in other cities, by a sustaining fund obtained by appeals to the public.

The fifteen orchestras that travel cover wide areas and bring symphonic music in many communities where it was formerly a stranger. Virtually, every part of the United States is now covered by these organizations.

The average quality of performance is admitted to be high. The most conspicuous bands are of course those of Chicago, New York, Boston, Philadelphia, Cleveland, Cincinnati, Detroit, Minneapolis, San Francisco, Los Angeles, but other orchestras that have made little stir in the musical world outside of their own communities often have attained by careful training to a surprising excellence. One thing that strikes every person examining the programs played by these organizations is their high grade. To compare the programs of the least celebrated of all these deserving organizations with the best programs played when Theodore Thomas began is to receive an impression of growth in musical taste that fortifies faith and annihilates pessimism. Many of these orchestras have been established in the face of overwhelming difficulties by a few men and women of high hearts and noblest ambitions. They have their reward in this remarkable national asset.

It may be worth while to point out that the third oldest grand orchestra in the United States is that of St. Louis. The West did not really lag behind the East in musical development.

B. THE THOMAS HIGHWAYS

FIRST

Outward	*Homeward*
New York	St. Louis
New Haven	Indianapolis
Hartford	Louisville
Providence	Cincinnati
Boston	Dayton
Worcester	Springfield, Ohio
Springfield, Mass.	Columbus
Albany	Pittsburg
Schenectady	Washington
Utica	Baltimore
Syracuse	Philadelphia
Rochester	New York
Buffalo	
Cleveland	
Toledo	
Detroit	
Chicago	

(With several tours to the Pacific Coast.)

SECOND

(*After removal to Chicago*)

Chicago	Pittsburg, Pa.
Milwaukee	Springfield, Ill.
St. Paul	Aurora, Ill.
Minneapolis	South Bend, Ind.
Duluth	Indianapolis, Ind.
Omaha	Grand Rapids, Mich.
Kansas City	Detroit, Mich.
Topeka, Kan.	
Nashville, Tenn.	
Mobile, Ala.	
Atlanta, Ga.	
St. Louis, Mo.	

C. INDEX NUMBERS

Of the Representative Popular Taste in Music, Compiled from the Current Programs of Each Period (excepting those of the New York Philharmonic.)

1852
Master Marsh, the Boy Drummer
The Concertina Soloists
"The Firemen's Quadrille"
"Trip by Railroad," as played by the Silver Cornet Band
"General Taylor's Funeral March"

1862
"Battle of Prague"
"Earthquake Polka"
"Skinners' Quickstep"
"Firefly Polka"

1872
"Linnet Polka"
Strauss's "Aurora Ball Polka"
Strauss's "Blue Danube Waltz"
"Carnival of Venice"
Selections and Overtures from Italian Operas
The Beginning of Wagner

1882
"Tell" Overture
Liszt's Second Rhapsody
"Midsummer Night's Dream" Overture
Mendelssohn's "Spring Song"
"Funeral March of a Marionette"
"Tännhauser" Overture
"Lohengrin"
"Träumerei"
Beginning of Saint-Saëns

1892
Wagner—especially
"Flying Dutchman"
"Tristan und Isolde"
Händel's Largo
Music from "The Ring"
Schubert's Unfinished Symphony
Second Movement from Beethoven's Second
Standard concertos

1902

Wagner
Beethoven's symphonies, overtures, and concertos
Schumann
Tschaikowsky
Richard Strauss
Brahms

D. CHICAGO AND EUROPE

This list of first performances by Theodore Thomas with the dates on which the same compositions were for the first time played in Europe was compiled by Mr. Bernhard Ziehn and first appeared in the first volume of Mr. Upton's book, at page 228. It will be observed that it covers only seven years of Thomas's work and is limited to Chicago.

FRANCK, "Les Éolides," Chicago, 1895; Vienna, 1903.
STRAUSS, R., "Eulenspiegel," Chicago, 1895; Vienna, 1903.
BRUCKNER, Symphony No. 7, Chicago, 1893; Dortmund, 1903.
CHARPENTIER, "Impressions d'Italie," Chicago, 1893; Frankfurt a/M., Sondershausen, 1903.
LISZT, "Mephisto Waltz," Chicago, 1893; Hanover, 1903.
TSCHAIKOWSKY, "Francesca da Rimini," Chicago, 1896; Vienna, 1903.
FRANCK, "Le Chasseur Maudit," Chicago, 1898; Hanover, 1903.
GLAZOUNOW, "Le Printemps," Chicago, 1898; Munich, 1903.
D'INDY, "Istar," Chicago, 1898; Sondershausen, 1903.
DUKAS, "L'Apprenti Sorcier," Chicago, 1900; Dresden, Munich, 1903.
FRANCK, Symphony, D minor, Chicago, 1900; Frankfurt a/M., 1903.
BRUCKNER, Symphony No. 3, Chicago, 1901; Dessau, Leipzig, 1903.
FIBICH, "Evening," Chicago, 1901; Vienna, 1903.
SCHILLINGS, Prologue to "King Œdipus," Chicago, 1901; Stuttgart, 1903.
WEINGARTNER, Symphony No. 2, Chicago, 1901; Berlin, 1903.
HUMPERDINCK, "Dornröschen," Chicago, 1902; Berlin, 1903.
HAUSEGGER, "Barbarossa," Chicago, 1902; Bremen, 1903.
SIBELIUS, "Christian II," Chicago, 1902; Munich, 1903.

E. THE MEN THAT STOOD BY

Original guarantors of the Chicago Orchestra that made it possible and gave Theodore Thomas his new field.

J. McGregor Adams	John M. Clark
Allison V. Armour	Charles Counselman
George A. Armour	R. T. Crane
Philip D. Armour	Columbus R. Cummings
S. E. Barrett	N. K. Fairbank
A. C. Bartlett	Charles Norman Fay
Henry W. Bishop	Henry Field
T. B. Blackstone	Marshall Field
E. W. Blatchford	Charles W. Fullerton

Lyman J. Gage
John J. Glessner
T. W. Harvey
William G. Hibbard
H. N. Higinbotham
Charles L. Hutchinson
Ralph N. Isham
Albert Keep
Edson Keith
S. A. Kent
Henry W. King
Walter C. Larned
Victor F. Lawson
L. Z. Leiter
J. Mason Loomis
Franklin MacVeagh
Ezra B. McCagg

Cyrus H. McCormick
O. W. Meysenburg
Thomas Murdoch
Eugene S. Pike
Henry H. Porter
O. W. Potter
George M. Pullman
Norman B. Ream
Martin A. Ryerson
Byron L. Smith
Albert A. Sprague
Otho S. A. Sprague
Charles H. Wacker
John R. Walsh
Norman Williams
Carl Wolfson

F. MR. THOMAS'S LAST PROGRAMS

(Being those for the 1904–1905, the Fourteenth Season of the Chicago Symphony Orchestra, which he founded)

First Concert, November 4, 1904, Overture, "Carnival," op. 92, Dvořák; Symphony No. 5, "From the New World," E minor, op. 95, Dvořák; Overture, "In the South" ("Alassio"), op. 50 (new), Elgar; "Siegfried's Rhine Journey," from "Die Götterdämmerung," Wagner; Rondo, "Till Eulenspiegel's Merry Pranks," Strauss.

Second Concert, November 11. Overture, "Academic Festival," op. 80, Brahms; Symphony No. 2, D major, op. 36, Beethoven; Scena "Abscheulicher! wo eilst du hin?" and aria, "Komm Hoffnung," from "Fidelio," Beethoven (Mme Louise Homer); "The Country Wedding," op. 26, Goldmark; Songs, "Träume," "Der Engel," "Stehe still!" and "Schmerzen," Wagner (Mme Homer); Vorspiel to "Die Meistersinger," Wagner.

Third Concert, November 18. Overture to "Benvenuto Cellini," Berlioz; Symphony No. 6, "Pathétique," B minor, op. 74, Tschaikowsky; Concerto for pianoforte, F minor, op. 16, Henselt (Mrs. Fannie Bloomfield-Zeisler); Overture to "Tannhäuser," Wagner.

Fourth Concert, November 25. Concert overture, "Cockaigne," Elgar; Serenade for wind choir, op. 7, Strauss; Symphonic variations, op. 78, Dvořák; Suite from the ballet, "Casse-noisette," op. 71a, Tschaikowsky; Symphonic poem No. 2, "Phaëton," op. 39, Saint-Saëns; "Heart Wounds," and "Spring," Grieg (string orchestra); "Intermezzo" and "Perpetuum Mobile," op. 39, Moszkowski; Vorspiel to "Lohengrin" and "Ride of the Valkyries," from "Die Walküre," Wagner.

Fifth Concert, December 2. Overture, "In Italy," op. 49 (new), Goldmark; Variations, op. 36, Elgar; Suite for violin and orchestra, op. 180, Raff (Mr. Leopold Kramer); Symphony No. 2, C major, op. 61, Schumann.

Sixth Concert, December 9. Overture, "Egmont," Beethoven; Symphony No. 1, C minor, op. 68, Brahms; Variations, sur un thème rococo, for violoncello and orchestra, op. 33, Tschaikowsky (Mr. Bruno Steindel); Symphonic poem No. 3, "Les Préludes," Liszt.

Dedicatory Concert, December, 14. "Hail! Bright Abode," from "Tannhäuser," Wagner (chorus and orchestra); Dedicatory address (Hon. George E. Adams); Overture, "Tannhäuser," Wagner; Tone poem, "Death and Transfiguration," Strauss; Symphony No. 5, C. minor, Beethoven; "Hallelujah," from "The Messiah," Händel (chorus and orchestra.)

The regular concerts of the season were resumed the same week in Orchestra Hall, the seventh concert being given, as had been Mr. Thomas's custom for several years, in celebration of Beethoven's birthday, with the following Beethoven programme:

Seventh Concert, December 16. Symphony No. 4, flat, op. 60; Romanza for violin, F major, op. 50 (Mr. Leopold Kramer); Overture, "Coriolanus," op. 62; Overtura, grande fugue, tantot libre, tantôt recherchée, B flat, op. 133 (string orchestra); Symphony No. 7, A major, op. 92.

Eighth Concert, December 23. Overture. "In der Natur," op. 91, Dvořák; Larghetto from Second Symphony, Beethoven; "Contrasts" (The Gavotte A. D. 1700 and 1900), Elgar; "Suite Pastorale," Chabrier; "Love Scene," from "Feuersnot," Richard Strauss; "Wald Fantasie," op. 83, Zoellner; "Träume," Wagner; Symphonic poem No. 1, "Le Rouet d'Omphale," op. 31, Saint-Saëns;Waltz,"Village Swallows," Joseph Strauss; Suite, "Sylvia," Delibes.

Ninth Concert, December 30. Symphony, C major (Köchel, 551), Mozart; Concerto for oboe, G minor, Händel (Mr. Alfred Barthel); Symphony No. 8, B Minor ("Unfinished"), Schubert; Scherzo, "A Midsummer Night's Dream," Mendelssohn; Overture, "Genoveva," Schumann.

Mr. Frederick Stock, assistant conductor of the orchestra, was leader at the ninth concert, Mr. Thomas having been stricken with the illness which resulted fatally. The tenth concert was postponed on this account, and memorial concerts were given at Orchestra Hall and the Auditorium, with this program:

Memorial Concerts, January 6 and 8, 1905. Chorale, Bach; Symphony No. 3, "Eroica" (first two movements), Beethoven; "Siegfried's Death March," from "Die Götterdämmerung," Wagner; Tone poem, "Death and Transfiguration," Strauss.

Tenth Concert, January 6, 1905. Symphony, No. 4, F minor, op 36, Tschaikowsky; Concerto for pianoforte, No. 2, F minor, op. 21, Chopin (M. Vladimir de Pachmann); Scherzo, "L'Apprenti Sorcier," Dukas; Tone poem, "Death and Transfiguration," op. 24, Strauss.

Eleventh Concert, January 13. Symphony, G major (B. & H. Edition, No. 13), Haydn; Symphonie concertante for violin and viola, E flat (Kochel, 364), Mozart (Mr. Ludwig Becker and Mr. Franz Esser); Variations, "Chorale St. Anthony," op. 85, Brahms; Overture, "Leonora," No. 3, Beethoven.

Twelfth Concert, January 20. Suite, "Impressions d'Italie," Charpentier; "La Fiancée du Timbalier," op. 82, Saint-Saëns (Miss Muriel Foster); Chorale and variations for harp and orchestra, op. 74, Widor (Mr. Enrico Tramonti); Vorspiel to "Lohengrin," Wagner; Concert overture, "Froissart," op. 19 (first time), Elgar; "Sea Pictures," op. 37, Elgar (Miss Foster); "Italian Serenade" (first time), Hugo Wolf; Suite from the ballet, "Casse-noisette," op. 71a, Tschaikowsky.

Thirteenth Concert, January 27. Concert overture, "Euterpe," Chadwick; "Endymion's Narrative," Converse; Concerto for violin, D major, op. 77, Brahms (Mr. Fritz Kreisler); Symphony No. 4, D minor, op. 120, Schumann; Rondo, "Till Eulenspiegel's Merry Pranks," Strauss.
Fifteenth Concert, February 10th. Symphony in D (Kochel, 504), Mozart; Concerto No. 5, E flat, op. 73, Beethoven (Eugen D'Albert); Symphonic variations, op. 78, Dvořák; Overture, "In the South" ("Alassio"), op. 50, Elgar.

G. WORKS INTRODUCED INTO THIS COUNTRY BY THEODORE THOMAS

This list was compiled after Mr. Thomas's death and is reprinted from the second volume of Mr. Upton's book, *Theodore Thomas, a Musical Biography.* The compositions cited were marked on his programs by Mr. Thomas himself as "new," "first time," or "first time in America." It is not known exactly what these markings signified, but so large a proportion of these compositions undoubtedly were played for the first time in America by the Thomas Orchestra, that the list may be taken as representative of his work in that line, even though it may contain a few errors. It was a matter of pride with him to be the first conductor to present in America every orchestral work of merit, especially those by American composers.

ALBERT
    Symphony No. 1, D major, "Columbus," op. 31, Brooklyn, October 27, 1866.
D'ALBERT
    Prelude to "The Ruby," Chicago, January 3, 1896.
    Overture, "Der Improvisator," Chicago, October 14, 1901.
    Vorspiel, "Kain," Chicago, January 30, 1903.
AUBER
    "Grand Inauguration March," New York, September 18, 1862.
BACH (Johann Sebastian)
    Toccata in F (Esser arrangement), New York, January 13, 1865.
    "Passacaglio" (Esser arrangement), New York, April 8, 1865.
    Suite No. 3, in D, New York, October 26, 1867.
    Eight-part Chorus, "I Wrestle and Pray," New York, March 13, 1869.
    Suite in B minor, New York, November 27, 1874.
    "Magnificat" in D, Cincinnati, May 13, 1875.
    Suite No. 1, in C, New York, March 25, 1876.
    Prelude, adagio, gavotte, and rondo (Bachrich arrangement), New York, January 24, 1880.
    Ciaconna (arranged by Raff), Philadelphia, February 24, 1887.
    Fugue in A minor (Hellmesberger Edition), New York, December 6, 1887.
    Gavotte, sicilienne, and bourrée (string orchestra), New York, April 14, 1888.
    Bourrée, gavotte, réjouissance, Suite No. 4, Chicago, November 1, 1901.
BACH (Carl Philipp Emanuel)
    Symphony in D major, New York, September 18, 1862.
BALAKIREW
    Symphonic poem, "Thamar," Chicago, October 23, 1896.
BARGIEL
    Overture, "Prometheus," Brooklyn, October 28, 1865.
    Symphony in C, op. 30, New York, January 13, 1866.

"Trois Danses Allemandes," op. 24, New York, August 6, 1869.
Intermezzo, Chicago, July 28, 1887.

BEETHOVEN
Concerto No. 2, for piano, Brooklyn, January 21, 1865.
Concerto for piano, violin, and violoncello, New York, February 18, 1865.
Concerto for piano, No. 3, Brooklyn, December 8, 1865.
Choral fantasia (complete), New York, January 13, 1866.
Overture in C, op. 115, New York, December 2, 1866.
Music to "Prometheus," New York, December 15, 1867.
Twelve minuets, New York, August 6, 1874.
Serenade, op. 8, New York, July 13, 1875.
Rondino, for two oboes, two clarinets, two bassoons, and two horns, Chicago, July 14, 1885.
Cavatina, from String Quartet, op. 130, Brooklyn, October 26, 1886.
Grand Fugue, op. 133, New York, March 29, 1888.
"Ritter Ballet," New York, January 17, 1889.

BENNETT
Symphony in G minor, New York, September 7, 1875.

BERLIOZ
Overture, "Corsair," New York, March 7, 1863.
Symphony, "Harold in Italy," New York, May 9, 1863.
Second part from dramatic symphony, "Romeo and Juliet," New York, December 3, 1864.
Overture, "Benvenuto Cellini," Brooklyn, November 9, 1867.
"Tristia," op. 18, New York, February 5, 1885.

BIZET
Egyptian dance from "Djamileh," Chicago, April 24, 1896.

BOËLLMANN
Variations symphoniques, for violoncello, Chicago, November 14, 1902.

BORODIN
"Sketch of the Steppes," Brooklyn, March 23, 1886.

BÜLOW
Ballad, "The Minstrel's Curse," op. 16, New York, February 15, 1868.

BUNGERT
Symphonic poem, "Auf der Wartburg," New York, February 28, 1888.

BRAHMS
Serenade in D, op. 11, New York, May 29, 1873.
Variations on theme by Haydn, Brooklyn, April 11, 1874.
Theme and variations, from Sextet, op. 18, Brooklyn, December 19, 1874.
Hungarian dances, New York, February 6, 1875.
Second Symphony, D major, op. 73, New York, October 3, 1878.
"Tragic" overture, New York, November 12, 1881.
"Academic" overture, New York, November 29, 1881.
Rhapsody, op. 53, New York, January 6, 1883.
Third Symphony, F major, op. 90, New York, November 15, 1884.

BRISTOW
Overture, "Great Republic," Brooklyn, May 10, 1879.

BROUELET
Suite, "Scènes Fantasistes," Chicago, July 19, 1890.

BRUCH
   Symphony in E flat, op. 28, New York, March 13, 1869.
   "Honors of War to Patroclus," from "Achilleus," New York, April 1, 1886.
BRUCKNER
   Symphony, No. 7, E major, Chicago, July 29, 1886.
   "Te Deum," Cincinnati, May 26, 1892.
   Symphony, No. 4, "Romantic," E flat, Chicago, January 28, 1897.
BRUNEAU
   Symphonic poem, "La Belle aux Bois Dormant," Chicago, November 7, 1903.
   Entr'acte symphonique, "Messidor," Chicago, February 24, 1903.
BUCK
   "Centennial Medication of Columbia," Philadelphia, May 11, 1876.
CATEL
   Overture, "Semiramide," New York, December 12, 1868.
CHADWICK
   "Columbus Ode," Chicago, May 26, 1892.
   "Pastoral Prelude," Chicago, January 25, 1895.
CHAMINADE
   "Concertstück," Chicago, February 8, 1895.
CHANSSON
   Symphonic poem, "Viviane," Chicago, October 21, 1898.
CHARPENTIER
   Suite, "Impressions of Italy," Chicago, November 25, 1893.
CHERUBINI
   Introduction to Act III, from "Medea," New York, October 26, 1867.
   Entr'acte and ballet music, "Ali Baba," Brooklyn, January 16, 1879.
COLERIDGE-TAYLOR
   Ballad in D minor, Chicago, February 13, 1903.
CONVERSE
   "Festival Overture," Brooklyn, January 25, 1868.
COWEN
   Scandinavian Symphony, New York, November 11, 1882.
   Welsh Symphony, No. 4, B flat minor, New York, April 11, 1885.
   Symphony, No. 5, New York, February 28, 1888.
   Overture, "The Butterfly's Ball," Chicago, October 28, 1902.
CUI
   "Tarantella," New York, October 28, 1886.
DAVID (Ferdinand)
   "Festival March," New York, July 30, 1874.
DELIBES
   Ballet, "Sylvia," New York, March 24, 1886.
   "Scène de Bal," New York, April 30, 1886.
   Ballet, "Coppelia," New York, January 15, 1887.
DOHNANYI
   Symphony in D minor, Chicago, January 16, 1904.
DUKAS
   Scherzo, "L'Apprenti Sorcier," Chicago, January 13, 1899.
DUPARC
   Symphonic poem, "Leonore," Chicago, November 13, 1896.

DVOŘÁK
"Slavonic Rhapsody," No. 3, op. 45, Cincinnati, February 4, 1880.
Symphony in D, op. 60, No. 1, New York, January 6, 1883.
"Scherzo Capriccioso," Brooklyn, November 8, 1884.
Overture, "Husitzka," New York, November 15, 1884.
Symphony, D minor, op. 70, No. 2, New York, January 9, 1886.
Cantata, "Spectre's Bride," op. 69, Brooklyn, March 20, 1886.
"Légende," New York, March 1, 1887.
Suite, op. 39, New York, March 31, 1887.
"Slavonic Dances," op. 72, Second Series, New York, November 12, 1887.
"Symphonic Variations," op. 78, Chicago, July 19, 1888.
Tone poem, "The Golden Spinning Wheel," Chicago, January 1, 1897.
Symphonic poem, "The Wild Dove," Chicago, October 20, 1899.
Overture, "Mein Heim," Chicago, November 15, 1901.

ELGAR
Concert overture, "Cockaigne," "In London Town," Chicago, March 15, 1901
"Variations," op. 36, Chicago, January 3, 1902.
Military Marches, "Pomp and Circumstance," Chicago, November 28, 1902.
Incidental music and funeral march from "Grania and Diarmid," Chicago, November 7, 1903.
Concert overture, "Froissart," op. 19, Chicago, January 20, 1905.

FUCHS (Robert)
Symphony in C major, New York, December 10, 1885.

FRANCHETTI
Prelude to "Asrael," New York, January 24, 1888.

FRANCK (César)
Symphonic poem, "Les Eolides," Chicago, November 8, 1895.
Symphonic poem, "Le Chasseur Maudit," Chicago, February 8, 1898.

GADBY
Orchestral scene, "The Forest of Arden," New York, October 26, 1886.

GADE
"Spring Fantasia," op. 23, New York, January 16, 1869.
"Noveletten," op. 53, New York, January 4, 1877.

GERMAN
Three Dances, "Henry VIII," Chicago, October 25, 1895.

GERNSHEIM
"Tarantella," from Symphony in F, Brooklyn, March 23, 1886.

GLAZOUNOW
"Oriental Rhapsody," Chicago, November 13, 1896.
Second Concert Waltz, Chicago, October 29, 1897.
Symphony, No. 6, in C minor, Chicago, October 19, 1900.
Tableaux musicales, "Le Printemps," Chicago, November 4, 1897.
"Ruses d'Amour," op. 6, Chicago, March 15, 1901.
Overture, "Solennelle," Chicago, December 6, 1901.
Suite, "Moyen Âge," op. 79, Chicago, January 23, 1904.

GLEASON
Symphonic poem, "Edris," Chicago, April 17, 1895.

GLINKA
Overture, "Rouslane et Ludmila," New York, July 10, 1873.

GLUCK
>Overture, "Paris and Helen," New York, January 8, 1875.

GOETZ
>Concerto, B flat, for violin, New York, April 15, 1882.
>Opera, "The Taming of the Shrew," New York, January 14, 1886.

GOLDMARK
>"Wedding March and Variations," from "Country Wedding," op. 26, Brooklyn, February, 16, 1878.
>Overture, "Penthesilea," op. 31, Cincinnati, December 3, 1879.
>Symphony, No. 2, in E flat, op. 35, New York, November 17, 1888.
>Overture, "Spring," op. 36, New York, March 9, 1890.
>Overture, "Prometheus Bound," op. 38, New York, December 6, 1890.
>Overture, "Sappho," op. 44, Cincinnati, May 23, 1894.
>"Scherzo," op. 45, Chicago, December 28, 1894.

GOUNOD
>Ballet music, "Queen of Sheba," New York, July 1, 1867.
>Larghetto and scherzo from Second Symphony, New York, June 27, 1871.
>Overture, "Le Médecin Malgré Lui," New York, May 14, 1874.
>Overture, "Mireille," New York, May 20, 1874.
>Oratorio, "Redemption," New York, December 6, 1882.
>Oratorio, "Mors et Vita," St. Louis, October 30, 1885.

GRADNER
>"Eine Lustspiel Ouvertüre," op. 28, New York, December 25, 1887.

GRIEG
>Concert overture, "In Autumn," New York, November 24, 1888.
>Suite No. 1, "Peer Gynt," op. 46, New York, January 24, 1889.
>"Symphonic Dances," op. 64, Chicago, January 17, 1899.

GRIMM
>Suite in canon form, op. 10, New York, December 30, 1866.
>Second Suite in canon form, op. 16, New York, May 22, 1873.

GUIRAUD
>"Carnival," Chicago, July 20, 1877.

HALVERSON
>"Boyard's March," Chicago, December 13, 1895.

HAMERIK
>"Nordish Suite," op. 22, New York, September 3, 1873.
>"Christian Trilogie," Baltimore, May 1, 1884.

HÄNDEL
>"Royal Fireworks Music," New York, October 21, 1868.
>Concerto in F, for string orchestra, Chicago, April 17, 1896.

VON HAUSEGGER
>Symphonic poem, "Barbarossa," Chicago, October 31, 1902.

HAYDN
>Theme and variations, "Kaiser Franz Hymn," Brooklyn, November 9, 1867.
>"Oxford Symphony," New York, March 4, 1875.
>"Surprise Symphony," G major, Brooklyn, January 20, 1881.

HILLER
>"Dramatic Fantasia," New York, May 21, 1874.

HLARAC
"Chopin Suite," New York, March 3, 1888.
HOFFMAN
"Hungarian Suite," New York, May 14, 1874.
HOFMANN
"Frithjof Symphony," New York, February 6, 1875.
"Pictures from the North," Chicago, July 11, 1877.
"Overture to a Drama," Chicago, July 12, 1882.
HOHNSTOCK
Overture, "Hail, Columbia," Brooklyn, March 4, 1865.
HORNEMANN
Fairy overture, "Aladdin," New York, July 16, 1871.
HUBER
"Tell" Symphony, New York, February 11, 1882.
"Romischer Karneval," Chicago, July 21, 1887.
HUMPERDINCK
Dream music from "Hänsel und Gretel," Chicago, November 15, 1895.
Tone picture from "Dornröschen," Chicago, October 14, 1902.
D'INDY
"Wallenstein's Camp," from "Wallenstein Trilogie," Chicago, October 19, 1900.
"La Forêt Enchantée," Chicago, December 6, 1901.
Introduction symphonique to "L'Étranger," Chicago, October 31, 1903.
JADASSOHN
Serenade in canon form, New York, September 11, 1873.
JARNEFELT
Symphonic poem, "Korsholm," Chicago, November 21, 1902
JENSEN
"Wedding Music," op. 45, Jersey City, January 21, 1886.
JOACHIM
March No. 1, in C, New York, June 27, 1871.
March No. 2, in D, New York, July 21, 1871.
Hungarian Concerto, Brooklyn, January 10, 1874.
Concerto for violin, G major, New York, January 10, 1891.
KAUN
"Festival March and Hymn," Chicago, January 7, 1898.
Symphony in D minor, op. 22, Chicago, January 14, 1898.
Overture, "Der Maler von Antwerpen," Chicago, February 3, 1899.
1. Symphonic poem, "Minnehaha," Chicago, February 6, 1903.
2. Symphonic poem, "Hiawatha," Chicago, February 6, 1903.
KLEIN
"Liebeslied," New York, April 14, 1888.
"Hochzeits Klange," New York, April 14, 1888.
KRUG (Arnold)
Prologue to "Othello," New York, November 14, 1885.
KUCKEN
Quadrille, "Nuss Knacker," New York, June 20, 1872.
LACHNER
Suite in D minor, op. 113, New York, December 3, 1864.

LAMOND
  Overture, "From the Highland," Chicago, December 28, 1893.
LAZZARI
  Prelude, "Armor," Chicago, March 3, 1899.
LISZT
  Symphonic poem, "Mazeppa," New York, November 11, 1865.
  Concerto for piano, No. 1, in E flat, New York, December 2, 1865.
  Mephisto Waltz (after Lenau), Brooklyn, December 8, 1866.
  March, "Vom Fels zum Meer," New York, July 5, 1867.
  Symphonic poem, "The Ideal" (after Schiller), New York, January 11, 1868.
  Symphonic poem, "Prometheus," New York, April 3, 1869.
  "Goethe March," New York, May 9, 1870.
  Symphonic poem, "Orpheus," New York, June 20, 1872.
  Symphonic poem, "Héroïde Funèbre," New York, August 8, 1872.
  "Rhapsodie Hongroise," No. 1, New York, May 27, 1875.
  "Rhapsodie Hongroise," No. 6, "Pesther Carneval," New York, June 22, 1875.
  "Second Mephisto Waltz," Chicago, July 18, 1882.
  Concerto, "Pathétique," New York, March 16, 1886.
MacCUNN
  Concert Overture, "Land of the Mountain and the Flood," Chicago, November 11, 1892.
MACKENZIE
  Scotch Rhapsody, "Burns," op. 24, Brooklyn, November 3, 1883.
  Oratorio, "Rose of Sharon," New York, April 16, 1885.
  Overture, "Twelfth Night," op. 40, New York, March 9, 1889.
  "Benedictus," New York, March 14, 1889.
  Nautical Overture, "Britannia," Chicago, January 25, 1895.
  Three dances from "Little Minister," Chicago, October 21, 1898.
MASCAGNI
  Intermezzo, "L'Amico Fritz," Chicago, October 21, 1892.
MASSENET
  "Scènes Pittoresques," New York, July 29, 1874.
  "Variations," op. 13, Chicago, July 20, 1877.
  Marche "Héroïque," New York, October 26, 1886.
  "La Vierge," for string orchestra, New York, October 28, 1886.
  Suite, "Esclarmonde," Chicago, April 15, 1891.
  Ballet Music, "Thaïs," Chicago, November 15, 1895.
MEHUL
  Overture, "Horatius Cocles," Chicago, July 5, 1877.
MENDELSSOHN
  "Trumpet Overture," Brooklyn, November 9, 1867.
  "March," op. 108, New York, May 21, 1869.
  Overture, "Wedding of Comacho," Chicago, May 1, 1875.
MEYERBEER
  "Inauguration March," New York, June 25, 1874.
MOLIQUE
  Concerto for violoncello, op. 45, Brooklyn, April 13, 1867.
MOSCHELES
  Quartet for pianos, "Les Contrastes," New York, May 13, 1862.

MOSZKOWSKI
  Suite, No. 1, op. 39, New York, March 22, 1887.
  Suite, No. 2, op. 47, New York, November, 15, 1890.
  "Boadil," Chicago, October 21, 1892.
  "Torchlight Dance," op. 51, Chicago, February 3, 1894.

MOZART
  Symphony in G minor, Brooklyn, April 7, 1863.
  Symphony concertante, for violin and viola, New York, April 8, 1865.
  Symphony, No. 3, in D major, Brooklyn, January 20, 1866.
  Concerto for two pianos, in E flat, New York, February 10, 1866.
  Andante, variations, and menuetto (from the First Divertimento), New York,
    August 29, 1866.
  "Turkish March," New York, August 29, 1866.
  First, Second, and Third Motets, New York, December 12, 1868.
  Symphony in E flat, Brooklyn, April 17, 1875.
  Introduction and Fugue, for strings only, New York, August 5, 1875.
  Nocturno, from Serenade, op. 8, New York, April 1, 1881.
  Overture and ballet music, "Idomeneo" Chicago, July 11, 1882.

MÜLLER
  "Festival March," New York, May 26, 1867.

NICODÉ
  Symphonic Variations, New York, January 10, 1885.
  "Jubilee March," New York, October 28, 1886.

PAINE
  "Centennial Hymn," Philadelphia, May 11, 1876.
  "Columbus March and Hymn," Chicago, May 26, 1892.

PHELPS
  "Hiawatha Symphony," New York, May 10, 1880.

PRAEGER
  Symphonic poem, "Life, Love, Strife, and Victory," New York, April 14, 1888.

PRATT
  "Court Minuet," New York, March 23, 1886.

RAFF
  Symphony, "An das Vaterland," New York, February, 18, 1865.
  Suite in C, op. 101, New York, January 12, 1867.
  Overture, "Dame Kobold," New York, August 1, 1872.
  "Lenore Symphony," Boston, December 5, 1873.
  Sixth Symphony, in D minor, op. 189, New York, January 8, 1875.
  "Sinfonietta," op. 188, for wind instruments, New York, June 24, 1875.
  Suite No. 2, in F, op. 194, New York, February 26, 1876.
  Suite for piano and orchestra, op. 200, New York, November 20, 1877.
  "Die Jahreszeiten," for chorus, piano, and orchestra, Brooklyn, March 20, 1886.
  "Festival March," New York, November 4, 1886.
  Concerto for violoncello, op. 183, New York, March 17, 1888.

RAMEAU
  "Romaneska," Chicago, July 20, 1877.
  Gavotte, tambourin, minuet et passepied, from "Castor et Pollux," New York,
    February 7, 1885.

Reinecke
Overture, "King Manfred," after Uhland, New York, May 24, 1868.
"Festival Overture," New York, June 13, 1871.
"In Memoriam," New York, August 13, 1874.
Variationen über "Ein feste Burg ist unser Gott," New York, November 12, 1887.
Reyer
"Waking of the Valkyrie," from "Sigurd," New York, December 8, 1888.
Rheinberger
"Wallenstein's Camp," New York, August 10, 1871.
Overture, "Demetrius," New York, March 11, 1881.
"Passacaglio," op. 132, New York, April 14, 1888.
Concerto in G minor, for organ and orchestra, Chicago, February 22, 1895.
Rheinhold
Prelude, minuet, and fugue, op. 10, New York, January 24, 1879.
Concert overture, op. 32, New York, January 10, 1883.
Rietz
"Festival March," New York, July 9, 1867.
Reitzel
"Eine Volksthümliche Suite," New York, December 24, 1884.
Rimsky-Korsakow
Suite of characteristic dances, from "Miladi," Chicago, January 8, 1897.
Symphonic poem, "Antar," Chicago, November 29, 1901.
Ritter
Symphonic waltz, "Olafs Hochzeitsreigen," Chicago, January 30, 1903.
Roentgen
Ballad on a Norwegian Folksong, Chicago, December 11, 1896.
Rubinstein
"Faust," ein musikalisches Charakterbild, op. 68, New York, January 16, 1869.
Overture, "Dimitri Donskoi," New York, July 19, 1871.
"Don Quixote," Humoreske, op. 87, New York, May 30, 1872.
Ivan IV, Charakterbild, New York, January 24, 1874.
"Ouverture Triomphale," on a Russian hymn, New York, September 17, 1874.
Dramatic symphony, No. 4, D minor, op. 95, New York, March 4, 1875.
Fifth Symphony, New York, December 10, 1881.
Ballet music from opera, "Nero," New York, July 16, 1881.
"Bal Costumé," first series, op. 183, Chicago, July 18, 1883.
"Vine" ballet, New York, February 7, 1885.
"Fantasia Eroica," Brooklyn, April 18, 1885.
Bal Costumé, second series, Chicago, July 5, 1886.
Oratorio, "Paradise Lost," Brooklyn, March 12, 1887.
Scenes from opera, "Nero," New York, November 12, 1886.
Concerto No. 2, op. 95, for violoncello, New York, February 9, 1887.
Opera, "Nero," New York, March 14, 1887.
Overture, "Antony and Cleopatra," Brooklyn, January 17, 1891.
Second and third tableaux of "Moses," Cincinnati, May 25, 1894.
Saint-Saëns
Symphonic poem, "Phaeton," op. 39, New York, October 9, 1876.
Tarantelle for flute and clarinet, op. 6, New York, June 24, 1873.
"Marche Héroïque," op. 34, New York, May 21, 1874.

"Danse Macabre," op. 40, New York, January 29, 1876.
Ballet music from "Samson and Delilah," St. Louis, March 15, 1877.
Suite, op. 49, Chicago, July 24, 1877.
"Suite Algérienne," op. 60, New York, April 1, 1881.
Ballet, "Henry VIII," Chicago, July 20, 1886.
Concerto for piano, No. 3, op. 29, E flat, New York, November 12, 1885.
Third Symphony, C minor, op. 78, New York, February 19, 1887.
Symphony, No. 2, op. 55, Chicago, November 16, 1900.
Symphonic poem, "La Jeunesse d'Hercule," op. 50, Chicago, November 15, 1901.
Overture, "Les Barbares," Chicago, October 31, 1902.
"Coronation March," Chicago, January 30, 1903.
Symphonic poem, "Le Rouet d'Omphale," op. 31, New York, June 5, 1875.

SCHARWENKA (Philipp)
Fantasia, "Liebsenacht," op. 40, Chicago, July 21, 1887.
"Arkadische Suite," New York, January 28, 1888.
"Frühlingswogen," op. 87, Chicago, January 29, 1892.

SCHARWENKA (Xavier)
Concerto for piano, op. 56, No. 2, New York, February 1, 1883.
Symphony in C minor, op. 60, New York, December 12, 1885.
Concerto for piano, op. 32, No. 1, B minor, Chicago, March 24, 1893.

SCHOLZ
Symphony in B flat, op. 60, New York, March 13, 1886.
Suite, "Wanderings," op. 74, Chicago, November 16, 1893.

SCHUBERT (Franz)
Fantasia, op. 15 (Liszt arrangement), New York, May 13, 1862.
"Reiter March" (Liszt arrangement), Brooklyn, October 27, 1866.
Entr'acte, "Rosamunde," New York, March 13, 1867.
Overture, "Rosamunde," New York, July 7, 1867.
"Unfinished" Symphony, B minor, New York, October 26, 1867.
"Twenty-third Psalm," New York, December 12, 1868.
Overture in Italian style, op. 170, New York, May 12, 1869.
March in B minor (Liszt arrangement), New York, August 17, 1871.
Overture, "Alfonse and Estrella," New York, June 11, 1874.
Impromptu in C minor, op. 90, New York, May 27, 1875.
Overture, "Teufel's Lustschloss," New York, May 28, 1875.
Octet, for string instruments, New York, August 10, 1875.
Symphony in C, No. 10, New York, August 20, 1875.
Divertissement à la Hongroise, op. 54, arranged by Erdmannsdörfer, New York, January 17, 1888.
Overture in E minor, New York, January 24, 1889.

SCHUMANN (Georg)
Symphonic variations, op. 24, for orchestra and organ, Chicago, October 20, 1900.
Variationen und döppelfuge, op. 30, Chicago, December 26, 1903.

SCHUMANN (Robert)
Overture, "Bride of Messina," New York, April 8, 1865.
Overture, "Genoveva," Brooklyn, April 13, 1867.
"Träumerei," New York, August 13, 1867.
"Gipsy Life," op. 29, New York, March 13, 1869.
"Paradise and the Peri," Chicago, February 18, 1874.

"Bilder aus Osten," op. 66 (orchestrated by Reinecke), New York, May 27, 1875.
"Concertstück," op. 92, New York, December 4, 1875.
"Marche Funèbre," from quintet, op. 44 (orchestrated by Godard), New York, November 4, 1886.
Fantasia for violin, op. 138, New York, March 28, 1889.

SCHYTTE
"Pantomimes," op. 30 (orchestrated by Müller-Berghaus), Chicago, July 21, 1886.

SEIFERT
"Festival March," New York, June 15, 1875.

SGAMBATI
"Te Deum Laudamus," Chicago, December 28, 1893.

SHELLEY
"Grand Sonata," for stringed instruments, New York, March 2, 1888.

SIBELIUS
"Two Legends," from "Kalevala," Chicago, December 6, 1901.
Suite, "King Christian II," Chicago, November 14, 1902.
Symphony, No. 2, D major, Chicago, January 2, 1904.
Tone poem, "Eine Sage," Chicago, April 30, 1904.

SINDING
Symphony in D minor, Chicago, December 8, 1893.
"Rondo Infinito," Chicago, January 5, 1900.
"Episodes Chevaleresques," Chicago, January 19, 1900.

SINGER
Fantasia, for piano and orchestra, New York, April 3, 1869.
"Festival Ode," for chorus and orchestra, Cincinnati, May 14, 1848.

SIX RUSSIAN COMPOSERS
Variations on a Russian theme, Chicago, October 24, 1903.

SMETANA
Ouverture zur Oper, "Die verkaufte Braut," New York, November 12, 1887.
Symphonic poem, "Sarka," Chicago, October 25, 1895.
Symphonic poem, "Vyschrad," Chicago, April 24, 1896.
Symphonic poem, "Richard III," Chicago, November 13, 1896.

STANFORD
Serenade in G, New York, January 19, 1884.

STOCK
Symphonic variations, Chicago, February 26, 1904.

STRAUSS (Johann)
"Blue Danube Waltz," New York, July 1, 1867.
Waltz, "From the Mountains," New York, July 7, 1867.
Waltz, "Bürgersinn," New York, July 14, 1867.
Polka Mazurka, "Lob der Frauen," New York, July 14, 1867.
Waltz, "Wein, Weib, und Gesang," New York, July 20, 1869.
Waltz, "Seid umschlungen Millionen!" Chicago, October 21, 1892.

STRAUSS (Richard)
Symphony in F minor, New York, December 13, 1884.
Symphonic fantasia, "Italy," Philadelphia, March 8, 1888.
Vorspiel from opera "Guntram," Chicago, November 1, 1895.
Rondo, "Till Eulenspiegel's Merry Pranks," Chicago, November 15, 1895.
Tone poem, "Thus Spake Zarathustra," Chicago, February 5, 1897.

Tone poem, "Don Quixote," Chicago, January 6, 1899.
Tone poem, "Ein Heldenleben," Chicago, March 9, 1900.
Tone poem, "Macbeth," Chicago, October 25, 1901.
Love scene from "Feuersnot," Chicago, February, 14, 1902.

SUK
Ein Marchen, "Pohadka," Chicago, November 22, 1901.

SULLIVAN
"Overture di Ballo," New York, May 20, 1873.
Overture, "Tempest," New York, July 16, 1874.
Cantata, "On Shore and Sea," Chicago, June 6, 1877.
Overture, "In Memoriam," Chicago, November 4, 1886.

SVENDSEN
Symphony, No. 1, in D major, New York, June 12, 1873.
Symphonic Overture, "Sigurd Slembe," New York, September 18, 1873.
Fantasia, "Romeo and Juliet," op. 18, New York, March 11, 1881.
"Norwegian Artists' Carnival," New York, January 12, 1886.
"Festival Polonaise," New York, March 1, 1887.
Legende "Zorahayda," op. 11, New York, March 14, 1889.

TSCHAIKOWSKY
"Marche Slave," New York, November 2, 1886.
Suite No. 3, op. 55, New York, November 24, 1885.
Suite, "Mozartiana," New York, February 4, 1888.
Introduction and fugue, op. 43, New York, January 24, 1889.
Suite No. 1, Brooklyn, March 15, 1889.
Overture fantasia, "Hamlet," Brooklyn, February 14, 1891.
Suite, "Casse-noisette," op. 71, Chicago, October 22, 1892.
Suite du Ballet, "La Belle au Bois Dormant," op. 66a, Chicago, 19, 1900.

URSPRUCH
Overture, "Der Sturm," Chicago, January 2, 1903.

VOLBACH
"Es waren zwei Königskinder," Chicago, January 23, 1903.

VOLKMANN
"Festival Overture," op. 50, Chicago, April 3, 1869.
Serenade in F, op. 63, New York, January 10, 1842.
Serenade in D minor, Brooklyn, January 10, 1874.
Concerto for violoncello, op. 33, Chicago, March 17, 1893.

WAGNER
Overture, "Flying Dutchman," New York, May 13, 1862.
Vorspiel, "Die Meistersinger," New York, October 20, 1866.
"Kaiser March," New York, June 22, 1871.
"Huldigung's March," New York, September 8, 1871.
Introduction and final scene from "Tristan und Isolde," Boston, December 6, 1871.
"Ride of the Valkyries," New York, September 17, 1872.
"Wotan's Departure," and "Magic Fire Scene," Philadelphia, January 8, 1875.
Introduction and Siegmund's Love Song from "Die Walküre," New York, September 14, 1875.
"Centennial March," Philadelphia, May 11, 1876.
"Siegfried Idyle," New York, February 28, 1878.
Vorspiel, "Parsifal," New York, November 11, 1882.

Flower Girl Scene from "Parsifal," Philadelphia, February 24, 1887.
"Dreams" (orchestrated by Theodore Thomas), New York, January 17, 1889.

WEBER
"Invitation to the Dance" (Berlioz arrangement), New York, February 10, 1866.
Overture, "Abu Hassan," New York, May 14, 1874.
Symphony, No. 1, in C, New York, June 17, 1875.

WEIDIG
Scherzo Capriccioso, op. 13, Chicago, January 5, 1900.

WIDOR
"Chorale and Variations," for harp and orchestra, Chicago, November 28, 1902.

WOLF
Symphonic poem, "Penthesilea," Chicago, April 23, 1904.
"Italian Serenade," Chicago, January 20, 1905.

ZELLNER
Symphony, op. 7, New York, June 12, 1873.
"Melusine," op. 10, New York, August 21, 1874.

ZÖLLNER
"Midnight at Sedan," Chicago, December 11, 1896.

INDEX

INDEX